Currency Lads & Lasses

Currency Lads & Lasses

Behind the Faces on Australian Banknotes

GEOFF HOCKING

Lothian BOOKS

Thomas C. Lothian Pty Ltd
132 Albert Road, South Melbourne, Victoria 3205
www.lothian.com.au

First published 2004

National Library of Australia
Cataloguing-in-Publication data:

Hocking, Geoff, 1947–.
Currency lads and lasses: Behind the faces on Australian banknotes.

ISBN 0 7344 0532 4

1. Banknotes — Australia.
2. Australia — History. I. Title.

994

Cover and text design by Geoff Hocking
Printed in China by SNP Leefung Printing Limited

WARNING TO INDIGENOUS PERSONS

This book contains images of deceased Aboriginal persons.

Permission has been granted to the author to reproduce these photographs by the descendants of those deceased persons shown.

Thanks go to Melva Kartinyeri and the Raukkan Community Council.

Contents

The Currency Lads may fill their glasses,
And drink to the health of the Currency Lasses;
But the lass I adore, the lass for me,
Is a lass in the Female Factory.

She got death recorded in Newry Town,
For stealing her mistress's watch and gown;
Her little boy Paddy can tell you the tale,
His father was turnkey of Newry jail.

TRADITIONAL BALLAD — *1832*

Farewell, emigrants leaving England for Australia
Pen-and-wash drawing by Thomas Rowlandson, c. 1800

(Rex Nan Kivell Collection NK561. By permission, National Library of Australia)

Introduction

EACH SOCIETY DEFINES ITS SENSE OF SELF IN SYMBOLIC ways. Almost all salute a national flag, sing a patriotic song, revere a revolutionary hero or tell tall tales and true about legendary characters.

Currency Lads & Lasses recalls the lives of those featured on Australia's banknotes, those who helped create the spirit of the nation and made a difference to the way all Australians live today, whatever their origin.

These are the lives of the men and women who met the challenge of this wide brown land; they are the lives of the dreamers, the schemers and those who chanced their luck, and of those who fought tooth and nail for their beliefs and the rights of their fellows to live in equality and freedom under the Southern Cross.

Australia is a nation unique among all others. Its national flag bears the flag of a foreign power, yet the flags that reach into the heart of Australians are considered too comical, too trivial or too politicised to be treated seriously at all. Our 'revolutionary' heroes are invariably drunkards or desperadoes, hanged by the neck or hounded from office; our mythical characters seem larger than life.

When Phillip Adams cynically commented to a group of Melbourne students in the mid-1970s, 'No matter how hard you do try, remember, Australia, rhymes with failure', he was rather facetiously ignoring the incredible success over the years of thousands of ordinary Australians. Sometimes this success may be just the business of survival in a harsh and unforgiving land, or simply the success of a secure home and a happy family.

While there have certainly been many spectacular failures — Burke and Wills never made it back, and almost every early aviator perished somewhere over the ocean — our greatest defeat, on the rugged clifftops at Gallipoli, has melded so successfully into the very fabric of the Australian soul that it has become the nation's defining moment of glory.

The stories told in this book celebrate the lives of a select few; unique Australians who are neither princes nor princesses, revolutionaries nor mythical creatures. *Currency, Lads & Lasses* honours them all. These stalwart pioneers lived as an example to all Australians to be proud, to stand together and be counted — whatever colour, creed, gender, level of education or place of birth — as one people, in success and in failure.

— *Geoff Hocking, 2004*

Painted by Sir Joshua Reynolds.

Engraved by W. Dick

Joseph Banks Esqr

Sir Joseph Banks

1743–1820

Sir Joseph Banks is featured on the face of the $5 paper note, first issued in 1966.

The first man of science in New Holland — the father of Australia

JOSEPH BANKS WAS BORN INTO A LIFE OF PRIVILEGE. HE WAS the son of William Banks, a wealthy country squire and member of the House of Commons, and Marianne Banks, described as 'a lady remarkable for her charities and piety'. Marianne gave birth to their son on 13 February 1743 in their London residence in Argyle Street.

Joseph first went to school at Harrow and then, at the age of thirteen, he was sent to Eton, the perfect training ground for boys set to rule, or at least set for a life of influence, wealth and power. He was not a particularly distinguished scholar, but was an energetic lad, good at sports. Fond of long rambles in the countryside, Joseph loved the outdoors. He complained that he would much prefer to learn the nature of the flowers and plants that he came across on his rambles than the Latin and Greek he was forced to study.

Young Joseph Banks became totally absorbed in the pursuit of knowledge of the natural world. Long before Charles Darwin was to propose his theory of evolution, the concept of 'natural order' had popular currency among men of science and contemporary philosophy. Joseph remained a lifelong proponent of this philosophy, and his investigations into and classification of the hundreds of species that he recorded and discovered remain unchanged even 200 years after his time.

Such was his desire for new discoveries that he even used his pocket money to pay the women who collected plants for drug-makers. They brought him specimens of any unusual plants they had discovered, and shared with him their knowledge of the natural properties of all they gathered.

At home from school on holidays, Joseph discovered a copy of *Gerarde's Herbal* among his mother's old books. This discovery was a turning point in his life. Not long after, Joseph enrolled at Christ Church, Oxford, where he pursued his desire for knowledge of all things natural. He was disappointed to discover that the only professor of botany attached to the university had given just one lecture in his thirty years there. Joseph decided to pay for his own lecturer, and with a group of like-minded fellow students secured the services

OPPOSITE:

Mr Joseph Banks, Esq.

Mezzotint by William Dickinson, after a painting by Sir Joshua Reynolds, c. 1771-3, published 30 January 1774, (London)

Banks sat for this portrait first in 1772 and again after his voyage to Iceland in 1773.

(Rex Nan Kivell Collection NK10667. By permission, National Library of Australia)

ABOVE:

Arms of Sir Joseph Banks, Bt

Hand-coloured engraving, c. 1803

Banks was born into a tradition of wealth and privilege; his gentleman father was a member of the English parliament.

He first studied at Harrow and Eton, then went 'down to Oxford', where he indulged his passion for botanical investigation.

(National Library of Australia Collection)

of Israel Lyons of Cambridge. Joseph Banks's career as a botanist began in earnest.

After his father died in 1761 Joseph's mother moved to London. Joseph, still not of age, would have to wait a few more years before he was able to take full advantage of his inheritance, but this didn't stop him making the most of any opportunity that came his way. When he learned that an old friend was making a voyage to Newfoundland and Labrador he jumped at the chance to join the excursion. He sailed aboard the *Niger* on 22 April 1766, and at the end of the voyage brought back to England cases of specimens to add to his growing collection. Ever ready to find a place for himself on other such exciting

ABOVE:

Captain James Cook, Sir Joseph Banks, Lord Sandwich, Dr Daniel Solander and Dr John Hawkesworth

Oil on canvas by John Hamilton Mortimer, c. 1771

The sitters for this romantic portrait of the intrepid explorers of the South Seas can be identified as, from left to right: Dr Daniel Solander (friend of Banks), Sir Joseph Banks, Captain James Cook, Dr John Hawkesworth and Lord Sandwich.

However, the title identifies them in the order that posterity may have them placed, with James Cook, the discoverer of Australia, pre-eminent among this group of otherwise privileged and learned gentlemen.

It was Sandwich who had suggested that his young botanist friend should lead the expedition to observe the transit of the planet Venus across the face of the sun in 1769. It was Sandwich again who prompted Banks to join Cook's second voyage in 1772.

When Banks pulled out from this second trip at the last minute he wrote a long letter to Sandwich detailing his reasons and thanking him for his continued support over the many years they had been friends; members of the Royal Society could ill afford to lose favour. Patronage was all-important for these men with unusual ideas, no matter how wealthy they themselves were.

(National Library of Australia Collection)

voyages of discovery, Joseph Banks continued to keep his ear to the ground.

The transit of Venus

In the early years of the eighteenth century the astronomer Edmund Halley had suggested that it would be possible to measure the distance of the earth from the sun by accurately observing the passage of the planet Venus across its face; this 'transit of Venus' was to take place on 3 June 1769.

The Royal Society had been pressing the Admiralty to mount an expedition to observe the phenomenon. The Admiralty finally agreed and proposed that sightings be taken from several different locations; it was decided to send observers to Hudson Bay, Lapland and to Wallis's newly discovered islands of Tahiti.

There was some considerable debate as to who would be the right person to take charge of such a venture and it fell to Able Seaman James Cook, who had proved to be an excellent sailor, had shown great ability in the charts he had made of the Gulf of St Lawrence during the Seven Years War, and had continued this work, making 'remarkably accurate charts of Newfoundland', after hostilities had ceased.

Cook was given the rank of lieutenant for this expedition to the islands and chose for his vessel a broad-hulled Whitby collier that was re-registered by the Royal Navy, and renamed the bark HMS *Endeavour*. When she set sail for the South Seas, with her crew of eighty-four, she also carried eleven passengers who had paid their own way to be the first to travel into largely uncharted waters on behalf of the Royal Society and in the interests of scientific discovery.

Most notable among this eleven was the wealthy young gentleman of science Joseph Banks, and quite a retinue of his friends and servants. Accompanying Banks on this voyage was his botanist friend and colleague, Danish scientist Dr Daniel Solander; Mr Parkinson, his painter of natural history; Mr Buchan, landscape artist; Mr Charles Green, who had been sent by the Royal Astronomical Society to

The fortunate Mr Cook

James Cook, the second son of an agricultural labourer, was born in the village of Marton-in-Cleveland, Yorkshire, on 27 October 1728.

At the age of seventeen, after a disagreement with the shopkeeper with whom he had been employed, he was discharged and bound as apprentice to Walker's shipping firm in Whitby. It was on Walker's vessel, the *Freelove*, that he learnt the arts of navigation and seamanship.

Cook volunteered to join the Royal Navy, 'having a mind to try his fortune that way', when the Seven Years War broke out in 1755.

It was his success in navigation and mapping during this war that brought him to the notice of the Admiralty. As a result Cook was chosen above many thought to be superior, raised to the rank of lieutenant and offered command of the South Sea expedition.

He chose the *Earl of Pembroke,* a Whitby-built collier, for this expedition, which was re-registered by the Royal Navy and named the *Endeavour*.

ABOVE:
Portrait of James Cook
Oil on canvas — copy of Nathaniel Dance's portrait in the National Maritime Museum, Greenwich, England, c. 1800
(National Library of Australia Collection)

BELOW:
HMS Endeavour *off the coast of New Holland*
Watercolour by Samuel Atkins, c. 1794

(National Library of Australia Collection)

make the necessary observations on its behalf; and a couple of Negro servants. As far as the Royal Society was concerned, this voyage was Banks's expedition; Banks had put up most of the money. Cook was merely the sea dog that would ensure the safe arrival of the scientific party.

Observing the transit of the planet was the primary reason for Cook's expedition. Banks and the Royal Society were only interested in scientific, botanic and ethnographic study. And there was another reason for this voyage.

Since time immemorial, there had been reports of a great southern land in the South Pacific. Scores of ships had sailed across these oceans looking for the new land, Terra Australis Incognita, but none had returned to claim its discovery. Discoveries of island groups and coral atolls were all that they had made. The *Dolphin* had been twice around the world, first in 1764-6 and again in 1766-8, and many of Cook's crew on the *Endeavour* had been on these voyages. The discovery of the islands of Tahiti by Captain Wallis was the impetus for sending Cook there to observe the planetary phenomenon.

The *Endeavour* slipped from its moorings in the River Thames on 21 July 1768 and set sail for the Pacific. The journey took the *Endeavour* west across the Atlantic and then south along the coast of South America. It stopped at Rio de Janeiro for supplies in November and then headed south again, until it sailed into the Bay of Good Success, on the southernmost tip of the continent, where it stopped to gather wood and fresh water. The men of science, Banks and Solander, went ashore to look for water and to talk with the natives. They decided to climb a nearby mountain and nearly died of the cold. The two Negro servants who had accompanied them on their ill-fated journey of discovery perished on the mountainside.

The *Endeavour* then sailed out across the South Pacific Ocean until it reached the islands of Tahiti, in April. It was headed for

Otaheite, later known as Venus Fort, which had been discovered by Captain Wallis in the *Dolphin* on his 1766–8 voyage.

Not long after their arrival Banks and Solander, never ones to avoid adventure or to hang back in fear of danger, immediately went ashore and pitched a tent, all the while under close inspection by the natives who had gathered around. The explorers traded with the natives, wary that they may be attacked by them, but although both Solander and Monkhouse had their pockets picked, there was little to make them afraid.

In search of fresh specimens for investigation Banks had taken off with a musket cradled in the crook of his arm. Banks was followed by a throng of inquisitive natives. Just as they crossed a creek Banks raised the musket and shot three ducks with one charge. Several of his followers, shocked at this display of seemingly magical powers, fell to the ground as though they too had been shot. Those who had gathered on the shore around Banks's tent were fascinated by the display of firepower; one, braver than the rest, leapt forward and snatched a musket from the hands of a marine guarding the tent. This fellow ran into the woods but was felled by a musket ball from the other guards standing by the tent.

Following this incident, the explorers of the bark *Endeavour* constructed a crude fort to afford them protection while they awaited the transit of the planet.

On the evening of 20 April 1769 Lieutenant Cook wrote in his journal: 'Mr Banks and Dr Solander lay ashore tonight for the first time, their marquees being set up within the walls of the fort and fit for their reception'.

3 June 1769—The long-awaited day had finally dawned and after the passage of the planet had been successfully observed Cook made his journal entry:

> This day proved as favourable to our purpose as we could wish. Not a cloud was to be seen the whole day, and the air was perfectly clear, so that we had every advantage we could desire in observing the whole of the passage of the planet Venus over the sun's disk. We very distinctly saw an atmosphere or dusky shade round the body of the planet, which very much disturbed the times of the contact.[1]

Cook, Solander and Mr Green all observed the passage and all three recorded different times. However, compared with the complete failure of the Hudson Bay and Lapland expeditions it may be considered that they had been extraordinarily successful.

Mr Banks goes native

Joseph Banks was keen on all things natural. He dedicated his life to the study of not only plants and animal species but also the habits of the native peoples encountered on his voyages.

Once, when planning to observe a local ceremony, he blackened his skin with powdered charcoal, and adorned his nether regions with only a loincloth. Upon his return the boys of the ship's company were greatly amused as he lay in a creekbed while they scrubbed him clean.

Relationships with the local inhabitants were always of great interest to Banks, who found their habits and customs to be curious, to say the least. They soon became aware of the collecting habits of Banks and his men and would bring gifts of plants to his marquee.

On one occasion two young women came before Banks and lay upon the ground a cloth, offered presumably as a gift; 'one of the women then stepped upon the cloth, and with as much innocency [sic] as one could possibly conceive, exposed herself, entirely naked, from the waist downwards ... turned herself once or twice around'.[2] After her little ceremony was over she rolled up the cloth and the two women went and embraced Banks.

His reaction went unrecorded.

BELOW:

Venus Fort, Otaheite

Engraving by Samuel Middiman, published by Stanfield Parkinson, London, 1773

This fort was constructed in the South Sea islands at Otaheite for the men of science on board the *Endeavour* to enable them to secure themselves during the observation of the transit of Venus in 1773.

(National Library of Australia Collection)

The *Endeavour* left the island on 13 July 1769, three months after the expedition had first stepped ashore. At the request of Mr Banks, whose fascination with the natives and their place in 'the natural order' never left him, they carried with them the native chief and priest Tupia, and his servant boy. Tupia's son had been taken back to Paris with Louis Antoine de Bougainville some years before, and had made a great hit as the 'noble savage' in the salons of that great city of enlightenment.

Cook had been handed sealed orders before the *Endeavour* had left England's shores; his task was now to look for, and finally discover, the Great South Land that must lay beyond the islands of New Zealand, which had been discovered by the Dutch explorer Abel Tasman over a century earlier, in 1642.

Cook's secret orders

Without the knowledge of the professional party on board the *Endeavour*, Cook had received the following, sealed, instructions from the Admiralty before he set sail:

> Whereas there is reason to imagine that a continent or land of great extent, may be found to the southward of the tract lately made by Capt. Wallis in His Majesty's ship the *Dolphin* ... you are therefore in pursuance of His Majesty's pleasure hereby required and directed to put to sea with the bark you command, as soon as the observation of the planet Venus shall be finished, and observe the following instructions.
>
> You are to proceed to the southward in

BELOW:
Cook's landing at Botany A. D. 1770

(National Library of Australia Collection)

order to make discovery of the continent above-mentioned until you arrive in the latitude of 40°, unless you sooner fall in with it; but not having discovered it, or any evident signs of it, in that run, you are to proceed in search of it to the westward, between the latitude before mentioned and the latitude of 35° until you discover it or fall in with the eastern side of the land discovered by Tasman and now called New Zealand.[3]

Cook's course was clear: he had been instructed to search for terra incognita, and as a consequence take Banks, Solander and retinue along for the ride. For Banks, it was really a case of being in the right place at the right time. After circumnavigating both islands of New Zealand, Cook struck out west until the southern coast of continental 'terra incognita' was finally sighted on 19 April 1770. This was named Point Hicks, in honour of Lieutenant Hicks, who first sighted land at the latitude of 38°. Cook then sailed up the east coast until a landing was attempted on 28 April.

With the *Endeavour* lying at anchor two miles from the shore, Cook, Banks, Solander and the native Tupia launched a yawl and attempted to make a landing. They first tried to battle the pounding surf, but retreated to try again the following day.

The landing party stepped ashore at Botany Bay on 29 April 1770. The honour of being the first European to stand on Australia's sunny shores fell to Isaac Smith, a nephew of Cook's wife. Mr Banks, Dr Solander, Lieutenant James Cook and Tupia stepped ashore immediately after him.

BELOW:

The bay at Endeavour River where the ship was careened to effect repairs to the hull, after Cook struck the coral reef on 10 June 1770

Engraving by Ignaz Klauber, Amsterdam, c. 1795

(National Library of Australia Collection)

They had been watched by a pair of natives, who threw a couple of spears in their direction. The landing party responded with a return of musket fire; Cook wounded one man in the arm and the natives hastily retired to the safety of the scrub. It was an inauspicious beginning for the settlement that would eventually become the colony of New South Wales.

Mr Banks and Dr Solander were out and about as quickly as they could taking samples of plants, shooting birds and chasing whatever animals they could find. They had stumbled into a cornucopia of flora and fauna that had never been seen by European eyes.

When, sailors fishing in the bay on 5 May netted two large stingrays weighing, in total, more than four hundredweight, Cook was moved to name the bay Stingray Harbour. But given the large number of plant specimens Banks had gathered, he was persuaded to name it Botany Bay. (A score of balladeers who followed the settlement of the colony of New South Wales are no doubt thankful for Banks's intervention in this matter.)

Banks and Solander had cut, dried and filled almost two hundred pages of their pressing books with botanical specimens in the few days they had been at anchor, and had collected many more ready for classification. They were aware then that they had in their possession scores of plants previously unknown to botany, and they were excited in their belief that they had been present at the discovery of natural phenomena new to science.

The *Endeavour* sailed north, keeping the eastern coastline in sight. Cook would not have known that he was sailing inside the waters of a great barrier reef until at 11 pm on

10 June 1770 the ship ran aground where the coral reef converges on the Queensland coast at what is today known as Cooktown.

The *Endeavour* was careened ashore in order that repairs could be made to the smashed hull. During this time Banks was again out and about making the most of this subtropical layover. It was while at 'Endeavour River' that they had their first close encounter with a 'kangaru', which they killed. After making some drawings and consigning an appropriately detailed description of the dead beast to their journal, the gentlemen then skinned, cooked and ate a hearty meal of kangaroo.

Three years had passed since the *Endeavour* had left England, and the Admiralty feared that harm had come to the ship, its crew and the gentlemen on board. When the ship sailed back into harbour on 12 July 1771, their fears turned to joy and congratulations. However, although the voyage had been an outstanding success in scientific terms, there had been considerable loss of life: thirty-eight men had died on the voyage, including Buchan and the two Negroes in Banks's party.

All those who had served aboard the *Endeavour* enjoyed great notoriety; the tales of their discoveries reached all corners of the land. The president of the Royal Society presented Banks and Solander to King George III, who was fascinated by Banks's description of the qualities of the new land discovered in the king's name. Banks was overflowing with praise for the opportunities for agriculture he felt sure existed in New Holland: he had seen new plants, billowing grasslands, native fauna abounded and good soils beside safe harbours, which, in his opinion, made this new land eminently suitable for colonial settlement.

Cook prepared for a second voyage, again to the South Seas. Banks agreed to join him, but was this time eager to ensure that he was accommodated in a manner befitting a man of his rank and scientific eminence. At the last moment he pulled out of the expedition, claiming that the Royal Navy had not prepared the vessel in accordance with his wishes. As he was putting up much of the money, he had every right to demand that he was adequately provided for, but Cook felt that some coolness had developed between them and left without him in May 1772.

Two months later Banks joined another expedition, to Iceland, where he collected plant specimens and samples of animal and marine life to add to his growing collection at home in England.

Banks and Cook, the two companions of the first voyage to the Pacific Islands, were never

First — catch your kangaru

Endeavour River, 15 July 1770:—

Yesterday Lieutenant Gore shot one of the peculiar animals that was first seen about three weeks ago, thought at first to be something like a dog, though it 'jumped like a hare or a deer'.

It was a small one ... the head, neck and shoulders very small in proportion to the other parts. It was hair lipt, the Head and Ears were most like a hare's of any Animal I know; the tail was nearly as long as the body ... Its progression is by Hopping or Jumping 7 or 8 feet at each hop upon its hind legs only, for in this it makes no use of the Fore, which seem to be design'd for Scratching in the ground, etc. The skin is cover'd with a Short, hairy furr of a dark Mouse or grey colour. It bears no sort of resemblence to any European animal I ever saw.[4]

Cook also noted in his journal that after Banks had made sketches of the animal, the gentlemen sat down and made a meal of it, exclaiming that it was 'excellent food'.

to meet again; Cook was murdered by natives on the island of Hawaii on 15 February 1779.

Banks was elected to the Dilettante Society in 1774 and on 30 November 1778 he was elected president of the Royal Society, an office he held for the next forty-two years.

His contribution to the world of science was officially recognised in 1781 when he was made a baronet.

Sir Joseph Banks never lost his affection for the land he had seen for only a short while. At best he was in Australia for three months, but his fame had been made by his part in the discovery of that island continent.

In May 1785 a committee to find a suitable site for the settlement of a colony was established under the chairmanship of Lord Beauchamp. When Banks appeared before the committee he said that he had:

> ... no doubt that the Soil of many parts of the eastern Coast of New South Wales, between the latitudes of 30° and 40° south, is sufficiently fertile to support a Considerable Number of Europeans who would cultivate it in the Ordinary Modes used in England.[5]

Banks recommended that his beloved Botany Bay was in every way 'adapted to [that] purpose'. He told the committee that the natives were only in small numbers, and that although they were inclined to hostility they were really not to be feared. He said that they appeared to own nothing and were not interested in anything the Europeans had to offer except food. He was confident that the natives in the area would soon 'abandon the country to the newcomers'.

Banks continued to expound the possibilities for colonial settlement. The committee

ABOVE:
The great South Sea Caterpillar, transform'd into a Bath Butterfly
Hand-coloured etching, published 4 July 1795 by H. Humphrey, 37 New Bond Street, London

The caption to this satirical cartoon reads:

> This insect first crawled into notice from among the weeds and Mud on the Banks of the South Sea; & being afterwards placed in a Warm Situation by the Royal Society changed by the heat of the Sun into its present form—it is noticed and Valued Solely on account of the beautiful Red which adorns its body and the Shining Spot on its Breast; a Distinction which never fails to render Caterpillars valuable.

The sun referred to is the Crown; the red represents The Order of the Bath, which Banks received in 1795. The satirist is showing the metamorphosis of a caterpillar into a beautiful butterfly — Banks transformed by honour of the king. Crawling from the mud, however, was a bit cheeky, and not altogether fair play.

Banks was typical of a privileged, dilettante class in the romantic era of George III whose members claimed the world as their oyster and had the means to enjoy devouring it. The popular press took pleasure in satirising their globe-trotting activities.

(Rex Nan Kivell Collection NK1603. By permission, National Library of Australia)

was assured that the climate was similar to Europe, the coast abounded with fish, grass was abundant and the soil should also support the cultivation of grains and vegetables. He added that although he had seen no useful quadrupeds, birds were plentiful, and that the timber grown there was suitable for all purposes of building ships and houses.

Three years later Captain Arthur Phillip set out from Portsmouth with a small fleet of eleven vessels, which carried more than 1400 officers, merchantmen, Royal Navy seamen, marines and convicts to establish a penal settlement in New South Wales. This First Fleet arrived on 18–20 January 1788 and marked the beginning of the Australian nation.

Sir Joseph Banks continued to exert his influence on the development of the colony; many who had settled there, or who had been transported, looked to him for advice and encouragement. A succession of colonial governors sought his counsel and he was instrumental in the appointment of at least one to that post.

Banks put forward the name of William Bligh, writing to him and offering him the position of Governor of New South Wales. Banks continued to support Bligh through all his disagreements with the argumentative pastoralist John Macarthur. It may have been his support for Bligh that turned him against Macarthur and the establishment of an Australian wool industry; Banks had opposed sheep breeding in the colony, believing the pastures unsuitable.

In June 1799 the first fabrics made in New South Wales were sent to England by Governor Hunter and Irish convict Andrew Cunningham, for Banks's appraisal. Cunningham had woven linen from flax he had grown from wild seed, and a bolt of cloth from local wool.

In October 1800 Governor King sent a box to Banks containing samples of wool grown by pastoralist John Macarthur, as well as other boxes containing botanical and geological samples. The number of sheep in the colony had grown to 6000 and breeders were anxious to create a viable industry for the supply of the much-needed fibre to rival the Spanish wool producers.

In the face of this evidence of the success of sheep breeding and wool production in New

LEFT:
Portrait of Sir Joseph Banks
Watercolour, artist unknown, c. 1812
Sir Joseph Banks's long and distinguished career meant that he was in the public eye over a very long period. With more than forty years as president of the Royal Society, he saw scores of portraits, cartoons and engravings made of his likeness to feed the endless public hunger for heroes of the realm.
(National Library of Australia Collection)

South Wales, it is strange that Banks remained opposed to the industry. When Macarthur was held to be responsible for the insurrection against Governor Bligh in 1808, it did nothing to soften Banks's attitude to Australian wool.

In 1800, when it was proposed that botanic gardens be established near Government House in Parramatta 'for the purpose of scientific research and the improvement of horticulture in the settlement', Banks supported the appointment of George Caley to their management. Caley was to gather specimens to send back to Banks for his research and for the living collection at Kew Gardens, and the Parramatta gardens were to be used for the acclimatisation of European species in the colony.

In 1801 Banks engaged botanist Robert Brown to accompany Matthew Flinders on his voyage in the *Investigator* to do just as Banks had done when he first travelled with Cook thirty years earlier. When Brown returned five years later he brought with him a variety of specimens from parts of Australia that Banks had never seen. Flinders had sailed from the west to the east, following the Great Australian Bight, from December 1801 to May 1802.

On Flinders's voyage, which took in a complete circumnavigation of the continent, were the landscape painter William Westall, the

Eponymous plants

The almost primordial form of the banksia family was astonishing to European eyes used to the soft, subtle forms and gentle textures of English flora.

The harshness of the Australian climate, and the island continent's isolation, prevented botanical invasion from overseas. Consequently, the evolution of indigenous plant species was unique and totally suited to its environment.

Banks revelled in the opportunity to be at the very genesis of the botanical discoveries of Australia, his own name given to one of the most extraordinary of all plants he found.

ABOVE:
The Banksia, [Banksia gibbosa]
Engraving, published by I. Debrett, 29 December 1789

This illustration of the seed pods of a unique plant from the genus *Banksia* was published in *Journal of a voyage to New South Wales* by John White in 1790.

(State Library of Victoria Collection)

BELOW:
Banksia coccinea [Scarlet banksia]
Hand-coloured engraving by Ferdinand Bauer, published in Illustrations florae Novae Hollandie, *London, 1813*
(State Library of Victoria Collection)

astronomer John Crosley, natural history painter Ferdinand Bauer, and Banks's man, naturalist Robert Brown.

At the turn of the century Sir Joseph Banks began to slow down. Once a vital, energetic, outdoors type of fellow, he now suffered severely from gout, especially in the winter months; by 1804 he was almost unable to walk. He had to be pushed to meetings of the Royal Society in a bathchair.

Although his mind was still active and his interest in scientific matters was as vigorous as ever, Banks's power over his physical world was slowly slipping away from him. Realising that he could not go on much longer, he resigned from his presidency of the Royal Society in May 1820. The society refused to accept, and in honour of his long service to the scientific community he was asked to withdraw his resignation.

But his time was at an end; he died only a few months later. At seven in the morning on 19 June 1820 the 'father of Australia' breathed his last.

RIGHT:
Sir Joseph Banks
Engraving after Thomas Lawrence, 1810

Banks was awarded the title of baronet in 1781 in recognition of his contribution to the world of science. He had been president of the Royal Society for thirty-two years when this portrait was drawn.

He had become a gentleman of great influence, whose opinions on many matters, especially concerning the development of the colony beneath the Southern Cross, was sought right up to the end of his life.

Banks never lost interest in Australia. His voyage to New South Wales had put him at the forefront of scientific discovery; his expertise had consolidated his pre-eminence.

(Collection: National Portrait Gallery, Canberra)

John Macarthur

1767–1834

The scheming father of Australia's wool industry

John Macarthur is featured on the face of the $2 paper note, first issued in 1966.

Opposite:
Gentleman John Macarthur
Oil on canvas, artist unknown

Macarthur was a charmer, a scheming rogue who had a good eye for a fine fleece, and a good mind to market it.

With five rams and two ewes obtained from the flocks of King George III in Kew, England, Macarthur bred the foundations of the Australian wool industry.

(Dixson Gallery, State Library of New South Wales Collection)

Above:
Elizabeth Macarthur 1766-1850
Oil on canvas, artist unknown
(State Library of New South Wales Collection)

But for the fact that John Macarthur laid the foundations of the great Australian wool industry, there is little else in his inglorious record to recommend him. Macarthur was a scheming, pettifogging, devious and often seditious individual with pretensions to aristocracy and a disdain for any official who dared to thwart his desires.

The truth is, he spent so much time away from his farm, both fighting against a succession of colonial governors and back in England to face court martial for sedition, that it was his wife Elizabeth who truly created the breed known today as the Australian merino.

Yet it is John Macarthur who stands large today, remembered as the founder of the Australian wool industry, just as he stood larger than life in the affairs of the colonial penal settlement of New South Wales.

John Macarthur was born in Plymouth, Devonshire, England, in 1767. He was the son of Alexander Macarthur, who had once fought for Prince Charles Edward at the battle of Culloden in 1745 and who had taken refuge in the West Indies until the memory of old alliances had died down. Alexander had returned to establish a business in Plymouth shortly before the birth of his son John.

With this background it seemed that John Macarthur was destined for service in the military. He was educated at a private school, joining the service as an ensign in 1782. On half-pay due to the lack of any wars that needed the attention of the British Army, he began to study

Elizabeth Macarthur (née Veale)

There is no doubt that it was really Elizabeth Macarthur who was responsible for the care and breeding of the Australian merino.

The daughter of an English country gentleman, Elizabeth had sufficient knowledge of country matters to carry on the work started by her husband before his many absences in court and overseas.

She had settled immediately into Australian colonial life, taking great pleasure in her property, Elizabeth Farm. In a letter written in September 1798 she described the countryside of New South Wales as like an English park. She wrote: 'we enjoy here one of the finest climates in the world. The necessaries of life are abundant, and a fruitful soil affords us many luxuries … the fruit and vegetable gardens are extensive and produce very well. As well [we] have 120 acres planted with wheat …'[1]

It is a pity that her husband apparently spent so little time enjoying it.

for the bar, but was recalled to duty in 1788, the year of the First Fleet and the founding of the penal colony of New South Wales.

He had just married Elizabeth Veale, the daughter of a country gentleman, when he was commissioned as lieutenant to the newly formed New South Wales Corps, a body made up of all those military officers considered unsuitable for any other commission than to guard the convicts being sent out to Botany Bay. The private soldiers were gathered from the streets of London; probably the only difference between them and the lags they were guarding was the uniform they wore.

But before they had raised anchor, Macarthur was already showing the kind of feisty, argumentative and petulant character that was to mark him for all his time in New South Wales. He quarrelled with his captain before they departed and challenged him to a duel. They faced each other, the duel was fought but neither was injured. This may have been the first but it was certainly not the last time in Macarthur's long career that he was prepared to face down an adversary.

Macarthur and the New South Wales Corps set sail on the *Neptune* on 14 November 1789; with Elizabeth and their first child on board, it was the first ship to carry an educated and free woman to New South Wales.

The *Neptune* finally dropped anchor in Port Jackson on 28 June 1790. Before the year was over Macarthur had again quarrelled with a fellow officer and challenged him to a duel. This time Lieutenant John Macarthur faced Captain Nicholas Nepean; neither was injured and reconciliation ensured that the matter went no further. Once again Macarthur had vented his displeasure, once again he had not faced any repercussions from higher military authorities. This began a pattern of behaviour that was to see him before the courts time and again over the ensuing years.

The New South Wales Corps had control over virtually all trade and commerce in the new settlement. Although there was already a handful of free settlers who had been granted farming lands around the district, and they were prospering with the assistance of convict labour, the corps controlled the import and export of all goods, and, in the absence of any hard currency, usually paid the settlers for their produce with promissory notes or liquor.

On 25 February 1793 the *Shah Hermuzear* arrived in port from Calcutta with a mixed cargo including 100 Bengal sheep. This hardy, hairy and fast-growing breed, more valued for its meat than for its wool, was quickly snapped up by various farmer–officers eager

The New South Wales Corps

The commander of the recently formed New South Wales Corps, Major Francis Grose, arrived in the colony on 14 February 1792, on board the *Pitt*. He was accompanied by the final company of men who would replace the soldiers of the First Fleet.

The members of the corps were a mixed bag. Some of the officers were well connected from famous regiments, and many noncommissioned officers were veterans of the American wars. Their numbers were raised under a bonus system which benefited the officers for each man they enlisted. As a result quite a lot of the privates were not of the highest military standards, and had poor records; some had even been released from military gaols, prepared to suffer virtual exile for their 'freedom'.

Macarthur, who had abandoned England, leaving behind him a debt of over £500, had arrived two years earlier with Captain Nicholas Nepean and Captain James Hill.

The fellow who was to become his nemesis over the years to come, former military officer Richard Atkins, was also on board the *Pitt*. Atkins was also fleeing from debt; his was £800.

to add them to their breeding stock. Macarthur was prominent among them; he had taken a great interest in the science of animal husbandry and it was from these, and other animals he was to avail himself of some years later, that he was able to build the breed that began the Australian wool industry.

By the end of the following year, Macarthur expanded his land-holdings to 250 acres with the grant of some land along the Parramatta River, where he built the substantial homestead he named Elizabeth Farm in honour of his wife. On this excellent grazing land he was the first in Australia to cut the earth with a plough. He began to grow wheat with seeds he had imported from India and from Ireland, and experimented with the crossbreeding of sheep for the production of wool.

ABOVE:

Captains Hunter, Collins & Johnston, with Governor Phillip, Surgeon White &c. Visiting a Distressed Female Native of New South Wales at a Hut near Port Jackson

Engraving published by Alexander Hogg, 31 August 1793 (London)

(Rex Nan Kivell Collection NK2799. By permission, National Library of Australia)

Gentlemen of destiny

Most of these military officers were to play a significant role in the battles with Macarthur. Some stood against him; Hunter withstood Macarthur's attacks for years over his appointment of Thomas Atkins to the magistrate's bench, and his rulings on the monopoly over the sale of wines and spirits.

Others stood beside him; Johnston, who had been the hero of the Castle Hill insurrection by Irish prisoners in 1804, became the acting governor after he and Macarthur plotted successfully for the overthrow of Governor King's successor William Bligh in 1808.

But agricultural success was not enough for John Macarthur. He enjoyed the privileges afforded the military circle in the penal colony, and was protective of the power he and his fellow officers continued to exert over all the affairs of the colony. Control over the importation, supply and sale of all wines and spirits was central to their power, so on 23 January 1796 Governor Hunter came face to face with the corps after he banned the distillation of spirits. In direct defiance of the governor, the corps responded with the destruction of the house of carpenter's foreman, John Baughan, whose crime was to have caused the arrest of a fellow officer for leaving his post.

Hunter attempted to bring the perpetrators of this vengeful attack to justice but could establish no evidence against them until the free settlers, now in a state of alarm, afraid of the power assumed by the military men, prevailed upon surgeon and magistrate William Balmain to press Baughan to prosecute those responsible for the destruction of his house.

Macarthur intervened. He wrote to Balmain 'on behalf of his fellow officers', demanding to be told what advice he had given to the carpenter. Balmain taunted Macarthur in reply, accusing Macarthur of being 'a base rascal and an atrocious liar and villain', and waited upon his reply to this obvious challenge. Macarthur did not respond—he had fought enough duels—but his fellow officers wrote to Balmain offering to meet him one by one. This was the cowards' retreat; they knew well enough that Balmain could not engage them all. When Baughan finally agreed to prosecute, a general court martial was ordered.

Macarthur, feeling that this time he had gone too far, wrote to Hunter and expressed 'contrition and sincere concern for what had happened'. The corps offered to compensate Baughan for his loss; the warrants for their arrests were withdrawn.

Hunter continued to undermine their monopoly over the supply of alcohol in the colony. In April he issued ten new licences to allow the establishment of public houses. This again placed him head to head with the corps.

But it was Macarthur's pen that created more strife for him than anything else. When deputy judge advocate Richard Atkins reported the theft of some turnips from the governor's Parramatta garden, but refused to give up the man's name 'unless called to do so by a superior power', Macarthur admonished him, writing: 'It never has and I hope never will be, any part of my practice to conceal fraud, or screen offenders from punishment',

Land grants for the corps

By the end of 1791 the total amount of cleared land suitable for cultivation around Sydney and Parramatta was almost 1000 acres. The total of all livestock in the colony was six horses, sixteen cows, fifty-seven sheep and twenty-five pigs.

The government, both in England and in New South Wales, was keen to see productive settlement and encouraged noncommissioned officers and common soldiers to settle on lands granted to them after the expiry of their term of duty. Commissioned officers and free settlers were already able to negotiate land grants based on their particular circumstances, and in most cases, their influence with the governor and their social standing.

The rules for the granting of lands to noncommissioned officers and soldiers were as follows:

> To every non-commissioned officer, an allotment of 130 acres of land, if single; and 150, if married. To every private man, eighty acres, if single; one hundred, if married; and ten acres for each child at the time of granting the allotment; free of all taxes, quit-rents, and other acknowledgments, for the term of five years.[2]

Noncommissioned officers and privates were also induced to stay on in the corps by a further grant which doubled their allotment, plus £3 in their pocket—if they behaved well for five years. They could then pick up quite a considerable

obliquely advising Atkins that he was being derelict in his duty. His biggest insult to Atkins was in failing to address the letter to 'Richard Atkins Esquire'. Affronted by this slight, Atkins replied that any further letters sent to 'Mr Richard Atkins' would be returned unopened.

An earlier altercation between these two men had poisoned their relationship. In 1796 Macarthur had been convinced that Atkins, while dining with the governor, had criticised Macarthur's control of stores. As a result of this slight Macarthur had resigned from his post as inspector of public works, claiming that he no longer enjoyed 'the confidence which your Excellency was once pleased to express'. Although Governor Hunter had denied the accusation made against Atkins, in Macarthur's case a slight was an invitation to open warfare, even if it was totally imagined.

Judge Advocate Atkins (Esquire) was instructed to reveal the name of the turnip thief, and Macarthur was chided for forgetting his manners. Even though he had suffered a polite reprimand, this small victory encouraged Macarthur to broaden his attack on Atkins. He charged that Atkins 'had drawn bills

parcel of land free of taxes for the next decade, upon discharge from the corps. Upon discharge they would also receive 'a supply of clothing, a year's provisions, with seed-grain, tools, and implements of agriculture'.[3]

Thus, the First Fleeters became the first landholders in the colony. They had the pick of the best holdings and many built fortunes on the backs of the convicts they were charged with guarding.

For the officers there seemed little to prevent them from becoming true gentlemen; but for many, greed and pretensions to grandeur brought them into conflict with one another, and with a succession of governors who found the New South Wales Corps to be a constant adversary and a law unto itself.

ABOVE:

The residence of John Macarthur Esqre. near Parramatta. New South Wales

Hand-coloured aquatint published by J. Souter, 'Views in Australia', *1 April 1825 (London)*

Macarthur certainly selected an excellent site for the setting of the property he named 'Elizabeth Farm'. The homestead remains Australia's oldest building.

(State Library of New South Wales Collection)

BELOW:
Parramatta River
Watercolour drawing by John Hughes, 1826
The artist John Hughes was a lieutenant in the 3rd Regiment who had arrived in the colony in 1825.
Drawn on 12 July 1826, his watercolour of a bend in the river shows the original cottage at Vineyard (Rydalmere) as it was before it was rebuilt in 1836 by Hannibal, the nephew of John and Elizabeth Macarthur.
It was Hannibal Macarthur who stayed with Elizabeth while John was away fighting his battles, and together they built up the flocks which made all their fortune.
(State Library of New South Wales Collection)

without credit, was often drunk on duty, ill-treated convicts and [had] removed an official letter from a file'.

Almost forgetting how this whole affair had started, the pair fired off letter after letter to one another. To bring the unseemly argument to a head, Atkins demanded that the matter be brought before the court to put to rest the charges made against him. The Reverend Samuel Marsden heard the depositions made on behalf of Atkins; in each case they refuted Macarthur's allegations.

A letter from Hunter further encouraged Atkins. It concluded: 'I shall be glad to find that your public conduct has been less censurable than we have been informed'. Buoyed by this support from Hunter, Atkins fired off an attack on Macarthur, which ended with the words: 'the repugnance I feel at descending to an epistolary or any other altercation with a man of your principles'.

Macarthur took his opportunity to have the last word. He dipped his pen once again into the well of sarcasm. He wrote in reply: 'I am thankful for your letter as it has afforded me an opportunity of bringing to punishment a man [Corporal John Townsend] who is a disgrace to the British name and [a] dishonour to humanity'.

In the end Townsend, the 'turnip thief', was duly tried, and acquitted. It had been a right royal fuss over nothing.

In the same week as Townsend's farcical trial, both Hunter and Macarthur had written to the Home Secretary, each putting their own case as to how the colony should be governed. Macarthur's letter was in the manner of complaint, Hunter's one of rebuttal.

Macarthur proposed that he alone had the superior knowledge of agriculture and that he would be able to feed the colony himself if only the governor would give him more land and 100 more men to work it. He complained that too many in the colony capable of work were idle, that most fed off the government expense and that little public infrastructure was being created. He added an attack on Atkins to his proposal, claiming that vice in the colony was openly encouraged by such officials whose own example was 'openly dissipated and abandoned'.

On 15 April 1800 Lieutenant Governor King arrived in the colony from England with a dispatch recalling Governor Hunter and notifying him of his replacement by King.

Although Hunter had spent most of his service in the colony at loggerheads with the officers of the New South Wales Corps, they all lined the road to the wharf and 'attended [him] with every mark of respect, attachment and regret'. It is a shame that they refused him the same when he was in office.

Philip Gidley King

Macarthur was rarely happy with any of the vice-regal appointments to Government House. He rarely approved of any of the succession of Governors sent to Parramatta and railed against each and every one until they were either recalled or requested an end to their posting. He was not about to change tack for Philip Gidley King.

Macarthur continued to undermine the office of the governor. He allowed rumours to spread abroad about the contents of a letter written by Lieutenant Colonel William Paterson to Sir Joseph Banks, which was critical of King. Paterson had foolishly let Macarthur see this letter, and Macarthur made sure that King was aware of its content.

Paterson then knew that he must challenge Macarthur lest it be thought that he too had fallen into the pastoralist's sphere; not to do so would further destabilise the colony. He challenged Macarthur to a duel.

When they faced each other Macarthur shot Paterson in the shoulder and was immediately placed under house arrest. Although King ordered his release some time later, Macarthur demanded that he be re-arrested and sent to England for court martial; he wanted to save his name from 'public disgrace'. The ship that carried the prisoner to England also carried the indictment against him. Curiously, this rather large document never reached England's shores; the part Macarthur had played in its disappearance can only be speculated.

LEFT:

Philip Gidley and Anna Joseph King, and their children Elizabeth, Anna Maria and Philip Parker

Watercolour by Robert Dighton, 1799

Dighton painted this family portrait in the year that King was to leave for New South Wales to take up his appointment as governor.

Anna Maria and Philip Parker King, who had both been born on Norfolk Island, stayed in England, not seeing their parents again until 1807, after King was recalled from the colony to be replaced by William Bligh.

(State Library of New South Wales Collection)

ABOVE:
Camden Park House
Watercolour by Conrad Martens, 1843
This painting of the Macarthur property at what was once known as 'the cowpastures' was commissioned shortly after the house was completed in 1843.

The finished work was sent to relatives in England by James Macarthur's wife Emily, daughter-in-law of John and Elizabeth Macarthur.

It was brought back to Australia at the turn of the century and returned to Camden in 1931. It remained there until 1947.

(State Library of New South Wales Collection)

At Macarthur's court martial, the lack of any official complaint against him laid the prosecution low. Macarthur was at best a charming rogue, at worst a scheming liar; in the English court his charm was most in evidence. He soon won over those meant to discipline him and had the Colonial Office eating out of his hand. He had taken samples of his wool and impressed all who saw them with the quality of his New South Wales fleece.

In England, Macarthur was also warmly received by the Privy Council for Trade and

Macarthur's flocks

Macarthur began to breed his flocks by crossing the small Bengal sheep, which had been brought to the colony by Governor King in 1793, with the larger Cape breed. Although he was excited by the results and sent a sample of cloth woven from the improved breed to England in 1798, he was still not completely satisfied.

At the time, England was hostile to both France and Spain and could no longer rely on wool from those regions. Macarthur saw the opportunity to succeed if he could only create the right sort of flocks to satisfy the British demand for wool.

The sheep that had been brought out to Australia were only suitable for butchering, their wool coarse and unsuitable for the needs of British weavers. He wanted to import some of the Spanish merino breed from England which had been a gift from the Spanish royal court to the English king. After the Privy Council for Trade and Foreign Plantations Committee had declared itself in favour of Macarthur's vision for a merino stud in the colony, he was able to purchase seven rams and two ewes from a stud sale at the King's own farm in Kew.

Given the state of relations across the Channel, the English royal court was probably also pleased to be able to put some of the Spanish beasts into

Foreign Plantations, which agreed to support him in the development of a new colonial wool industry.

He resigned his commission in England and returned to Australia aboard the *Argo* in June 1805; this time he came as a gentleman farmer. He had been the beneficiary of a very successful trip to England for his court martial.

Rather than being disgraced, Macarthur returned with his lands enlarged; a further 5000 acres had been granted to him by Lord Camden. He had also acquired seven rams and two ewes from the King's own stud at Kew, the Spanish merino stud animals that he had long desired.

Lord Camden, the highest colonial authority, had commissioned him to establish a wool industry in Australia. In October 1805 Governor King approved the grant of 5000 acres of excellent grazing land at 'the cowpastures', later renamed Camden, and 30 more convicts to help Macarthur farm it.

The arrival of Bligh

By the time Governor William Bligh arrived in 1806 as his replacement, Governor Philip Gidley King had become a disappointed and dissolute gentleman unable to rein in the excesses of the Rum Corps. Bligh immediately set himself on a course that would bring him face to face with the imperious Macarthur.

On the day that he arrived and even before he had stepped ashore, Bligh noticed barrels of rum being unloaded from a nearby schooner. He was furious at the sight of the cause of so much corruption and dissipation being carried ashore before his very eyes. On the evidence of this first sighting of the colony he described the place as 'a sink of iniquity'.

The officers of the New South Wales Corps, now effectively under Bligh's command, had been accustomed to acting as a de facto administration in their own right. They controlled all aspects of the law, they were the judges, and they made up the juries and the military courts. They were effectively the law, and they were a law unto themselves.

In the absence of any real currency, rum became the tradable item. Labourers were paid in rum; a few barrels of rum could buy an acre of wheat. The corps still had the sole rights to control the sale of liquor and therefore controlled the economy and all trade in and out of the colony. Most of the officers in the garrison were amassing solid fortunes from their commission to New South Wales. Pity the poor governor who sought to change this well-established status quo.

the hands of the one breeder who was confident of creating a product that would rival the dominance of Spanish wool.

The experiment with breeding from the merino exceeded all expectations. Before long Macarthur was proudly exclaiming the qualities and quantity of the improved fleeces that came from his flocks:

> ... as a proof of the extraordinary and rapid improvement in my flocks, I have exhibited the fleece of a coarse-woolled ewe that has been valued at nine-pence a pound, and the fleece of her lamb, begotten by a Spanish ram, which is allowed to be worth three shillings a pound. When I left Port Jackson, the heaviest fleece that had then been shorn weighed only three pounds and a half; but I have received reports of 1802, from which I learn that the fleece of my sheep had increased to five pounds each, and was softer than the wool of the preceding year. The beauty of it indeed is such to cause it to be estimated at six shillings the pound.[4]

Macarthur had built his flocks up to four thousand by 1802. The Reverend Samuel Marsden had about half that number and several other colonists had flocks from three to eight hundred head each.

The age of Australian wool had begun.

But Bligh thought he could. He tried to rally the support of the free settlers and others outside the military circle.

Bligh often treated his subordinates as children, and he had a reputation as a short-tempered and abusive man; he had just faced court martial for abusing one of his officers aboard the HMS *Warrior* and had been censured for his 'ill-tempered language'. Despite this, he was popular with the settlers, who were ever at the mercy of the Rum Corps.

Right from the start Bligh was made aware of division within the colony. In an unusually obsequious attempt to curry favour, Macarthur presumed to welcome Bligh to the colony 'on behalf of the free citizens'. The fact that he had not informed the free citizens of his address on their behalf infuriated them. The Sydney settlers claimed that Macarthur was an 'unfit person to step forward on such an occasion'. The disgruntled group of Hawkesbury settlers petitioned the governor for a 'bill of rights' that would protect them from the clutches of the corps.

Bligh saw a colony divided: on the one side the settlers, and many officials; on the other, Macarthur and the New South Wales Corps.

When Bligh attempted to curb the excesses of the corps, he came up against a body of men unused to interference in their affairs and unwilling to surrender their privileges. Although Macarthur was no longer a serving officer, he was never prepared to subordinate his activities for the governor's pleasure.

When Bligh dismissed principal surgeon Jamieson from his office of magistrate in September 1807, Macarthur began a prolonged attack on the governor in defence of his ally. Macarthur was charged with sedition and brought to trial.

Even before he was brought to trial Macarthur was agitating to annoy the governor. In defiance of the advice of Surveyor General Grimes who had told him that the governor would not permit any building on leased land, he constructed a fence on some Crown land he had leased under King's

RIGHT:

Rear Admiral William Bligh

Watercolour on ivory by Alexander Huey, 1814

Bligh was one of the most notorious of the naval officers of his generation. A short-tempered, often belligerent and abusive man, who treated his crew as if they were his children, he suffered a mutiny on board his ship HMS *Bounty* in 1789.

The insurrection against his authority was led by John Adams and his crew, who had fallen in love with the islands of the Pacific, and with its bare-breasted, bronzed beauties, and saw no joy in returning to mist-shrouded, miserable old England. They rose up against Bligh and his officers, setting them adrift in a longboat in the middle of the ocean.

It is a credit to Bligh's ability as a navigator that he sailed back to civilisation without loss of life.

(National Library of Australia Collection)

administration on Church Hill in Sydney Town.

In fact, Bligh wanted to resume control of such leases and had offered leaseholders plots in other parts of the settlement in lieu. Few wanted to move — some had built dwellings on the land — and Macarthur, ever eager to be in the vanguard of a fight against the governor, threw up his fence.

Bligh ordered the removal of the fence and offered Macarthur some land at the end of Pitt's Row, 'a place where the common gallows stood, and which was surrounded by all the vile and infamous characters of the town of Sydney'. Bligh knew the value of a well-placed insult, and so did Macarthur.

In October, Macarthur entered court yet again; this time his complaint was the confiscation of two stills that he had imported into the colony. Bligh had seized the stills as they arrived on board the *Dart* on 9 March, just a month after he had issued a general order prohibiting distilling.

Although Macarthur had removed the stills from the stores, purportedly to take out goods that were packed inside them, they had been reimpounded by Naval Officer Robert Campbell. It was Campbell who stood opposite Macarthur in court defending the accusation of unlawful seizure. Macarthur gave a stirring speech in praise of 'unbridled private enterprise in the cloak of defence of liberty'.

When the sedition trial began on 25 January 1808, other events had overtaken the original charge. Atkins had circulated a public notice that announced the escape of a prisoner on board Macarthur's jointly owned ship the *Parramatta.* This serious breach of the regulations demanded the loss of the bond of £800 posted by all ship owners as a surety against absconders. When the ship returned to port, Naval Officer Campbell refused to pass the ship's papers and placed the *Parramatta* under arrest.

Macarthur accused Campbell of virtually dispossessing him of the *Parramatta* and simply gave up the ship; he notified the master and crew, saying, 'I have abandoned the said schooner, and [state] that neither you nor them are henceforth to look to me for pay or provisions'.

A week later the crew, desperate for provisions, came ashore. They went to Atkins and informed him of Macarthur's move to subvert his obligation to the bond. Atkins immediately wrote to Macarthur demanding that he appear before him in court the following day to 'shew cause for such conduct'. Macarthur replied that he was no longer responsible for the *Parramatta* and that for

Macarthur calls in old debts

As part of a sustained attack on Governor Bligh, Macarthur attempted to embarrass those close to him. In July 1807 he began by claiming the payment of £341 10s on a promissory note from Andrew Thompson, the colony's largest grain grower and a close associate of the governor.

Thompson had signed the note for 99 bushels of wheat, which was valued before the Hawkesbury floods of 1799 at £34 10s. Macarthur's claim was based on the post-flood price, but was thrown out by the governor based on a recent order that all notes were to be honoured in currency, not goods.

Macarthur then turned his attention to Judge Advocate Atkins. In December he demanded that Atkins pay £26 6s on a bill drawn on him in February 1793. He wrote to Bligh, laying before him the history of his claim and warning him of 'the unhappy effects it might produce on the morals of the colony if it should appear that a judge resists the payment of a just debt'.

Macarthur had once again dipped his pen in the well of sarcasm — and added a little vitriol.

BELOW:
Arrest of Governor Bligh, 26 January 1808
Pencil and watercolour by John Smart, 1808

Major Johnston and John Macarthur, followed by the troopers of the New South Wales Corps, marched on Government House on 26 January 1808, coincidentally the twentieth anniversary of the arrival of the First Fleet.

Bligh had secreted himself beneath a cot in the servants' quarters; he later claimed that he was actually attempting to hide his private papers beneath a mattress stored there.

The popular view among the troops was that he was trying to hide himself beneath the cot; his daughter was the only member of the household who put up any resistance at all to his arrest.

(National Library of Australia Collection)

further information he should refer to Campbell, who had seized the boat.

Eventually, Macarthur was arrested for breach of regulations and came before the magistrate's bench, which included Major Johnston and Naval Officer Campbell; he was bailed and committed for trial before the Criminal Court.

Macarthur's old adversary Richard Atkins was appointed judge advocate for the trial; Macarthur objected. He harangued Atkins in court until Atkins actually left the building to seek advice from Bligh, claiming that Macarthur was defaming him in court. This left Macarthur in court in the charge of six of his former fellow officers, who all agreed that the defendant had a point and asked Bligh to replace Atkins. When the governor refused, in the absence of the judge advocate, they simply closed the court, claiming that they were holding Macarthur in their protective custody, as he was fearful for his life.

Bligh summoned Major George Bain Johnston to Government House to defuse the situation, but Johnston politely declined, pleading ill health. As his last act of this day Bligh issued an escape warrant against Macarthur.

26 January 1808

On 26 January 1808, the twentieth anniversary of the arrival of the First Fleet, Provost Marshall William Gore ordered the arrest of Macarthur. The court again wrote to Bligh requesting the removal of Atkins from the bench, and as a conciliatory gesture, suggested a return of Macarthur to his original bail conditions.

But it appears that events had moved too quickly for any peaceful resolution to this already heated impasse. Bligh ignored the court's requests.

By mid-afternoon the officers had again assembled; this time they were to charge Gore

for his arrest of Macarthur. Atkins advised Bligh that this action had brought the officers into a direct challenge of the authority of the judiciary and therefore the government itself. He declared that the officers were attempting to incite rebellion.

Bligh summoned the officers to come before him one by one the following day, but this order would never be carried out.

Major Johnston made a remarkable recovery from his malaise of the previous day and rode in from his property to Sydney, where he met with several merchants and officers. He then rode on to the barracks and called the men to arms. Macarthur was released and joined him for a march on Government House.

With a fife-and-drum band playing 'The British Grenadiers', their bayonets fixed and muskets charged, the rum-primed New South Wales Corps straggled along behind Johnston and Macarthur as they stormed the steps of the governor's residence.

Bligh offered no resistance to the 'rebels'—he was clearly outnumbered—and it was only his daughter, the recently widowed Mary Putland, who attempted to defend the office of the governor. She stood her ground and dared the troops to 'stab me to the heart, but to respect the life of my father'. Her father, however, was nowhere to be found. After a thorough search of all quarters, Governor Bligh was eventually discovered beneath a bed in one of the servants' rooms. He later claimed that he had been attempting to hide his official papers in one of the mattresses stored there. He said that he had planned to lay low until he could make his escape to the Hawkesbury district, to rouse the settlers there he believed would support him in a stand against Macarthur. Very few believed this; the image of the governor cowering beneath a servant's cot was a much more satisfying image for the troops and officers of the Rum Corps.

The troops who discovered Governor Bligh allowed him to dress in full regalia before he was brought down to meet Major Johnston and Macarthur. Johnston then arrested Bligh, and, assuming the commanding role of governor himself, took control of the colony. In order to ensure his absolute authority and to re-establish order, martial law was declared.

That night, even under the rigour of martial law, the streets of Sydney were filled with licentious and drunken revelry. Liquor was liberally, indeed profusely, served to all the soldiers, while bonfires blazed in all parts of the town, and scenes of riot, tumult and insubordination ensued.

The trial of John Macarthur continued, ending on 6 February with his acquittal. The

D'Arcy Wentworth vindicated

In August 1807 surgeon D'Arcy Wentworth, father of emancipist William Wentworth, was another 'victim' of the tyranny of Governor Bligh. Wentworth was charged with the misuse of convict patients and suspended from his position at Parramatta Hospital. He had been accused of transferring convicts who had come into his hospital as patients to his own employ after they had recovered. They remained on the hospital books and were therefore maintained by the government purse for Wentworth's profit. Wentworth was publicly reprimanded with a court martial, Bligh added the further insult of suspension from duty.

Although he denied the charges made against him, Wentworth was not permitted to defend himself.

In February 1808 D'Arcy Wentworth was fully absolved of all charges brought against him by Bligh's administration. Bligh had been deposed, and 'hard on the heels of the "retrial" of John Macarthur … another victim of the "tyranny" of Governor Bligh [was] vindicated', by new judge Captain Anthony Fenn Kemp of the New South Wales Corps.

arrest warrant was declared invalid and his speech to the magistrates not held to be seditious. A week later he was appointed colonial secretary in the administration of the self-promoted Lieutenant Governor Johnston.

In time, the officer who had the unfortunate duty of arresting Macarthur on 26 January was transported to Norfolk Island for seven years, convicted of perjury.

The arrival of Foveaux and Macquarie

Lieutenant Colonel Joseph Foveaux, who had been on his way to take command of Norfolk Island, arrived in the colony on board the *Sinclair* on 29 July 1808. As the most senior of all legitimate serving officers in the region, he simply assumed command of the colony of New South Wales from Major Johnston. It was almost six months since Bligh had been deposed and Foveaux saw no reason to reinstate him or to dispense with the administration of Johnston and Macarthur, until such time that advice could be received from London.

Part of the ensuing advice was the recall of the New South Wales Corps to England. Lord Castlereagh, Secretary of State for War and the Colonies, decided that having a fixed corps in the settlement was 'productive of many evils'. Castlereagh believed that the colony could not be managed until the officers and troops who had played such a decisive role in the insurrection against Bligh were disbanded.

Foveaux was concerned that Bligh was delaying his departure and possibly attempting to gather strength from some of the settlers for a possible pitch to regain control.

Bligh was under house arrest for over a year; his continued presence in the colony was an embarrassment to the rebels and a continued nuisance to Foveaux and to Lieutenant Colonel William Paterson, whom Foveaux had requested to assist him in government. Theoretically, Bligh remained the supreme commander of all the king's ships in the South Pacific, and in this capacity he had ordered Foveaux to arrest the 'rebels' as soon as he landed — but to no avail.

In December 1809 the new governor, Colonel Lachlan Macquarie, arrived on the *Dromedary*, escorted by the *Hindustan* and his own regiment. On 31 December the company marched up from the docks to Government House, where he took command.

RIGHT:
Colonel William Paterson, 1755-1810
Artist unknown.

Lieutenant Colonel Foveaux requested the assistance of Lieutenant Colonel Paterson in re-establishing order in the colony.

As this was the same man whom Macarthur had fought and severely wounded in a duel, it is no surprise that Macarthur's hold on the affairs of the colony was short-lived.

When Colonel Lachlan Macquarie arrived in 1809, plans for Macarthur's removal from any position of influence were already well under way. Macarthur and his fellow conspirator Johnston were soon dispatched to England to face trial for their insurrection against Bligh.

(State Library of New South Wales Collection)

BELOW:
Vineyard at Camden
Watercolour by Elizabeth Macarthur-Onslow, c. 1860
Macarthur didn't waste his time in England; among other things he spent time studying the science of oenology, a study that his son William later took up with great benefit to the fledgling Australian wine industry.
(National Library of Australia Collection)

Macquarie was not going to be outdone by Macarthur. In over thirty years of service this 47-year-old son of a poor Scottish farmer had risen through the ranks to the position of deputy adjutant-general of the British Army; he was now governor of the colony of New South Wales.

Macquarie set about his reforms. Atkins was removed and replaced by Judge Advocate Ellis Bent. The New South Wales Corps was replaced by the 73rd Regiment, whose most recent posting was on the Indian subcontinent, and Major Johnston and gentleman farmer Macarthur were dispatched aboard the *Admiral Gambier*, bound for trial in England. This time Macarthur was facing the charge of treason.

Macarthur's last stand

As Macarthur was now a private citizen, he was originally set to face trial in Sydney; Major Johnston faced court martial in London. This arrangement didn't suit Macarthur at all. He had few friends among the settlers; his only supporters were in the New South Wales Corps, and they had long departed from the colony. Macarthur decided to take himself off to England to stand trial there, confident that his charming manners and financial success would once again win over the courtroom.

In 1811 Major Johnston was found guilty of mutiny and was cashiered out of the army. Macarthur remained in England in virtual exile, unable to return to the colony lest he be re-arrested. Lord Castlereagh instructed Macquarie that 'if examinations be sworn against him [Macarthur] charging him with criminal acts you will have him arrested and brought to trial'.

Macarthur stayed in England for a further eight years. Throughout this time his wife Elizabeth, with the assistance of their nephew Hannibal, ran the business of the farm. She perfected the breeding program that produced the fine Merino for which Australia became world-renowned, she managed the shearing and she sent the bales of wool for weaving to the mills of England.

After repeated petitions to the Colonial Office, permission was finally granted for the return of Macarthur to Australia, provided that he would not attempt to play any role in public affairs. Macarthur had not wasted his time in England: he had spent some time studying agriculture, with particular interest in oenology, a science that was put to good use on his return home. He returned to Australia in September 1817 accompanied by his two sons, William and James, who had been furthering their education in England.

Macarthur may have presumed to take up where he had left off, but those around him thought otherwise. It was apparent from his failing health and erratic behaviour that the once fiery adversary of a succession of vice-regal appointees had lost much of his influence, and even much of his control over his own farms,which had been so successfully managed by Elizabeth while he was absent.

Exclusives vs emancipists

Macarthur kept his own counsel for a while but eventually broke his silence in a letter to King's Commissioner John Thomas Bigge on 19 December 1821, outlining his scheme to establish an aristocracy of landowners to rule the colony. His rambling, often intemperate letter explained his scheme in favour of the 'exclusives' already established on their lands. He wrote of 'establishing a body of really respectable settlers, men of real capital, not needy adventurers … who have estates of at least 10,000 acres and reserves contiguous' and proposed that these exclusives would use the 'labour of any number of convicts or paupers Great Britain may send forth'.

Macarthur thought it would be a good idea to virtually enslave the multitude in the production of cheap wool, to enrich the few, like himself. Of course, Macarthur would be among the few who would benefit from such an enterprise. His plan involved giving landowners the powers to punish their labourers, including the withholding of food for up to a week. It was really the excesses of the Rum Corps revisited as capitalist enterprise, under the guise of aristocratic benevolence.

Few settlers agreed with his proposal. The new Governor Macquarie had laid the

RIGHT:

Major George Johnston, 1764-1823

Lithograph, artist unknown

Johnston had been the hero of the Castle Hill Rising of Irish convicts in 1804, when he stood up against the rebel leader Philip Cunningham. He placed his pistol against Cunningham's temple and asked him what he wanted. Cunningham replied: 'Death or liberty'. Johnston obliged him the following day, when Cunningham was hanged without trial. On the day of the uprising, fifteen of the convicts were shot, nine were hanged later, and many more were flogged.

Lieutenant Colonel Paterson commanded 150 armed troops from HMS *Calcutta* in the affray.

(State Library of New South Wales Collection)

foundations of continued support of the emancipist cause and native-born Australians such as William Wentworth railed against Macarthur and the exclusives. Governor Macquarie was to be the victim of continued attack by the exclusives. They argued against his support of the emancipists, and his desire to create a 'happy home' for every emancipated convict and bring principles of 'morality, virtue and temperance' to the colony.

Macquarie returned to England on 15 February 1822. It was other sheep-raising landowners such as the Reverend Samuel Marsden, as well as Macarthur, who had managed to raise concerns over Governor Macquarie's 'reasonable' treatment of the convict class.

The exclusives were pleased with the arrival of the new governor, Sir Thomas Brisbane, in December 1821. Brisbane was set to pursue a stricter policy on convict matters than Macquarie, and was keen to review the system of land grants. Over 340,000 acres were withheld from release until he determined new policy towards emancipists. Although Brisbane's conservative attitudes to penal reforms may have set the emancipist cause back a decade, it would appear that he was more like Macquarie than the exclusives would have wished, and did eventually pursue an enlightened course of action.

In October 1825, at the end of Brisbane's term, a public meeting was held to farewell him. William Wentworth praised the departing governor for continuing Macquarie's policies in regards to the emancipist cause, denouncing the exclusives as 'the yellow snakes of the colony' and the 'embodiment of privilege, monopoly and autocracy', all of which were the hallmark of the Rum Corps.

In the face of such an attack on his class, Macarthur re-entered the political arena in 1825, when in an apparent act of public clemency he was appointed to the Legislative Council.

But in council Macarthur was not the fire-eater of old; his erratic behaviour and continued outbursts destroyed any authority he had once assumed. When his son John Macarthur died in 1831 while studying in England, the flame seemed to go out of the irascible old man altogether. He gradually descended into madness and ended his days a lunatic.

John Macarthur died in a cottage on his estate, Camden Park, on 10 April 1834, aged 67. Three sons and three daughters survived him. Elizabeth lived on for another thirty-three years, running the farm as she had always done. In spite of all the troubles he had brought to her door, she had stood faithfully by her husband, supporting him to the end.

'Gentleman' George Johnston

Gentleman George Johnston returned to New South Wales on 30 May 1813. While he was away in England to face court martial he had left his property in the care of an agent. He was obviously confident that he could make his return, assume the lands granted to him as an officer in the New South Wales Corps and resume the life of the gentleman farmer. Johnston was granted land at Bankstown by Governor King in April 1815. Part of his property was bequeathed to his son David, who later served as a councillor in Liverpool. David Johnston also benefited by a grant of land in the Illawarra district from Governor Macquarie in 1827.

Although George Johnston built a prosperous life on the farm, the former hero of the Castle Hill Rising of 1804 had little further influence on public affairs. He died in 1823.

Mary Reibey

1777–1855

Mary Reibey is featured on the face of the $20 polymer note, first issued in 1994.

The transported horse thief from Lancashire achieved the two main aims of the emancipist: affluence and respectability

Opposite:
Miss Mary Reibey [née Haydock]
Portrait medallion, c. 1820

Transportee Mary Haydock was one of the prominent emancipists who helped to build the foundations of Sydney society.

Born in Bray, Lancashire, England, she was convicted of horse stealing in 1790, sentenced to seven years and was transported to Botany Bay in 1792.

She married Thomas Reibey two years later, and after his death in 1811 continued to develop and manage his various business interests, eventually becoming one of the largest property owners in Sydney in the first half of the nineteenth century.

(State Library of New South Wales Collection)

MARY HAYDOCK WAS BORN ON 12 MAY 1777 IN BRAY, Lancashire, England. When she was only two years old both of her parents died and Mary, along with her older sister Elizabeth, went to live with one of their grandmothers. In contrast to her quiet, shy sister, Mary was a tomboyish child who enjoyed the rough and tumble of play with her cousins. Her aunts would shake their heads and wonder what would become of this young girl who seemed so headstrong and unladylike. Her grandmother died when Mary was thirteen and she was sent out to work. She was put into service, which she hated so much that she decided to run away.

She disguised herself as a boy, took the name James Barrow and stole a horse. When she rode up to the door of the Swan Inn near Stafford and offered her 'uncle's fine brood mare with saddle and bridle' for sale for £17, some prospective customers became a little suspicious. Horse stealing was one of the more serious crimes at that time, and taking ownership of a horse without proper identification was a dangerous business. When it became obvious that the uncle

Right:
Convict hulks at Gravesend, England
Oil on canvas by Nicholas Condy, c. 1830

Convict hulks lay at anchor all along the southern coastline of England. Convicts such as Mary Haydock waited aboard these decommissioned battleships until a transport could be filled to take them to the penal colony of New South Wales.

Mary arrived in the colony aboard the *Royal Admiral* in October 1792.

(Rex Nan Kivell Collection NK6062. By permission, National Library of Australia)

didn't exist and the horse was stolen, 'James Barrow' was arrested and thrown into the all-male prison at Stafford. When Mary was brought into court, she was charged under the name of James Barrow. She was convicted of theft and sentenced to be hanged. It was only after she had been reprieved from the noose and her sentence changed to transportation to the colony of New South Wales for seven years, that her true identity was discovered.

Before she was to embark on her long journey into the unknown, Mary was brought before the prison doctor to be 'medically examined and cleansed'. During this examination her true gender and identity were revealed. It was only after being found out that she turned to her family for help.

Her teachers and her family petitioned the courts to let her go. They pleaded that she was 'a high-spirited and wilful lass who had been tricked into selling a horse by a passing scoundrel'. Whether this was true will never be known, but the judge, although insisting on her guilt, offered Mary her freedom only if she were taken back into the charge of her family. But nobody wanted her; her relatives didn't want this 'convict lass' to stain their own children. So she was left to the courts. Now fifteen years old, Mary, along with six other female and 289 male prisoners, climbed the gangway up into the transport ship in May 1792, bound for Botany Bay.

She arrived in the colony aboard the *Royal Admiral* in October 1792. She was lucky to have travelled aboard the *Royal Admiral*, as it

BELOW:

Letter written by transportee Mary Haydock to her aunt Mrs Hope in Blackburn, Lancashire, in 1792

(State Library of New South Wales Collection)

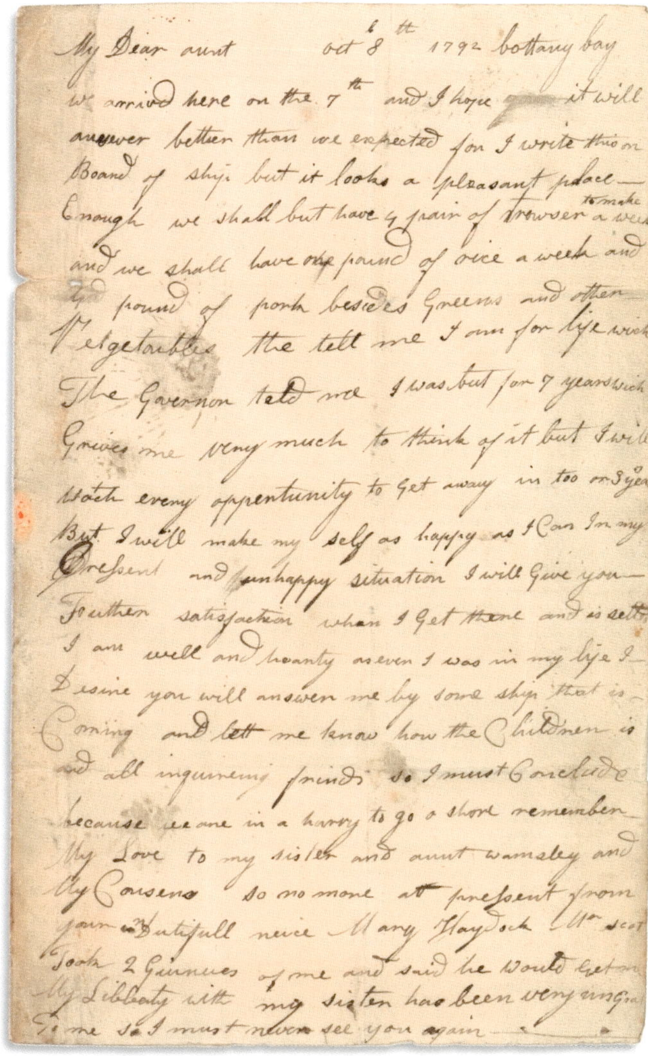

My Dear aunt oct 8 6 th 1792 bottany bay
we arrived here on the 7 th and I hope [illegible] it will
answer better than we expected for I write this on
Board of ship but it looks a pleasant place
Enough we shall but have 4 pair of trowser to make a week
and we shall have one pound of rice a week and
4 pound of pork besides Greens and other
Vegetables the tell me I am for life wich
The Governor teld me I was but for 7 years wich
Grieves me very much to think of it but I will
watch every oppertunity to get away in too or 3 years
But I will make my self as happy as I Can In my
Present and unhappy situation I will Give you
Further satisfaction when I Get there and is settl
I am well and hearty as ever I was in my life I
Desire you will answer me by some ship that is
Coming and lett me know how the Children is
and all inquiring friends so I must Conclude
because we are in a hurry to go a shore remember
My Love to my sister and aunt wamsley and
My Cousens so no more at present from
your dutifull neice Mary Haydock Mr scot
Took 2 Ginnues of me and said he would get me
My Libbarty with my sister has been very ungra
to me so I must never see you again

was one of the better convict transports; its captain was paid well to deliver healthy convicts and looked after his passengers, feeding them properly and allowing them plenty of exercise. The ship's doctor had also done his best to protect the young girls from the male passengers, other convicts and the crew on board, which was rarely the case in transports that carried females to the colony.

When she stepped ashore Mary was immediately placed into service again, this time as nursemaid in the household of Major Francis Grose, who had become commander of the colony's military garrison after the departure of Captain Arthur Phillip earlier that same year. Mary Haydock wrote home to her aunt on her arrival in the penal colony:

> ... they tell me I am here for life, which the Governor teld me I was but for 7 years wich Grives me vry much to think of it but I will watch every oppertunity to get away in too or 3 years ... Mr Scot Took 2 Ginnues of me and said he would get me My Libberty with my sister has been very ungrat ... to me so I must never see you again.[1]

She stayed in service for Major Grose until her 'oppertunity' arose even before 'too' years had passed. She was married to a former naval officer, Irish-born Thomas Reibey, on 5 April 1794. Thomas Reibey had first come to the

OPPOSITE:

View of part of the River of Sydney, in New South Wales. Taken from St Phillip's Church Yard

Engraving by John Eyre, published by Absalom West, Sydney, 1813

Macquarie had only been in the colony for four years when this drawing was made. He had taken over as governor following a period of constant bickering, legal battles and bitter petitions that had culminated in insurrection against Governor Bligh.

His administration brought great change, and Mary Reibey was one who benefited as a result of this visionary governor.

(State Library of New South Wales Collection)

BELOW:

Land-grant certificate given to Mary Reibey by Governor Macquarie in 1812

As another example of his support of the emancipist cause, in 1812 Macquarie granted Mary Reibey, and all her heirs, 'to have and to hold for ever 45 Rods of land lying and situated in the town of Sydney bounded on the South Side by Macquarie Street'.

Through such grants Macquarie changed both the look of the Sydney skyline and the pecking order in the colony. Through her hard work and canny business acumen Mary Reibey rose to be one of the most influential of the emancipists.

(State Library of New South Wales Collection)

colony with the East India Company in 1792 and returned two years later to take Mary for his bride.

Thomas Reibey received a grant of land along the Hawkesbury River, where he soon established himself as a trader of coal and cargo along both the Hawkesbury and Hunter Rivers and into Sydney. He was to become the first trader outside of the official military circle to establish himself in business in the colony. His business grew apace and before long he was engaged in the import and export of goods, skins, agricultural products and had also developed transport links throughout the colony and abroad.

At the time of the establishment of Reibey's business the colony was still reliant on goods, foodstuffs and other provisions to be brought in from the homeland; the late arrival or wreckage of a supply ship meant hardship and hunger for all. He formed a partnership with Richard Wills and they rapidly expanded their operations to include Bass Strait, the Pacific Islands, and then India and China.

Suffering the effects of sunstroke after one of his many trading voyages to India, Thomas Reibey died on 5 April 1811. When Wills died in the same year, Mary was left alone with seven children and a complex network of business and farming interests to manage.

Mary had spent many years managing the affairs of the business while Thomas was away on his frequent overseas excursions, so the task of continuing with the business did not daunt her at all.

She was a remarkable woman for her time. An independent businesswoman in a penal colony dominated by military men of rank, and an emancipated convict into the bargain, she must have been made of very strong stuff indeed. Mary Reibey was just one of many prominent emancipists in the penal colony whose aim was to wipe the convict stain from

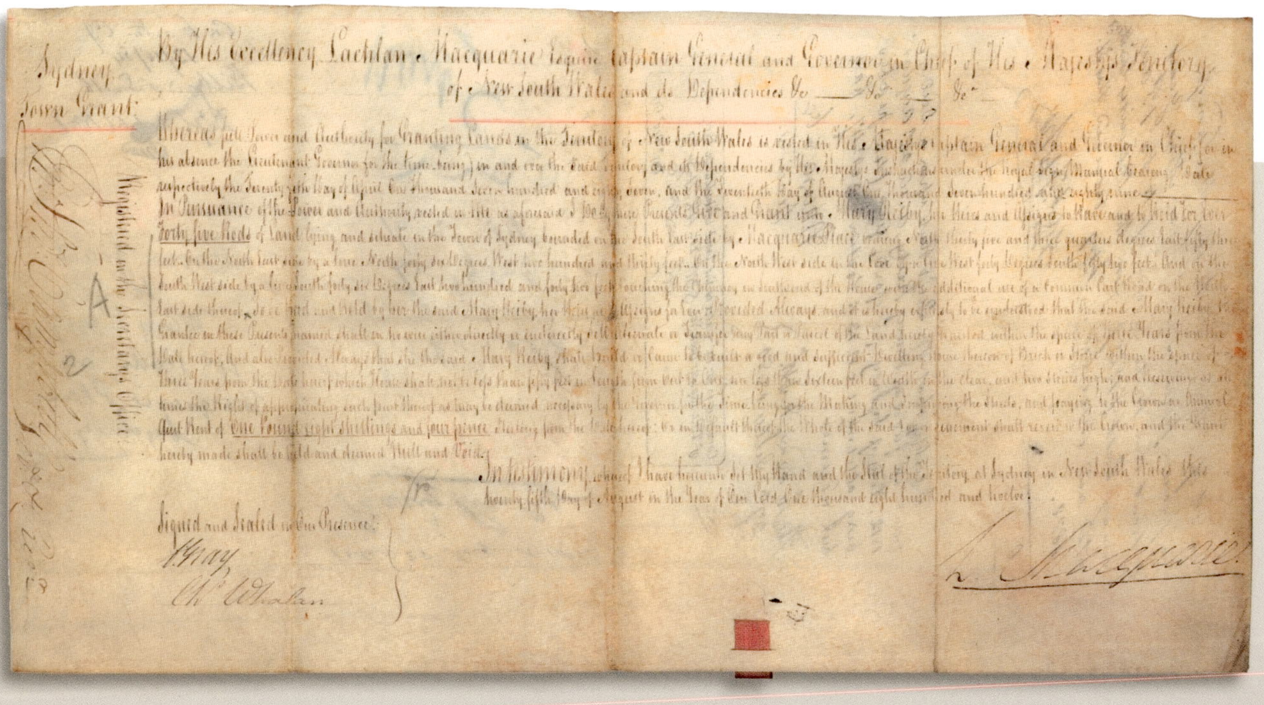
Sydney Town Grant

By His Excellency Lachlan Macquarie Esquire Captain General and Governor in Chief of His Majesty's Territory of New South Wales and its Dependencies &c. &c. &c.

all who had come to the colony in chains, had served their term and had made a new start.

Not all emancipists were ex-convicts: among their numbers were prominent Australian-born 'currency lads' who also supported the cause of the freed felon. Prominent among them was William Wentworth, who claimed to have been New South Wales's first 'native' son. Conceived on board a convict ship, he was born within sight of Australia's shoreline. He was the son of a convict lass and the assistant to the ship's surgeon D'Arcy Wentworth and, although freeborn, his mother's convict stain stayed with him all his life, no matter how hard he scrubbed away at it.

It was through the constant petition for 'equality of opportunity' by people like Wentworth that many ex-convicts were raised to a favoured place in colonial society.

All of the colonial governors were desperate to develop the settlement of Sydney Town. They needed to build the infrastructure that

ABOVE:

View of Sydney Cove taken from the north shore, Port Jackson, N. S. Wales

Watercolour attributed to Richard Read Snr, c. 1820

After the deaths of her husband, Thomas Reibey, and his partner Richard Wills, both in 1811, Mary Reibey continued to expand the business that the two partners had set on a sound footing.

Before long she had built her own warehouse on the Sydney docks, and added several more ships to her fleet of trading vessels.

Her waterfront property was situated behind the three-masted vessel to the left of the centre of this painting.

(National Library of Australia Collection)

would change the settlement from a ramshackle collection of poorly built huts hugging the craggy shoreline into a fine colonial outpost that would elicit the approval of the Crown. Their own fortunes rested upon success, and they had a seemingly never-ending supply of free labour with which to do it. What was lacking was a merchant or administrative class that was indebted to them. What was needed was a class of entrepreneurs who would work with the governor, rather than plot against him to serve their own greed and desire for nobility.

Governor Lachlan Macquarie favoured the emancipists, and in support of their cause he did his best to discourage the migration of free settlers to the colony. This was also a subtle way of ensuring his own support base. A man fond of power, Macquarie didn't want to see strengthened the influence of a 'freeman' class who could not be kept in line by military general orders or prison regulations.

He raised one emancipist after another to positions of influence. Much to the disapproval of the established men of rank, one ex-convict was appointed to the magisterial bench; another became the leading architect of his day; another, Simeon Lord, one of the wealthiest men in the colony; while another, William Redfern, was also made magistrate by Macquarie. All of these were transportees who had made good and all remained active supporters of the emancipist cause.

Macquarie also favoured Mary Reibey and liked to promote her as an example of one emancipist who had made a great success of herself under his patronage.

BELOW:
Port Jackson taken from the Flag Staff, Sydney
Watercolour by artist unknown, c. 1826

When Lachlan Macquarie arrived in the penal settlement which hugged the Port Jackson shoreline he envisaged a society that could rehabilitate the transportee. He believed that the convict who had served his, or her, time had it: 'within his power to recover what he has lost, and not only to become a worthy member of society, but to be treated as such'.

Mary Reibey certainly benefited by Macquarie's vision of a fair society that forgave the emancipated transportee who was prepared to make good.

(State Library of New South Wales Collection)

BELOW:

Mary Reibey's eldest son Reverend Thomas Reibey and his wife in the conservatory at Entally House

Stereoscopic photograph by John Smith

(The University of Sydney, Macleay Museum, Historic Photographic Collection)

Under this kind of vice-regal patronage Reibey expanded her husband's fleet of three schooners with the addition of two new vessels. She built a new warehouse in George Street, Sydney, and continued to develop Thomas's already established wine and spirits business. She acquired a further 200 acres of land near Sydney.

By 1816 Mary Reibey's wealth was already valued at £20,000. But she did not stop there. She was an entrepreneur accustomed to success. She invested in buildings in Sydney, eventually owning much of the lower George Street area. She had also once owned the Argyle Bond Stores in Sydney's Rocks district. The *Sydney Gazette* described her contribution to the Sydney skyline as 'elegant buildings, which considerably improved the City'.

Mary Reibey travelled back to England in 1820, where her daughters were to finish

LEFT:

'Entally' historic home (1820), Launceston, Tasmania

Printed postcard, c. 1960

Entally, named after a suburb of Calcutta in India, was built on the banks of the South Esk River near Halpern in Tasmania in 1819 by Thomas Haydock Reibey, the eldest son of Thomas Snr and Mary Reibey.

Shipping interests had taken Thomas to Tasmania as early as 1816. He settled there after the house, which includes its own chapel and is surrounded by an elegant garden, was completed in 1819. Thomas rose to become one of the island's most prominent citizens.

In 1883, a local newspaper described the house, as 'a house designed for comfort, [rather] than as a model for the exposition of any particular canons of architecture'.

(State Library of Victoria Collection)

BELOW:
Reibey Place, off Macquarie Place, Sydney
Photograph by Harold Cazneaux, c. 1910
(National Library of Australia Collection)

their education. Her relatives were so impressed by her wealth and social standing that her earlier disgrace was forgiven, and she was welcomed back into the affection of the family.

Mary Reibey, once condemned to the noose, had achieved the two main aims of the emancipist: affluence and respectability. After returning to Australia in 1828 she was able to live well off her investments in city properties. She set up her eldest son, Thomas Haydock Reibey, on a property in Tasmania called Entally, where he was to become one of the prominent citizens of that verdant island.

The success of Mary Reibey in the world of business, her property holdings and her charitable works, had earned her a revered place in respectable society. She was able to exert influence in those areas of social welfare that concerned her.

She was made a governor of the Free Grammar School in 1825, and was a founding member of the Bank of New South Wales, the first bank in Australia, which incorporated in August 1819. Each of these appointments alone were testament to her standing in the male-dominated colonial society.

After her retirement from business Mary Reibey built herself a new house in Newtown, where she lived until her death on 30 April 1855, aged 78 years. Five of her seven children had passed away before her.

In continuation of her charitable efforts in support of public education, the house at Newtown was used as a girls' school up until the early 1880s.

The emancipists

When Captain Philip Gidley King arrived in New South Wales he despaired at the state of the colony. He soon developed a poor opinion of the resources of the settlement and a much worse opinion of those who had been sent out to develop them. He despised the 'odious monopoly then exercised by the military and civil officers, and determined, so far as he was able, to destroy it'. In an attempt to change the pecking order in the colony, 'he encouraged and brought into notice the most deserving of the emancipated prisoners'.

Governor Lachlan Macquarie also believed that ex-convicts should be given every opportunity to reform. When he appointed the emancipist Thompson to the magisterial bench, he learned that he had been unwittingly duped by his adviser Lieutenant Colonel Foveaux, who had managed the colony after the removal of Governor William Bligh from office. Foveaux had hoped that Thompson would embarrass the governor and put an end to such appointments from the 'convict class'.

Foveaux remarked: 'I have placed a blister upon Governor Macquarie, which he will never be able to remove'. Macquarie replied that he had 'but two classes to choose from [in making appointments], those who had been transported and those — who ought to have been.' Macquarie believed that by encouraging convicts to take a place in colonial society he could 'make this country a home, and a happy home, to every emancipated convict who deserves it'. He allowed for them to be put on 'a footing of equality with the general population'.

Whereas former military men such as Macarthur had little to gain from sympathy with the emancipist cause, most of the free settlers supported the governor in any way that the control of the military circle could be broken.

But there were also established settlers and military officer-farmers (the 'exclusives') who refused to support the governor's aims. When Thompson was appointed to the magisterial bench, along with another emancipist, Simeon Lord, the Reverend Samuel Marsden refused to serve on the board with them. Supreme Court Judge J. H. Bent closed his court rather than allow ex-convict attorneys to stand before him.

Eventually, the emancipists won the support of the free settlers, and together with the governor sought to bring an end to rule of the colony by the 'exclusives'.

Macquarie resigned his post in 1822. As he departed for England he left Australia with this remark:

> I found New South Wales a gaol and left it a colony; I found a population of idle prisoners, paupers and paid officials, and left a large free community thriving in the produce of flocks and the labour of convicts.

Sir Thomas Brisbane replaced Macquarie and immediately set the clock back ten years.

Above:
Governor Lachlan Macquarie
(State Library of New South Wales Collection)

Macquarie replaced Bligh and soon brought the colony under control.

He stopped all trading by military and civil officers on the government payroll and encouraged the stimulation of a new merchant class by promoting the emancipist cause.

He was impressed by Mary Reibey's success and cited her as an example of the type of citizen that could be encouraged to contribute once freed.

However, it was his desire for power and control that led him to keep the convict class indebted to him. He was wary of the free settler who was outside his military jurisdiction.

J. CAR
IN
Invalid

Francis Greenway

1777–1837

Francis Greenway is featured on the face of the $10 paper note, first issued in 1966.

Macquarie's convict architect

AS THE RECORDER AT THE BRISTOL ASSIZES PLACED THE black cap upon his wig he intoned these fateful words: 'You shall be taken to the place whence you came—thence to the place of execution, where you shall be hanged by the neck until you are dead'.

The date was 23 March 1812, and 35-year-old 'architect and painter' Francis Howard Greenway was faced with a short future where no release from this grave prospect seemed at all possible.

Francis Greenway had been a hardworking and seemingly successful artisan and architect in the Bristol district, in the West Country of England, where his forebears had been builders and stonemasons of favourable repute for generations.

Francis, along with his brothers, Olive and John Tripp, had begun a building business, which, apart from providing speculating builders with plans and drawings, provided for the supply of all kinds of architectural ornamentation and specialised building materials.

Unwittingly, the Greenway brothers began their business venture at the end of a boom in the construction of grand houses and public buildings. The industrial revolution had made some men rich beyond their wildest dreams, while others became fodder for their dreary factory floors. The war with Napoleon had changed the face of Europe and the relationships between all of the major players.

As the war came to an end thousands of battle-wearied soldiers were cast back into an already troubled society, upsetting the delicately balanced English economy which had been built on colonial expansion and manufacturing dedicated to providing for the war. With thousands of under-employed returned men, the crime rate grew in the cities and towns, causing great uncertainty among the conservative establishment and the ruling classes. As a result, speculators began to look for security and withdrew their funds from unnecessary investments.

When some speculative work on a grand bathhouse and hot wells at Clifton on the Gloucestershire side of the River Avon fell through, the Greenway brothers were left exposed to their creditors.

The following notice appeared in the *Bristol Gazette* on 27 April 1809:

OPPOSITE:

Francis Howard Greenway

Dry-plate engraving, c. 1820

Born in the village of Mangotsfield near Bristol, in the West Country of England, in 1777, this son of a family of stonemasons, woodworkers, craftsmen and builders was fortunate enough to have been sent to study in a London architect's office, when it became apparent that he demonstrated considerable drawing and drafting skills.

Francis Greenway, who preferred to describe himself as 'architect and painter', ran a business with his brothers until an unfortunate collapse of building activity caused them to fall into bankruptcy.

An advertisement placed in the *Bristol Journal* of 26 January 1805 announced the expectation for success that had motivated the brothers in their venture:

> All orders for marble ornaments, chimney pieces, and every kind of ornamental stone work shall be carefully attended to, and executed in the most artist-like manner.
>
> Designs for houses, lodge-gates, and every part of domestic architecture may be seen at the office drawn by F. Greenway—who takes this opportunity of offering his services to the public in the capacity of architect, statuary, and landscape gardener.[1]

When they began in business England was at war with Napoleon and speculative building projects of the type that the Greenways were interested in were in the decline.

It was not long before the Greenways were in financial trouble.

(State Library of New South Wales Collection)

To Creditors
The creditors of Francis Greenway of the parish of Clifton, in the Co. of Gloster architect and Builder, are respectfully requested to meet on Monday next, at 12 o'clock at noon at the Royal York Hotel at Clifton, to take into consideration the state of his affairs and in the meantime to send an account of their respective demands on him to the office of John Cornish, Solcr., Small Street, Bristol. [2]

Obviously the news from this meeting of creditors did not go well, as the following week a similar call to arms was advertised in the *Bristol Mirror*, when the public at large was notified of an auction of all goods belonging to the household of Francis Greenway to be held on 8 May 'under a distress of rent'.[3]

The same day, an announcement was published in the *Mirror* that a commission of bankruptcy had been issued against the three brothers: Olive Greenway, John Tripp Greenway and Francis Greenway.

On 25 July 1809, amid a large crowd of bargain hunters, the auctioneer descended on the Greenways' yard at Limekiln Lane, where there was spirited bidding for the excellent materials that were the hallmark of the Greenway style: 'blocks of marble, chimney pieces, paving slabs, Painswick stone, Pennant and paving stones, Dutch tiles in casks, plaster figures and models of "the ancients", decorative sculptures and a pair of handsome chimney tunnels once intended for the country seat of Lord Clanricarde'.

While the bankruptcy was a devastating blow to the fortunes of the brothers, it was only Francis who seemed unable to avoid his total ruin. Olive re-established himself as a builder of quality and renown. John Tripp also stayed in the district, but little is known about him other than that he died unmarried and childless in 1831.

However, Francis was of a nature that could not bear defeat. He was so sure of himself that he embarked on a kind of crusade that he believed would salvage some dignity from his disaster.

He maintained that he had been underpaid on the completion of a contract he had undertaken for Colonel Richard Doolan, formerly of the East India Company. Greenway had been the creator of a building for Doolan for which the contract price was 1300 guineas. The colonel was not all that eager to pay the bankrupt Greenway, but his creditors entered into spirited negotiations with Doolan and the account was settled.

Francis Greenway maintained that a further £250 had been agreed upon in addition to the

OPPOSITE:
Hulks in the Medway
Oil on canvas by Hume Lancaster, c. 1837

From the mouth of the Thames estuary to the Hampshire coastal harbour of Portsmouth, the protected harbours of England's southern shores were home to thousands of convicted felons awaiting transportation to the colonies.

For all on board, the sullen grey skies over the chalky cliffs were their last memory of the land that had given them up.

The hundreds of rotting, decommissioned battleships which lay at anchor around the coast must have been a constant reminder of the harsh reality of British justice around the end of the eighteenth century.

But it seemed to have little impact, and the magistrates had no difficulty keeping them filled.

(State Library of Tasmania Collection)

original contract, but unfortunately for him that document could no longer be found. He claimed that the solicitor Mr Cooke had amended the original document in his favour, but that amendment was no longer available either. Greenway took this tale of woe to the arbitrators of the bankruptcy, but his cause was rejected. Curiously enough, there was nothing in this at all for Greenway, but he was a proud, and at times foolish, man; he became committed to trying to pay his creditors, in order to retain some dignity from his failure.

As the bankruptcy was almost settled, with great losses for all concerned, this extra £250 meant little at all, but Francis Greenway was trying to prove a point. He was to lose, badly. He advertised in the newspaper, offering a reward of ten guineas to anybody who could lay their hands on the missing document.

Lo and behold, the contract with its amendment was handed, anonymously, into the vestibule of the *Bristol Mercury* without any claim for the reward.

Greenway took the 'rediscovered' contract, with the amendment, to the assignees of his bankruptcy and insisted that Doolan be prosecuted for payment of the £250.

It was soon proved that the signature, however cleverly crafted to resemble solicitor Cooke's own hand, was a forgery, and Greenway was arrested in January 1812 and cast in to Newgate prison to await his trial.

Greenway was a man of great refinement; he had the artist's love of design and decoration, and the architect's passion for order and style. It is testament to his abilities that his talent survived the barbarity of the ensuing months.

On 23 March 1812 Francis Greenway stood in the dock at the Bristol Assizes charged with 'uttering as true a certain forged instrument, purporting to be an agreement between Colonel Doolan and the said Francis Greenway.'[4] He pleaded guilty to the charge, and must have been shocked to his very core when the recorder pronounced the sentence of 'death by hanging'.

While the courts were keen to clear the streets of criminals and make the towns safe for good citizens, Greenway's crime was not the dangerous kind. The newspapers came out in support of clemency; his friends and family sought a reprieve, which was duly granted by the court before the recorder had moved on from Bristol.

Greenway's sentence was revised to transportation to Botany Bay for fourteen years and he was taken to the hulks to await his removal to the other side of the earth.

Around the same time that Greenway was about to enter the hulks Lachlan Macquarie, Greenway's eventual 'saviour', already in Botany Bay, wrote to the secretary of state for the colonies with the following request:

> It would be highly necessary and very desirable that a government architect should be sent out to this country to plan and superintend the erection of public buildings, and I specifically entreat Your Lordship will send out a well-qualified person of this description to the colony as soon as possible. [5]

Transportation

Francis Greenway had to languish in the prison hulk *Captivity*, one of the many moored along England's coastline, for a further seventeen months before he finally set sail for Botany Bay on 26 August 1813. He was transferred to the transport ship *General Hewitt,* which had picked up 124 prisoners from the Thames, forty-eight more from the hulks in Sheerness, ninety-two from Portsmouth and then thirty-two more, including Greenway and his fellow inmates, from the *Captivity* at Langstone. Also on board were soldiers from the 46th (South Devon) Regiment and a number of free passengers, including fifteen women and seven children.

The *General Hewitt* was loaded to the gunwales. The Scottish owners, the McTaggarts, didn't believe in wasting any space on board. With the crew added to the number of passengers, both free and in chains, the total aboard numbered 515. They were set to inhabit the cramped and airless confines of

RIGHT:
A Fleet of Transports under Convoy
Hand coloured engraving, published in London, 1871

Groups of convicts, under escort to and from hard labour on land, were a common sight around the coastal ports were prison hulks were moored off shore.

Francis Greenway was transferred to the appropriately named hulk *Captivity*, to await transportation to Botany Bay. The thirty-two prisoners on the *Captivity*, moored at Langstone near Portsmouth, were trundled aboard the transport *General Hewitt*, then set sail for Botany Bay on 26 August 1813. It had been seventeen months since Greenway had stood in the dock.

The *General Hewitt* carried over one hundred crew, seventy soldiers from the 46th (South Devon) Regiment, 296 prisoners and a number of free passengers.

(Rex Nan Kivell Collection, NK1225. National Library of Australia)

the ship on a journey that was to last almost six months.

When the *General Hewitt* landed in Botany Bay on 7 February 1814, the entire human cargo, including crew and passengers, was in an incredibly filthy and debilitated state. Thirty-four of the original transportees had died on the voyage, their bodies slipped through the shrouds, delivered into the deep.They had perished from the ravages of the diseases of human filth: typhus, dysentery, brain fever and epilepsy brought on by the appalling conditions below decks.

Only twenty-five of the men from the *Captivity* were left. Greenway, although affected by the rigours of the hellish voyage, had survived; he stepped ashore still clutching a letter of recommendation to the Governor of New South Wales that had been given to him by his 'ever steady friend and patron',[6] Arthur Phillip, the first administrator of the colony.

The state of the bedraggled line of near-skeletons that climbed the gangplank out of the *General Hewitt* and onto Sydney's shores so infuriated Assistant Surgeon Redfern, himself an emancipated convict, that his report to Governor Macquarie instigated a regimen of

BELOW:
The Heads of Port Jackson N.S.W., from off the North Head — a squall
Oil painting by G.E. Peacock, 1846

When the *General Hewitt* entered the Heads in the first week of February 1814, Francis Greenway could not have dreamt that these towering cliffs were to see the beginning of the great change in his fortune.

He was granted a conditional pardon for his design for the construction of the South Head lighthouse (seen in the centre of this painting), the first navigation aid on the Australian coast. It used a whale-oil beam lantern to cast its warning light far out across the Heads.

Unfortunately the stone used in its construction was of inferior quality and it had to be replaced just over half a century later.

(State Library of New South Wales Collection)

BELOW:
New South Wales. View of Sydney, from the east side of the Cove. No. 2
Hand-coloured aquatint by John Eyre, 1810
Published by John Booth, Duke St, Portland Pl., London, 4 June 1810
This engraving of the Sydney skyline was drawn just prior to the arrival of Greenway. Under the direction of Governor Macquarie, Greenway gave the city of Sydney some of its most elegant buildings still in use today, more than 150 years after his death.
(State Library of New South Wales Collection)

change to the way in which transportees were shipped to the colony.

Even the captain of the *General Hewitt* had perished on the voyage; a victim of his own and the McTaggarts' parsimony in the lack of adequate provisions, and greed in overfilling the ship with its human cargo.

Macquarie rebuilds Sydney

Major-General Lachlan Macquarie was the first non-naval officer to govern New South Wales. He had arrived in the colony with his regiment, the 73rd, whose previous posting had been in India, and took over control from the regime of insurrectionists that had deposed William Bligh. He wrote that when he first began his administration he had:

> ... found the colony barely emerging from an infantile imbecility; the country impenetrable beyond forty miles from Sydney, agriculture languishing, commerce in its early dawn, revenue unknown, famine threatening, faction distracting and public buildings in a state of dilapidation and mouldering to decay. [7]

The arrival of the *General Hewitt* and its near-skeletal survivors had brought the solution to the last part of Macquarie's concerns at least. Greenway was fortunate that he was, at home anyway, known as a gentleman. He was well educated, well mannered and had held a noble profession. He was no common criminal, neither dangerous nor in need of rehabilitation by the flogger. Greenway was granted a ticket-of-leave almost immediately.

A factor in this matter was the entreaty by Greenway for his wife and children, who had followed him out to the colony, to be allowed to disembark from the ship *Broxbornebury* after an exceedingly unpleasant six-month-long voyage. Macquarie knew that a ticket-of-leave convict would be able to care for his own family rather than them depend on the government stores.

For all intents and purposes Greenway was now a free man. He was no longer required to wear the prison issue of grey and yellow that marked all his fellows as 'canaries' (prisoners of the Crown). He was able to find his own lodgings, and was expected to secure his own employment.

What he did for the first few months of this strange liberty is unknown, but it is known that in July 1814 Francis Howard Greenway was summoned to Government House by Governor Lachlan Macquarie and asked to copy some architectural drawings from a book belonging to Mrs Elizabeth Macquarie, who was quite possibly more interested in architecture and design than the governor himself.

Even after all his trials and tribulations Greenway was still a proud man; he held a very high opinion of his own abilities, and suffered no fool gladly. After the meeting he wrote to the governor with a carefully guarded admonishment, criticising the style of the building he was supposed to copy and entreating the governor to allow him to design something of his own. Possibly thinking he had gone too far, Greenway finished his letter with the following:

> I will immediately copy the Drawing Your Excellency has requested me to do, notwithstanding it is painful to my mind as a professional man to copy a Building that has no Claim to Classical Proportion or Character ... If your Excellency will grant me the power as an Architect to Design and Conduct a Public Work, I will exert myself in every way to do Your Excellency credit.[8]

Before the end of that year Greenway placed his first advertisement in the Sydney papers offering his services as an architect.

In March 1816 Macquarie appointed Greenway acting government architect on a salary

RIGHT:
Port Jackson Lighthouse
Watercolour from Richard Jones's scrap album, c. 1823

For a short while the Heads had two almost identical lighthouse buildings standing side by side: Greenway's South Head lighthouse, which was replaced due to the poor quality of materials used in its construction, and its twin, the Macquarie lighthouse of 1883.

When the Macquarie lighthouse was commissioned it used electricity to power its lamp, which was considered to be a great improvement. One vessel from the Marine Authority took to the sea at night to consider its report and exclaimed its 'vast superiority' over the first.

(State Library of New South Wales Collection)

BELOW:
St. Matthew's Church of England, Windsor NSW
Photograph, c. 1879
(State Library of New South Wales Collection)

of 3s per day. His first commission was to inspect and report on all existing buildings.

Macquarie wrote to Lord Bathurst in 1817:

> From the want of a scientific person to plan and superintend the Construction of all Government Public buildings, most of them have hitherto been very badly planned, and still worse executed.
>
> A Man named Francis Howard Greenway, who came out here as a Convict in the Year 1814, and who was originally an architect of some Eminence in England, having been strongly recommended by the late Governor Phillip, I have availed myself of his skill and scientific Knowledge as a Civil Architect, and accordingly for some time since employed him to act in that capacity, as an Assistant to the Inspector of Public Works, for which he receives 3s. per diem. [9]

It was his report on the inadequacy of the building techniques employed in the construction of the Rum Hospital that won Greenway the governor's support. By the end of 1817 Greenway saw the completion of his first architectural commission, the design and construction of the South Head lighthouse. For this work he received a conditional pardon, which was made absolute in June 1819.

After only seven years Greenway was a free man once more. This time, however, he almost had a blank canvas on which to execute his most elaborate creations. The Sydney he began with was without any style at all.

Abandoning the cautionary advice from London to take the expenditure on capital works into hand, Macquarie embarked on a vast, and ambitious, building program that transformed the skyline of the colony.

Following the building of the South Head lighthouse, churches were planned for Sydney, Windsor and Liverpool. A new factory and barracks for female convicts, a courthouse and houses for chaplains at Liverpool, Parramatta and Castlereagh were added to the list of commissions to be undertaken by the civil architect Francis Greenway.

Greenway eschewed the popular colonial style brought to Australia from India. His was a vision of classical proportion, of the Romanesque and the Italian Renaissance, with wide open spaces and Georgian-styled detail reminiscent of the colonnades of Bath and the unfinished 'hot wells' that were the root cause of his embarrassment.

His eclectic style brought together all the great traditions of classical form and embellished them with the craftsmanship and integrity of quality materials that was the hallmark of generations of Greenway builders.

One of Greenway's first major commissions was for the design and construction of Hyde Park Barracks, which he began in 1817. The large building on the outer perimeter of the township was to be a dormitory for the scores of homeless convicts who wandered the streets and slept rough every night. The

ABOVE:

Convict Barrack Sydney N. S. Wales

Watercolour by Joseph Lycett, c. 1820

When the new three-storeyed barracks to house male convicts was opened in Sydney on 4 June 1819, the occasion was celebrated by a dinner put on for the 580 convict inmates. To mark the great occasion they received plum pudding and punch in addition to their usual ration.

Up until the time this building was completed most convicts had to find their own accommodation, for which they paid rent taken from their earnings. In the new barracks, transportees worked the whole day without pay for the government in return for a full ration of food. They were also supplied with fresh clothes twice a week, although they still had to wear the broad arrow and a prison number.

Some of the married men were still allowed to live outside the barracks, and well-behaved men were able to take their leave at the weekends.

Barracks life was meant to reintroduce some discipline to the convict's day and to reduce the incidence of street crime that had been growing when such men were left to their own devices.

Some years later, after transportation had long ceased, reformer Caroline Chisholm sought permission from the government to use the barracks to house homeless migrant women.

(State Library of New South Wales Collection)

barracks kept over 1000 off the streets and supposedly away from mischief. Upon completion of the barracks in 1819, Governor Macquarie noted that the incidence of night robberies and burglaries dropped markedly.

A commission followed for St Matthew's Anglican Church at Windsor, one of five towns that had been set up by Governor Macquarie above the flood levels, which had been the nemesis of life in the early colony.

This simple church with its tower decorated by strikingly large urns and a small cupola was built by convict labour. Building commenced in 1817 and was finished three years later; the 'exclusive' enemy of the emancipist cause, the Reverend Samuel Marsden, consecrated the church. Its interior is large and open and the tall, rounded windows allow the nave to fill with light, flushing the well-crafted cedar joinery with a warm, soft glow. The integrity of the materials, the human scale and the craftsmanship shown in the detail of St Matthew's were the hallmarks of the Greenway builders of old. Francis transferred the qualities of the family firm to his work in the colonies.

In 1818 he created an obelisk for the governor, which still stands in Macquarie Place, Sydney. All distances and all roads in the colony took their measure from this marker. He also began work on a new factory for female convicts in 1818. It replaced a building constructed under the supervision of the Reverend Samuel Marsden before Macquarie had arrived in the colony.

Marsden was not at all happy to see the emancipist Greenway change the look he had given to Sydney and Parramatta; he had been the arbiter of public taste before Macquarie's administration and was solely responsible for the price paid and materials used in any public project. Under Macquarie, Marsden was to see his influence fade, and his pockets no longer so readily filled from the public purse from which funds had once flowed so freely in his direction.

Marsden's female factory had partly burned down some years before, and although he received a stipend of £50 per year for the spiritual guidance of the inmates still held there, he hadn't set foot in the place since 1810.

Upon landing in the colony it was customary for female convicts to come under the

RIGHT:
Front view of obelisk, Macquarie Place
Photograph, c.1870

King's Commissioner John Thomas Bigge, who had been sent to conduct a review into the affairs of the colony, questioned the value of the obelisk in Macquarie Place, among a long list of complaints about Macquarie's expensive tastes.

Bigge aimed an oblique broadside at Greenway when he criticised Macquarie: 'suffice to say the turnpike gate may be unsuitable, the obelisk unnecessary, the fountain absurd, the tower, lighthouse railing, etc. all useless extravagant expenditure', and all were the responsibility of the civil architect, 'but the Governor did not consider them so'.[10] On the contrary, Macquarie was proud of what he had achieved.

(State Library of New South Wales Collection)

BELOW:
Female penitentiary or factory, Parramatta, N.S. Wales
Watercolour by artist unknown, c.1826
(Rex Nan Kivell Collection NK12/47. By permission, National Library of Australia)

care of the magistrates Samuel Marsden and Hannibal Macarthur, two 'gentlemen' who showed no desire at all to see such cheap labour emancipated. Those they could not place into service were held at the factory, even after it had been partly destroyed by fire. The single-floor factory was above the gaol, and housed about thirty of the left-over hags and harridans of the transported convicts, the wayward girls and the uncontrollable:

> To the leaven of enciente girls, young mothers, and filthy hags who dwelt in these quarters the magistrates added a miserable assortment of sulky female misdemeanants. Thither went two young ladies who had been sentenced to be chained together for a month for polluting the ears of innocent Parramatta with unseemly eloquence; there was immured a little runaway, safe in double irons; there sulked in the corner a wretched maiden, due to remain were she was for two months, 'with a log chained to her leg' at the injunction of the gentle Mr Marsden.[11]

Although Marsden showed little interest in his 'parishioners', he did occasionally remark on the need for a new building, all the while positioning himself and his preferred contractors to take on the job if the governor ever saw fit to allocate a budget for it.

When Macquarie eventually called for tenders for a new female factory Marsden realised that he had been thwarted. He had been proposing a new building to be constructed with a budget of £14,000. Greenway and Macquarie set the budget at £4500. Just days before tenders were closed, Marsden's man, Mr Smith, called on the civil architect Francis Greenway and offered him a bribe of £500 to revise the tender to £12,000. Smith left this interview 'crimson in the face'.[12]

Governor Macquarie wasted no time re-creating Sydney; it was obvious by the number of capital projects commenced in the

years 1816 to 1822 that he was determined to leave behind a fine architectural legacy.

Greenway began work on the Supreme Court in 1820; it took eight years to complete. He created his elaborate designs for the servants' quarters and stables for the governor's residence in 1821. The opulence of style and the cost of Greenway's overwrought castellated designs for these buildings brought criticism of Macquarie's budgetary management from abroad. He was meant to be reining in the cost of running the colony, not building an estate for himself.

At the same time, Greenway had begun work on St James Church in King Street; it still stands today, the oldest church building in Sydney.

The Rum Hospital (so called because the builder was given 200,000 litres of rum as payment), which later became the home of the Parliament of New South Wales, was also completed in 1816. In the years between 1816 and 1822 Greenway had worked on either the design or restoration of forty-four buildings in and around Sydney.

However, Greenway, who had enjoyed the support of Governor Macquarie for almost a decade, was summarily dismissed from office on 15 November 1822. He had been alienating the men of influence around him,

ABOVE RIGHT:
St James Church, King Street, Sydney
Engraving by Samuel Calvert,
first published in the Illustrated Melbourne Post,
25 October 1864
(La Trobe Library Collection, State Library of Victoria)

St James Anglican church was a more imposing structure than St Matthew's at Windsor. Its Gothic spire was reminiscent of the grand cathedrals of old England; St Matthew's bell tower had more the look of the English country church. Much to Greenway's distaste, the classical-styled portico (shown at right) was added some years later.

RIGHT:
The north porch of St James Church, Sydney
Pencil-and-crayon drawing by Hardy Wilson, 1914
(National Library of Australia Collection)

BELOW:
Sydney branch, Royal Mint (Rum Hospital), Macquarie Street, Sydney New South Wales
Photographed by Charles Pickering, 1870

(State Library of New South Wales Collection)

including even Macquarie, by his refusal to rein in the excesses of his imagination, and consequently the costs of his designs.

The weakness of character that had once led Greenway to forge a solicitor's signature in an attempt to prove himself right also led to his eventual downfall in the colony.

Macquarie had promised Greenway that when he retired from his post in the colony of New South Wales he would reward him before he left to return home. Around the same time that Macquarie had made this offer to Greenway, Commissioner Bigge had been sent to New South Wales to conduct a review of all operations there. Pastoralist John Macarthur did his best to poison Bigge's mind against Macquarie, and against those emancipists that the governor favoured. The other prominent pastoralist, magistrate and cleric Reverend Samuel Marsden, did much the same: he also did his best to undermine Greenway. Bigge reported on Macquarie's architectural works and dismissed them as so much extravagant folly. He described Greenway's designs as 'too grand for an infant colony' and recommended that his work be curtailed.

When Macquarie's resignation was accepted in 1820, Greenway knew that he would have to move quickly before it was too late to gain his 'reward' from Macquarie. A new colonial secretary, Major Frederic Goulburn, had arrived in the colony and under his command Commissioner Bigge had been asking a few

BELOW:
St. Luke's & the parsonage, Liverpool N.S.W.
Dry-plate engraving, c. 1879
(State Library of New South Wales Collection)

too many difficult questions. Greenway knew that he would have to press his claim before both he and the former governor were brought into disgrace by Bigge.

He decided to levy an architect's percentage on all the work he had done for Macquarie. His bill came to the not inconsiderable sum of £11,232 15s. Even though a lot of this work had been done while he was still a convict (although emancipated and fully pardoned since his work on the barracks in 1819), the Greenways still lived off the public purse. They were provided with a house and land, a horse and forage, a supply of coal and three shillings a day.

Yet Greenway was a proud and conceited man who believed that he should be rewarded by his champion, for whom he had done so much excellent work. Before Macquarie departed his post, Governor Brisbane arrived to replace him. Greenway then attempted to claim his commission from Brisbane.

Before Macquarie left the colony, Greenway wrote to him, on 23 January 1822, again pressing his claim for his commission:

> ... I now, sir, call upon you to do justice to my family, and in justice to them I cannot relinquish my claims, and particularly when I see the greatest benefits lavished on those who have no claim but the merit of having duped and plundered the Government in various ways.
>
> I have laid these claims before His Excellency Sir Thomas Brisbane, the justice of which cannot be denied, and I have no doubt that everything will be done consistent with reason and justice between you ...[13]

Once again Greenway allowed his passion to take control of his head. In this letter he implied a criticism of the administration that had taken him from convict to respected emancipist, and once again his misdirected sense of self-righteousness was about to bring him undone. He may well have had a good case in demanding what he believed was duly his, but he really was in no position to be so persistently vocal about it.

He was called to Government House two days before Macquarie was due to leave. It can be imagined that Greenway was filled with expectation as he mounted the steps for this final interview with his old friend. But he was shocked when Macquarie turned on him 'in an almost extraordinary way and in such

language as he would not stain his paper with, threatening him and commanding him to withdraw his claims'.[14]

Foolishly, Greenway decided to sue the government for the comparatively trifling amount of £214 for travelling expenses incurred during his time as civil architect.

Macquarie sailed away on the *Surrey* on 15 February 1822, and it seems his reforming zeal sailed with him: the colony soon lapsed back into its old ways. Emancipists were swept from the magistrates' bench and no longer dined at Government House. The new officer in charge of all public works, Major Owens, had little time for the ex-convict Francis Greenway, who was becoming a persistent nuisance around government circles.

Greenway pestered Brisbane until on 15 November 1822 the new governor's patience seemed to desert him. When Major Owens reported to Brisbane that Greenway was neglectful of his duties and rendered not 'the least assistance to the office of Acting Engineer', Brisbane dismissed him.

History repeated itself on 11 March 1825, when a notice appeared in the Sydney *Gazette* announcing that on: 'Wednesday next 11th instant at the hour of 11 o'clock in the forenoon', all the possessions of the Greenway household were to be sold; chairs, tables, bedding, even Mary Greenway's pianoforte, were to be auctioned unless he was able to settle with his creditors.

On that same morning his old adversary Samuel Marsden was in the act of consecrating Greenway's last architectural masterpiece for Sydney — St James Church.

Without Macquarie's support, the days of Greenway's influence over the Sydney skyline were over. After a disappointing attempt at a return to private practice, he retired onto his property in the Hunter Valley where he died, almost penniless, in September 1837.

LEFT:
Lighthouse at South Head
Engraving
The Macquarie lighthouse was built as an exact replica of Greenway's first 'South Head' lighthouse, which fell into disrepair only half a century after it had been built.
(Private collection)

er del. T Fairland lith | Printed by Hullmand

Caroline Chisholm

Caroline Chisholm

1808–1877

Caroline Chisholm featured on the obverse of the $5 paper note, first issued in 1966.

The emigrant's friend

CAROLINE CHISHOLM WAS BORN CAROLINE JONES ON 30 May 1808. She was the youngest child of sixty-year-old yeoman farmer William and thirty-seven-year-old Sarah Jones. William Jones was a gentleman of property and influence within his community of Wooton, Northamptonshire, and his unusual generosity and goodwill to people of all kinds had a lasting effect on the path his youngest daughter's life would take.

Caroline remembered her father taking into their home and caring for a disabled soldier who had fought in the Napoleonic Wars. William Jones believed they all had an obligation to those who served their country in protecting ordinary people like themselves.

She also recalled the time when her father had offered sanctuary to a 'Romish priest' who was taunted as he passed through their village on his journey from one Catholic community to another. At that time there were hundreds of French priests who had taken refuge in England from the horrors of the French Revolution. Although William Jones was a member of the Protestant Church, he still considered the priest to be a man of the same God, and in the true spirit of Christianity he offered him shelter in his own home.

The priest stayed for several weeks, and for young Caroline this was to be one of the most formative experiences of her life. She was quick-witted and inquisitive and spent many hours in the priest's company, hearing stories of the places he had seen and the strife-torn homeland he had been forced to leave.

William Jones was criticised by some in the community for his generosity to this servant of Rome, but he persisted in his Christian duty. He believed that all men should be treated equally, and this example cast the die that foretold the future of his youngest child.

A new life abroad

In the early nineteenth century, England was in the middle of an almost bloodless revolution and the opportunities offered by emigration to the colonies were broadcast across the country. The customary use of agricultural land was being challenged as the old ways were cast aside. Lands once set aside for common grazing were undergoing irrevocable change as fields and meadows, commons and broadacres were enclosed by the hedgerows and fields that were the hallmark of the beautiful 'garden of England' for more than 200 years.

OPPOSITE:

Portrait of Caroline Chisholm

Lithograph by Thomas Fairland, published by M. I. Laidler, London, 1 February 1851

Caroline Chisholm (née Jones) was born in Wooton, Northamptonshire, in May 1808. She was the youngest child of sixty-year-old yeoman farmer William and thirty-seven-year-old Sarah Jones.

(Rex Nan Kivell Collection, U6422. By permission, National Library of Australia)

TO EMIGRANTS.

IE following GUTTA PERCHA ARTICLES will be found of great value to Emigrants, especially such as are proceeding to the

COLD DIGGINGS.

Joining Tubes, &c., and for securely

Attaching Gutta Percha Soles, will be forwarded (post free) on receipt of four postage stamps.

GUTTA PERCHA LINING FOR BOXES.

UCKETS. | LIFE BUOYS. | WASHING BOWLS.
RINKING MUGS. | FLASKS. | SYPHONS.

SOLES FOR BOOTS AND SHOES.

keep the feet dry is of the utmost importance to the Emigrant. This may be ed by the use of Gutta Percha Soles, which are perfectly waterproof, cheaper, and durable than Leather. They can be put on with ease by any one. This cannot be xtensively known amongst Australian Emigrants, as it is now difficult to find a aaker in that country.

DIRECTIONS TO EMIGRANTS

ining Boxes with Gutta Percha Sheet (so as to preserve the contents from injury by ater), also for Putting on Soles of Boots and Shoes, &c., may be had *gratis* on appli- to any of the Gutta Percha Company's Dealers.

DOMESTIC UTENSILS,

afactured from Gutta Percha, are not liable to break—a great desideratum on ship- , and equally so in countries where articles (manufactured of more fragile materials) ot be readily replaced.

GUTTA PERCHA TUBING.

IONS FOR PUMPS. JUGS. CARBOYS FOR GUNPOWDER. MINERS' CAPS.

old Washing Vessels of every variety of shape made to order.

THE GUTTA PERCHA COMPANY, PATENTEES,

, WHARF ROAD, CITY ROAD, LONDON.

Many were being put off 'their' land, which had once been held by the bond of blood, kin and community. Titled gentlemen, who had served their monarch, had developed large estates generously granted to them by a grateful Crown. For the dispossessed, emigration to the colonies seemed to offer the only alternative to a life of poverty or servitude.

There were many among the Jones's own family and friends who had already emigrated to America, and young Caroline sat at her father's knee, enthralled, as he read letters from the colonies to her.

When Caroline was six years old her father died after a short illness. She was devastated by the loss of the stalwart, robust yeoman who had always seemed so much in control of all he surveyed; he had always been commanding and protecting. Sarah Jones decided to stay on the farm and as well as looking out for herself and her children, she continued to provide for the needy just as William had done before her.

The following year, 1815, the English army defeated the French at the battle of Waterloo. The war with Napoleon was over and before long the roads were filled with columns of returning soldiers. Many were maimed, and Caroline watched as her mother cared for all she could in the manner that William would

ABOVE:

Quatre-Bras, 1815
The 28th Regiment at Quatre-Bras

Hand-coloured wood engraving, published in the Australasian Sketcher, *29 June 1885*

(State Library of Victoria Collection)

The success of Field Marshal Wellington over the army of Napoleon Bonaparte at the decisive battle of Waterloo in 1815 saw a change in the lives of all those in England.

Hundreds of battle-wearied soldiers fell back into the towns, creating massive unemployment in the cities and a crisis in rural areas. There was simply not enough work for all of these men to keep them occupied and out of trouble. A generation of men who had for a decade known little else than the rough discipline of the military camp was not going to settle easily back into civil servitude.

The crime rate, especially in the cities and coastal ports, soared to unprecedented levels and the magistrates' courts grew increasingly harsh; even the smallest of crimes became capital offences. The 'lucky' were transported; many others were hanged from the gibbet-post, even along the shoreline, as a warning to all who would ignore the Crown.

have wished. These were difficult times for those left in rural areas. Many young men who had been away to war never returned to work the farms, many young women went to work in the factories of the manufacturing centres of the southern Midlands, or sailed away from England's shores forever. They left behind a generation of older folk, left alone to eke out their declining years without their sons and daughters.

Sarah Jones took it as her Christian duty to care for these older folk as much as she was able. Accompanied by young Caroline and her sisters she took them meals, and would often sit and talk with them as they ate. Although Caroline was at times fearful that the family could ill afford this philanthropy, her mother would reply:

> The Lord will provide. Jesus has compassion on the multitude. He would not want us to let poor humans suffer from hunger. And if we are generous we will not want either. He said that even a cup of cold water given in his name would be rewarded.[1]

The Jones family was fortunate that William had invested wisely — life for them was not without its privileges. A governess was employed to teach the children, and Caroline was a good pupil. Arithmetic was one of her favourite subjects, for she had a quick mind and was not satisfied with just those lessons considered suitable for young females. But like most of her class she learned to play the piano, and went riding with her friends and her cousins. She also learned to speak French, and took dancing lessons to prepare herself for the day when she would be introduced into polite county society.

Caroline Jones was rarely impressed by the cut of the young men who sought to make her acquaintance. To her they seemed too shallow; while their interests lay in grain, horseflesh, and the vagaries of the weather, she had her mind set on greater things

Convinced that she had been prepared for a higher calling, she made the decision to carry on her parents' work. Although she had grown to be a striking young lass — of fair complexion, tall and graceful, with soft eyes and ringlets of auburn curls that fell against her cheeks — she was resolved to the fact that she might never marry. Until she met Scottish highlander Lieutenant Archibald Chisholm.

In the round of social engagements that peppered her social calendar Caroline attended some events to which officers from the Northampton Barracks were invited. At one such event Lieutenant Chisholm was partnered with Caroline for a brace of Scottish dances. In the break between sets she learnt

The emigration game

Even as a seven-year-old Caroline Chisholm played a game in which she sailed small boats filled with dolls, transporting them across imaginary seas in a washbasin on the stand in her bedroom. She recalled many years later:

> I made boats of broad-beans; expended all my money in touch-wood dolls; removed families, located them in the bed-quilt, and sent the boats back filled with wheat (of which I kept a store in a thimble case) back to their friends.
>
> At length I upset the basin, which I judged to be a facsimile of the sea, spoiled a new bed, got punished, and afterwards carried out my plan in a dark cellar with a rush-light ... I had a Wesleyan minister and a Catholic priest on board the same boat'.[2]

For one so young, Caroline had been exposed to a wide variety of opinions and, in her father's company, had met and learned to respect the ways and beliefs of all kinds of people, no matter what their nationality, religion, political inclination or status in life.

How prescient was the little game she played in the cellar beneath her father's house.

something about this rather reserved young man who was to become her partner for life. On furlough from several years in the Indian Army, Archy could see that there was little future left at home for the highlander. He had seen the sheep farmer with his purse full of English coin lure the rustic Scots away from the highlands and into the mills. Many had been evicted from the lands that they had defended against all-comers as the English landlords overran their hillsides with flocks of sheep. Three of Archy's brothers had already joined the East India Company and left the highlands forever.

The stalwart Lieutenant Chisholm began to court Miss Caroline Jones. Although he was several years older than she, and had little capital to bring to their match, she became interested in this man whose concerns for others so much reflected her own.

When he eventually admitted that he was a Roman Catholic he was surprised to discover that Caroline had some knowledge of his faith. She told him of her childhood days spent in the company of the French priest and of the way her father had taught her to respect the beliefs of others.

It was not long before Archy asked Sarah Jones for her youngest daughter Caroline's hand in marriage. When he proposed to her, Caroline asked him to wait a month before she would give her reply. He was sure that his love for her was requited, but nevertheless, she asked him not to see her for a full month and then to reconsider his proposal. She wanted him to be absolutely sure that he was prepared to share her life, which she had determined would be a life of service to others less fortunate than herself. Caroline was prepared to forgo her own happiness if it meant that she would have to deny her destiny and the example her father had set for her.

Archibald returned exactly one month later and he and Caroline agreed to be married. They were wed on 27 December 1830 in the Church of St Sepulchre, Northampton, the same church where she had been christened twenty-two years earlier.

Return to India

For the first year of their marriage the couple lived in the seaside township of Brighton, on the south coast. It was here that Caroline took fully to the congregation of the Catholic faith. For a young woman brought up as a Protestant, this decision to embrace Rome must have taken great courage, commitment and dedication. Caroline never lacked any of these virtues.

The female school

Upon arrival in Madras, Caroline Chisholm was distressed to discover the daughters of ordinary British soldiers running wild without schooling or adequate provision for their care. Many of these girls were orphaned, and half-English, half-Indian. The regiment had simply abandoned them to the streets. Some of these children were even seen caged in the street markets, for sale as slaves, or worse.

As they grew older, many were taken as soldiers' 'women' and the cycle of destitution, depravity and despair began all over again. Caroline knew her Christian duty. She sought assistance from the colonial governor, Sir Frederick Adams, who succumbed to her persuasive charms, subscribing twenty pounds himself towards the establishment of 'The Female School of Industry for the Daughters of European Soldiers'.

With an additional 2000 rupees collected from the officers and other gentlemen, Caroline was able to open her school in the district in the native quarter known as Black Town, which was well away from the fort where the Chisholms lived.

Such was Caroline's commitment to the service of others that the family moved away from the fort and into the school.

Archy was recalled to his posting in Madras and set sail for India in early 1832. Caroline followed a few months later.

The life of the officer's wife in Madras could have been one of comparative luxury, but Caroline never sought the easy life. Distressed at the number of mixed-blood girls left to run wild in the streets, she persuaded the governor to assist in founding a school for these abandoned 'daughters of the regiment', whom she considered to be in moral danger.

In 1834 Archy was posted to Vellore with the 30th Native Infantry. He returned to Madras the following year and the couple's first child, also named Archibald to honour his father, was born in May 1836. Their second son, William, was born at Hyderabad one year later.

In 1837, after five years in India, Archibald requested his release from this colonial posting. Although his health was suffering in the subcontinental climate, he could see no future in returning to the damp of Scotland. He had seen so many others who had gone home and were unable to settle under the grey and lowering skies of their class-ridden homeland. The highlands also offered little opportunity for their boys, so they set their sights on New Holland. It was said that there was plenty of land for the asking, and enough convict servants to provide the labour to secure a profitable future.

Bound for Botany Bay

On 23 March 1838 the Chisholms stepped aboard the *Emerald Isle* bound for Botany Bay. They had with them an Indian nurse for each of the boys and a third servant for themselves. The ship first docked at Mauritius, where it stayed a month for repairs. They then sailed on to Australia, landing first in Adelaide then Van Diemen's Land, before arriving in Sydney in September. Caroline and the boys waited on the wharf while the *Emerald Isle* disgorged its cargo, and Archy struck out for the town in search of lodgings. He soon returned, having secured some 'excellent rooms' in Jamieson Street; they were able to move into them the following day. The servants stayed on board ship until the family was settled then went back to Madras on the return voyage.

Although the streets of Sydney were still rough and ready, the young colony was just emerging from its frontier stage and growing into respectability and grandeur. The building program undertaken by Governor Macquarie had transformed the streetscape.

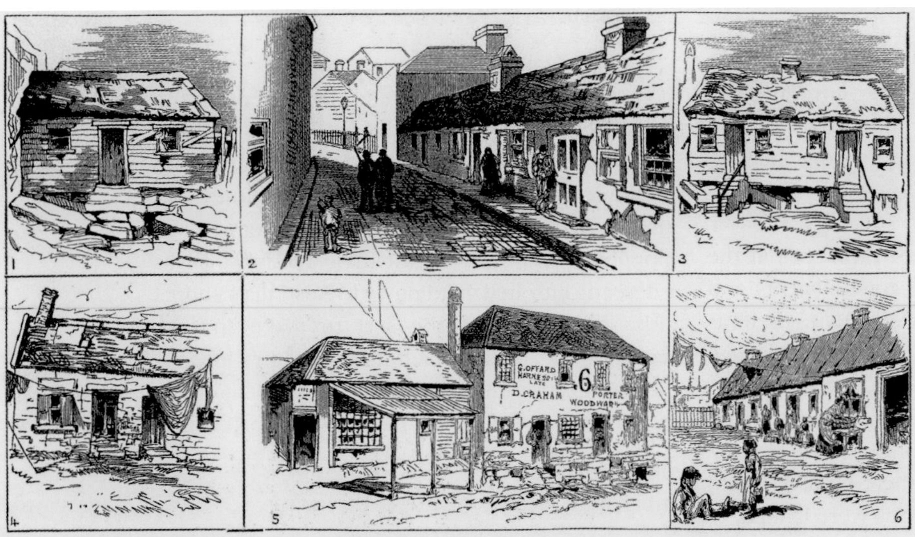

CITY IMPROVEMENTS IN SYDNEY: OLD BUILDINGS ORDERED FOR DEMOLITION.
1—DWELLING-HOUSE IN KENT-STREET. 2—DURAND'S-ALLEY. 3—DWELLING-HOUSE IN KENT-STREET (No. 2). 4—FOWLER'S-SQUARE. 5—CORNER KING AND CLARENCE STREETS. 6—BALDOCK'S-LANE.

LEFT:
Old Sydney buildings ordered for demolition

When the Chisholms landed in Sydney the town was just beginning to grow into grace and stature; yet there were many sadly decaying remnants left in the streets to remind the new settlers of Sydney's rough and ready past.

Governor Macquarie had spent a lot of his time in the colony attempting to rebuild Sydney, demolishing this type of architectural embarassment.

(La Trobe University Bendigo, Library Collection)

But teams of convicts, shackled together at the ankles, still shuffled through the streets on their way to hard labour breaking rocks on the roads; Aborigines could be seen begging; and soldiers languished in hotel doorways.

Proud squatters mounted astride their shiny beasts pushed their way through the crowds; bullock drays groaned up from the docks; carriages rushed by, oblivious to the shiploads of migrants wandering along lost in their new land, seeking lodgings, employment or simply somewhere to pass the night in safety.

It was not long before Caroline saw the need to put her Christian duty before all else, to practise her philanthropy and show her customary concern for the plight of others.

Passing through Hyde Park one day, Caroline and Archy saw a group of agitated men gathered beneath a clump of trees. The strongly built, ruddy-faced men were deep in conversation when Archy drew into their circle. The agitated discussion was being conducted in Gaelic; only one among them could speak any English. Archy listened for a while then turned to explain to Caroline that the men were 'bounty' migrants who had been unable to find any work in the colony:

> These men are Highlanders ... they say they came here as bounty immigrants—their passage is paid, but they cannot find work—they have no trades—no money, and no English—or very little ... Some of them

The bounty scheme

The bounty migration scheme was introduced in 1831 with the intention that individual free settlers were able to receive a bounty from the English government to pay the passage to the colony of any labour they required.

It was not long before the government put the scheme into the hands of 'immigration agents' and shipowners, paying the bounty directly to them, as settlers in the colony found it too hard to engage labour from so far away.

The main drawback with the revised scheme was that avaricious shipowners took little responsibility for the wellbeing of their human cargo, either on board ship or once they were landed.

The government also attempted to redress the imbalance of the sexes in the colony, but unfortunately the shipowners simply gathered girls from the streets or the workhouses. The journey out rarely saw redemption for these women, whose morality was already questionable. For most it was a descent into hell, landing onto Australia's shores girls who were not the sort to make an easy transition into 'genteel' service or country life.

By 1835 the scheme changed again when both men and women could migrate free of charge, such was the demand for labour.

OPPOSITE:
Chain Gang: convicts going to work nr. Sidney [sic] N.S.Wales
Steel engraving, published by E. & J. Backhouse, 1842
(Allport Library & Museum of Fine Arts Collection)

> have families in tents. I am just giving them something to buy food ...[3]

Caroline answered that the money wouldn't last them very long and observed that:

> They were such strong-looking men—they would be fit for hard work surely. The landlady said to me that she was often short of wood, yet there was dry timber about. Ask them if they would be woodcutters.

The highlanders replied that they were prepared to try their hand at anything. Caroline continued, with Archy translating her ideas into Gaelic so that they would understand:

> Then if they spent some of the money to buy axes and ropes—they might hire a cart and sell to the inns.[4]

Some days later it gave them both great satisfaction to see wood being delivered around Sydney in a handcart pushed by one of the ginger-haired highlanders.

Life on the Rocks

On other excursions around Sydney the Chisholms often passed through the area close to the Circular Quay known as The Rocks, an area which had been described to them as a fearful place—'unsavoury by day, unsafe at night'—inhabited by the worst criminal type, escaped convicts and women of ill repute and lost virtue.

The Rocks was a hellhole of gin shops, brothels and bawdy houses where the sailor, the drayman, the runaway soldier, or the swell on a spree could lose himself and, more often than not his purse as well, in debauchery.

Caroline was affronted by the way that 'bounty' ships simply abandoned their human cargo onto the quayside and into this district upon arrival in the colony, taking no further responsibility at all for the welfare of those they had carried, to their own financial benefit, so far from their home. She could see that there were many young girls simply dumped into this certain moral danger.

She resolved to do something positive about this unsavoury situation. Archy had found a property at Windsor, thirty miles out of Sydney on the Hawkesbury River, to which he intended to return as a 'gentleman farmer' after his time in the army came to an end. They settled into Windsor, where Caroline welcomed newly arrived migrant girls into their home. She then helped them find employment in the district. But it was not possible for her to house them all. She sought the

RIGHT:
Sir George Gipps, 1791-1847
Oil on canvas, artist unknown

Gipps served as Governor in the years 1838-1846. Although he was a reasonable man, it did take him some time before he agreed to assist Caroline Chisholm. He eventually granted her the use of the old barracks as housing for migrant girls.

Aware of the prejudice against women who sought to influence political affairs, and the resentment towards Catholics in the Anglican-dominated society, Caroline subtly got her way through her clever use of 'petticoat politics'.

(Mitchell Library Collection, State Library of New South Wales)

assistance of Governor George Gipps in the provision of a home for emigrant girls. She had her mind set on the disused Immigration Barracks, which stood in Bent Street.

Caroline was well aware of the prejudice against, and resentment towards, any female who interfered in political affairs. She was also aware of the open resentment of Catholics in the colonial society which was dominated at an official level by the Anglican Church. So Caroline wrote first to Lady Gipps, the governor's wife, to seek her support in her work: meeting every migrant ship that arrived from England, seeing the girls off safely and offering them what shelter she could find.

She needed to let others in the community know what she was trying to do, and to put pressure on the government to support her worthy cause. Summoning up all her courage, she sought help from the editor of the *Sydney Morning Herald*. By the time she went to petition the assistance of the paper, her intentions were already broadly canvassed throughout the colony.

Gipps was under pressure from the Colonial Office. The accounts of the colony were in the red. He was expected to make the Wakefield scheme of 'systematic emigration' work once and for all, reining in the excesses of the squatters who had grabbed as much good land and cheap labour as they could. In response, Gipps went overboard and offered so many bounty orders (sponsored emigration) that he was soon embarrassed by his ill-conceived attempt to control the labour supply. He really did not need to have the 'lunatic, Popish old-wife' of an Indian Army captain pestering him about the plight of a few boatloads of working girls.

When Caroline was first presented to Governor Gipps he was shocked, as he had:

> ... expected an old lady in a white cap and spectacles, who would have talked to him about [his] soul.

Instead, he was pleasantly surprised when he was introduced to:

> ... a handsome, stately young woman who proceeded to reason the question as if she thought her reason and experience, too, worth as much as mine.[5]

Although, at this first meeting, Caroline had acquitted herself well, Gipps was not won over. He thought she overestimated the power of her own opinions and he certainly did not want to commit the government purse to any crazy Roman Catholic scheme that would embarrass him further.

RIGHT:
Emigration in Search of a Husband

This lithograph published on 10 August 1833 bears the following inscription:

> What are you going to Sidney [sic] for pray ma'am. Vy they say as how there's lots of good husbands to be had cheap there—whereas the brutes in England can't see no charms in a woman unless she's got plenty of money to keep 'em in their idleness.

(National Library of Australia Collection)

So Caroline worked her way around him. She garnered support from the wives of leading citizens; first among them was Lady Gipps. While these women were not able to offer material support, their approval gave her proposals considerable credibility.

But Gipps was still not moved. Even some prominent Catholics suggested to Caroline that she should abandon her proposals; her public persistence was beginning to embarrass them.

Caroline was nearly at the end of her tether. She was getting nowhere and had almost exhausted all the avenues that had once seemed open to her. She was about to give up, when, walking along the cliff path on her way to church one Sunday morning she came upon an intoxicated young woman who looked as if she was about to throw herself into the crashing waves below.

Caroline recognised the lass as being Flora MacDonald, a once-striking beauty she had noticed causing quite a stir among a group of migrants in the Domain shortly after her arrival. Coincidentally, Flora's parents had been employed on the Chisholm estate in Scotland. Flora had travelled to the colony as a bounty migrant, where the score of young women on board were afforded little protection from sailors and male passengers on the hellish voyage out. On her arrival she had quite willingly allowed herself to be seduced by a gentleman lover, but had been used and discarded by this already-married man.

Flora could find no work in the economically depressed colony and fell into the only life possible to ensure her survival. Like so many other girls in the same predicament, she was living in a cave in the Rocks, hanging about the taverns at night, taking food and drink from any man who cared to take an interest in her. Flora had become so distraught with the course her life had taken that she had resolved to end it in the pounding waves that morning when Caroline Chisholm came upon her on the clifftop. Caroline stayed with Flora until she was assured that she would no longer do herself harm. Lodgings were secured and Caroline left her with the firm resolve that she would not give up:

> My spirits returned; I felt God's blessing was on my work. From this time, I never thought of human help; I neglected no steps to conciliate; I increased my exertions; but from that hour I was on the beach with Flora, fear left me.[6]

The newspapers began to assist Caroline's cause by reporting stories such as Flora's. They began to feed a tide of public opinion, which demanded that something be done.

The Wakefield scheme

Following the failure of a fledgling colony to gain a foothold in the Swan River district of Western Australia, there were many ideas for the best way to establish colonial communities and to encourage migration.

The prison system and transportation had been the most effective in ridding England of its unwanted and undesirable citizens, but there were many who sought to make a new start on the right side of the law.

Languishing in prison for the abduction of a young heiress, Edward Gibbon Wakefield developed his theory of systematic migration. He proposed that land be sold to prospective migrants at a price that would finance the further migration of free labourers and their families. He speculated that they, in turn, would earn enough to be able to buy their own patch, and this would then provide funds for further emigration.

The first example was the establishment of the colony of South Australia in 1834, which was a joint venture between London banker and shipowner George Fife Angas and the Crown. The scheme was scrapped in 1838 when it finally became apparent to all that the division of control between commerce and the Crown was unsustainable.

Caroline pressed the papers to continue to report similar stories until the Governor granted her the use of the barracks.

In October 1841 the Governor relented and the Female Immigrants Home was established in the old wooden Immigration Barracks in Bent Street, which had fallen into disrepair. Caroline spent the first night there accompanied by scores of rats that skittered around the rooms all night. Before long the barracks were cleaned up and became a temporary home to more than 100 girls a night, gathered from the recesses of the Rocks or from sleeping rough in the Domain.

Although Caroline was predominantly concerned for the welfare of her female charges, she also assisted many couples with children, who had the most difficulty securing any kind of employment where they could be housed together.

Into the country

Caroline next decided that she would write to influential gentlemen in the outlying regions: magistrates, clergymen, and government officials, anyone who would be able to assist her in finding employment for her charges. She composed a circular letter in which she announced her intentions and, with the assistance of Governor Gipps, the letter was posted free of charge throughout the country. It was not long before Caroline Chisholm was

ABOVE:

Circular Quay

Watercolour by F. Garling, 1839

It was the sorry plight of the abandoned migrant women found living rough in caves in the Rocks area adjacent to Circular Quay that first motivated Caroline Chisholm to petition the governor for his assistance.

She also sought assistance from the newspapers by supplying them with heart-rending stories of the girls she encountered. Public opinion encouraged Caroline in her work and the Governor soon offered his support as well.

(Mitchell Library Collection, State Library of New South Wales)

planning to take the first bullock dray loaded with emigrant girls out into the country and place them in rural employment.

Her first attempt failed. There were many who disapproved of Mrs Chisholm's plans to distribute her charges far and wide. There were many who resented her because she was a Catholic; they feared that the influence of 'papists' and the 'troublesome Irish' would turn the balance of power against the established classes.

While it was true that most of those who were helped by Mrs Chisholm in these early days were Catholic, and Irish Catholic in particular, these fears were largely unfounded. There were also many who resented girls of 'dubious virtue' being sent into the country; they feared a rapid decline in morality. These fears were also unfounded. Yet some did their very best to spread rumours of 'bushrangers and bunyips' to frighten away any young lasses unused to colonial life. They were successful — just the once.

BELOW:
The Green Hills from the [banks] of the Hawkesbury River
Watercolour, artist unknown, c. 1809

The Green Hills were later known as Windsor. This painting is from an album compiled by Lieutenant Governor William Paterson, who was in the colony from 1791 until 1810. Paterson had once duelled with Macarthur and came off second best.

Archibald Chisholm settled his family on a property at Windsor, intending to retire to the pastoral life after his time in the army was over.

(State Library of New South Wales Collection)

One evening, a 'pious' gentleman called upon Caroline unannounced, wishing to convey to her his fervent opinion on the dangers of travel into the rural districts. He was armed with numerous newspaper cuttings outlining the danger afoot for the unwitting traveller. He had news of murderous bushrangers, blood-thirsty Aborigines, rapes and all kinds of dastardly deeds that had occurred beyond the safety of the towns. He warned her that unless she ceased her activities he would write to the newspapers and tell such hair-raising stories that no single girl would ever climb aboard one of her drays and set out for a life in the bush.

Caroline was curious. This gentleman seemed slightly unhinged, as many obsessed with

RIGHT;
Bushing it
This engraving from Samuel Sidney's *Three Colonies of Australia*, published in London in 1852, is one of the few contemporary illustrations which depict Caroline Chisholm and her female charges camped out on the road.

(La Trobe University Bendigo, Library Collection)

BUSHING IT.

piety and righteousness at times do appear. She paced the floor of her room with him; taking him by the arm, she implored him to tell his story. It transpired that his sister had taken up with a 'gentleman', had been used, then cast aside.

Like Flora MacDonald, she had fallen by the wayside, and he was warning Caroline of the likely fate of those who fell onto that wayward path. Caroline respectfully insisted that the pious gentleman do his Christian duty and contact his sister, who was living in Sydney, take her back in to the fold of his family, and not deny her the love and support of the only family she had.

With Caroline's help, brother and sister were reconciled and he never wrote his troubling missive to the newspapers. However, the rumours of beasts and bushrangers were already broadcast and the girls on the first dray refused to go out at all. The dray was sent away empty.

Caroline kept the failure of her first attempt a secret and on the following morning she ordered two more drays and agreed to go with them as escort. From that day on Caroline rode with every shipment, escorting each group of emigrant girls, riding from farm to farm, station to township, securing employment for each girl as she went. She was meticulous in her arrangements with both employer and employee: she drew up contracts, in triplicate, which were distributed to all parties concerned, and kept careful records of where she had placed all her charges.

By 1841 Caroline Chisholm had established a network of employment agents in several country towns and set up a number of emigrant depots at Campbelltown, Liverpool and Parramatta where newly arrived emigrants could first be taken to help them get a foothold in the country.

After only a year she had settled hundreds of migrants into the country. She had depots at Bong Bong, Goulburn, Maitland, Moreton Bay,

The sad plight of Mary Teague

In September 1841 the *Chronicle* reported that in the first two weeks of that month 2557 emigrants had landed in Sydney. It also published a heart-rending letter telling of the sad plight of Mary Teague.

Mary Teague was a new arrival who had been arrested and charged with public drunkenness when she was found staggering along the Sydney streets.

She was publicly humiliated in the stocks, and was found three days later, lying in a ditch unable to move.

The fact that her unstable gait, the reason for her initial arrest, was the result of hunger and not alcohol — she had not eaten since she had left the bounty ship days before she was arrested — meant nothing to the constabulary. To them she was just another 'fallen' woman to be treated without rights or respect.

Caroline Chisholm pressed the newspapers to continue to report these stories until she was able to secure a place for the protection of these newly arrived emigrant girls.

LEFT:
Caroline Chisholm Barracks, East Maitland, New South Wales
Photograph by J. Houldsworth, c. 1986
(By permission, Australian Heritage Commission)

Port Macquarie, Scone, Wollongong and Yass. So successful was her method of distribution that the government saw little reason to continue with any scheme of its own. In fact, Governor Gipps was most relieved to be able to report to Earl Grey that almost all of his bounty migrants were settled and the pressure on the towns had been alleviated. He neglected to mention this success was almost entirely due to the hard work of Caroline Chisholm.

Even though she had carried hundreds of girls into the country, on some of the most dangerous roads in the colony, Caroline was never bothered at all by bushrangers. It may even be surmised that some protection was afforded her on her journeys, such was the chivalrous nature of most of the 'gentlemen of the roads', who were mostly young men whose own histories were not unlike those of Chisholm's charges.

While she was generally supported in her work, Chisholm's schemes for rural settlement were so successful that she did come under attack from some who had once been her strongest advocates.

Vehemently anti-Catholic, Presbyterian minister John Dunmore Lang was also keenly interested in assisted emigration, but of 'the right kind of people'—preferably Scots Protestants. Every success that Caroline had put her more and more at odds with Lang. After the editor of the Catholic *Chronicle* criticised Lang's discriminatory emigration policy, he fought back with a letter to the *Sydney Morning Herald* on 14 March 1846, critical of the assistance given by Chisholm to predominantly Catholic emigrants. Lang complained that no matter what she did she was considered 'an angel of light' and he 'a perfect fiend of darkness'.[7] He wrote:

> Mrs. Chisholm's past and future connection with immigration is regarded by this personage with unqualified approbation. And why so? Why simply because Mrs. Chisholm is a Roman Catholic, a zealous and devoted Roman Catholic who, he imagines will as a matter of course render her influence and efforts in that way subservient in some way

Procuring from the dock

The young girls on board the migrant ships must have wondered what they had struck when they witnessed a glaring stand-off between one of Sydney's fashionably dressed madams and the redoubtable Caroline Chisholm.

Caroline tried to stop the practice of allowing emigrants to stay on board ship for ten days after docking. She would have preferred to land all females immediately and take them to the security of her home or hostel.

Madams came aboard ship and made offers of 'employment' to any attractive young lass they took a shine too. It was just so easy to convince the newly arrived and innocent girls of a prosperous future in the colony. On many occasions Caroline had rushed to meet an incoming ship, and once on board stood her ground against any 'scarlet woman' who dared to climb aboard or recruit from the dock.

As evidence of the need to change the practice, Caroline Chisholm cited the case of one fifteen year old who was met at the dock, enticed to leave the ship and go straight to work—in a brothel. The girl had no inkling of her fate: she had only been instructed by her new mistress to walk in certain streets at certain times and 'a gentleman' would give her £2. Mrs Chisholm could do nothing to save her.

LEFT:
John Dunmore Lang

Presbyterian Minister J. D. Lang arrived in Sydney in 1822. A Scots-born Presbyterian, he was anti-Catholic with a vengeance. Although he started out in support of Mrs Caroline Chisholm and assisted emigration, he ended up her most strident opponent.

When she published her *Female Immigration and Voluntary Information from the People of New South Wales,* he countered with his *Australian Emigrant's Manual.*

She proposed a system of impartial colonisation; he proposed one for Protestants only. Lang believed that anyone not adhering to the strict tenets of his Presbyterian faith was on a sure path to eternal damnation. His attitudes were reflected in his emigration policy: if only the 'right' people were chosen, little else mattered. Chisholm sought to help all those in need regardless of circumstance.

Lang had only intended to stay in Australia until his Scots Kirk was built, but stayed, and continued to vent his spleen on his popish rival.

(State Library of New South Wales Collection)

> or other to the extension and prevalence of Romanism in this Colony and hemisphere.[8]

In reply, Chisholm denounced Lang, declaring that 'any attempt to conduct emigration on a sectarian basis will most assuredly fail; [his] proposal is an insult to the Colony, and if introduced would only tend to create discord and strife'.[9] Chisholm and Lang were alone in all of the colony for their interest in systematic emigration and yet their religious beliefs and subsequent socio-political affiliations pushed them further and further apart. Caroline Chisholm desired an impartial system of national colonisation, serving all equally; Lang desired the overthrow of the 'degrading despotism of Rome' in support of Protestant-only emigration from England to Australia.

In London with Dickens

As transportation of convicts to the Australian colonies had officially come to an end in 1853 (although the practice continued until 1868 when the *Hougomount* carried the last transportees to Western Australia), there was still a great demand for labour; there were plenty of willing employers among 'the great flock-owners [who] eagerly engaged the ticket-of-leave men, tamed somewhat by penitentiary discipline, and all unencumbered by wives and families ...'[10]

The case of the Carthaginian

The bounty ship *Carthaginian* arrived in Sydney in January 1842. Several of the female passengers were taken to Caroline Chisholm's home. Accustomed to tales of hardship at sea and unsavoury treatment of females at the hands of sailors and other male passengers, Caroline was generally not easily shocked. However, this time she was horrified to learn of the treatment meted out to one woman, Margaret Anne Bolton.

Margaret had been treated cruelly by the captain, Robert Robertson, and the ship's surgeon, Richard W. Nelson, when she had been accused of creating a nuisance and 'frightening' the other females on board by playing at ghosts.

Margaret was a bit priggish, she was not popular with the other passengers, and was somewhat peevish and inclined to be disdainful of others. But she certainly did not deserve to be so cruelly dealt with by her shipboard tormentors.

Although she denied the accusation made against her, the captain and surgeon dragged her up on deck, tied her to the mast and threw bucketfuls of icy-cold sea water over her, leaving her there to suffer in the elements for hours until one of the crew cut her free at around midnight.

By this time time she was too weak to walk back to her quarters. She was helped back to her bunk; unable to find the key to her seachest, she was

They were able to engage them at lower wages than the free emigrants, who with wives and children in tow had arrived at the same time. The government had been convinced that transportation was inconsistent with their efforts at free emigration; transportation tended to counteract the benefits of migration while emigration actually deprived transportation of its terror.

There were some who had even committed crimes in the hope that they would be transported for free to the land of plenty.

> In the latter end of 1848 the results of the distress in England and famine in Ireland were felt in Australia in the shape of an inflowing of free emigrants more numerous than had been received since the frantic mania of 1841 ... The gold discoveries [of a decade later] proved to everyone ... that transportation was not only odious to the colonists but absurd as a punishment.[11]

At a time of great unrest throughout Europe and the British Isles, the demand for emigration — to anywhere away from the squalor of British cities, the hunger and pestilence of the 'Emerald Isle', and revolutionary Europe — was greater than ever.

Caroline believed that the main problem with government schemes up until this point was that the wrong kind of people had been sent to the colonies. Few of the town dwellers had any experience with farming or rural labour, the refuse of the workhouses had little to offer except indolence and crime; the small number of decent women and families eager to emigrate did little to balance the needs of a growing, and decent, colonial society.

The Chisholms moved back to England, and set themselves up in the East End, in the heart of Charles Dickens's London. In grey and grimy crowded streets, with cockney-voiced barrow-boys and the constant roar and rattle of city traffic, the green fields and brilliant blue skies of Windsor on the Hawkesbury River seemed far, far away.

Caroline planned to assist the emigration of the wives and families of convicts who had been transported to Australia. When she arrived in England she had a long list of names of those who wished to be reunited.

With some financial help from the government Caroline Chisholm was able to assist the passage of hundreds who were eager to be reunited with loved ones in the colonies. She then began the work of establishing her vision for a national migration scheme, the Family Colonisation Loan Society.

Caroline's main aim was to help 'the poorer class to emigrate' and she drew support from unusual quarters indeed. After an introduction

forced to spend the night shivering on her mattress clad only in her wet nightdress and petticoat. She never fully recovered from her ordeal.

Caroline discussed the matter with Governor Gipps, informing him that she intended to prosecute the master and surgeon of the *Carthaginian*. Although Gipps warned her that a government prosecution was a grave matter, and one brought by a woman against a ship's master for the treatment of women under his care would be difficult to press, she went ahead with the prosecution and won the case.

Both captain and surgeon were found guilty of the charges brought against them; each was fined £50 and sentenced to six months in prison. The ensuing public outcry brought radical changes to the conditions on board bounty ships. As well as more care being taken in the selection of bounty migrants (several of Margaret's accusers on the *Carthaginian* were known to be 'women of the town'), it soon became practice for all ships to carry two qualified surgeons: one older, experienced man, and a younger man learning the ropes while at sea.

By making a test case of this, which was no doubt not an isolated incident, Caroline Chisholm had done a great service to the future welfare of all emigrants.

had been arranged by Elizabeth Herbert, the wife of the Right Honourable Sydney Herbert, Earl of Pembroke and Secretary of War, Caroline met the famed writer and journalist Charles Dickens, who threw his support behind her and her emigration scheme. Dickens visited her at her home and, accustomed as he was to the considerable degree of comfort that success and notoriety could bring, he was surprised that she lived in such a modest dwelling as she had taken in fashionable Islington, close to where he himself lived near to King's Cross Station.

Dickens knew the area well: he wandered these same surrounding streets at night, taking in the pubs and alleyways, his keen writer's eye recording for later use the romantic argot of the street, the sounds and smells 'where the lowest orders of Irish were wrangling "with might and main".'[12]

People came and went all throughout their meeting. A postman in a scarlet cloak rattled at the door and an armful of emigrants' letters, with postage to be paid, was carried in and interrupted Dickens in mid-speech. Dickens came away from his meeting with the Chisholms determined to help whatever way he could. He published many of the letters received from emigrants who had made successful new beginnings in the colonies, and helped to inform the British public of Caroline Chisholm and the work of the Family Colonisation Loan Society.

In Dickens's later serialised novel, *Bleak House*, the main character, Mrs Jellyby, is said to have been modelled on Caroline Chisholm herself. The emigration and colonial success of Mr Micawber, in *David Copperfield*, was taken directly from the experiences recalled in the emigrants' letters that appeared week after week in *Household Words*.

In 1851 Archibald Chisholm returned to Australia to set up as the colonial agent for the society—first in Adelaide, then in Melbourne. The agency helped the newly arrived, who

The way the scheme worked

Those wishing to emigrate formed themselves into cooperative groups and were required to save regular amounts until there were sufficient funds to send one family unit to Australia.

The fare for six adults and two children, or two adults and ten children, was £100. Once in the colony, the successful emigrants continued to save money into the society until others in their group could emigrate. The society also loaned money to assist emigrants to take their first steps. The more wage-earners who migrated, the quicker the loans were repaid and then more members could make the journey.

The scheme was very successful. Scores of hopeful 'new settlers' queued at the door of the Chisholm home begging for an interview with 'the emigrant's friend'. Caroline had her home almost totally turned over to the service of the emigrant. In one room she had a full-scale model of the migrant ship's berth so that emigrants could prepare themselves for the privations of the long journey to the colonies. Every migrant had to pass a stringent medical examination and only those fit to travel were allowed aboard.

Caroline Chisholm's ships had an unrivalled record for successful arrivals on Australia's shores.

BELOW:
Plan of an emigrant ship between decks

had emigrated with the society, to find suitable employment in the country.

The first emigrants assisted by the society sailed from England on 28 September 1850 aboard the *Slain's Castle*. Caroline ensured the safety of all aboard her vessels; emigrants travelled in family groups and single women were 'adopted' by married couples for the voyage. She encouraged family groups to form friendships on board, in the hope that once ashore they would offer support and a sense of community to one another.

Off to the diggings

It was not long before the society was almost made redundant. The discovery of gold in New South Wales in February 1851, and in the hills around Mount Alexander in Central Victoria in September, brought thousands of emigrants to Australia from all corners of the world without the need for any further encouragement from Charles Dickens or the British government.

This was not systematic, assisted emigration of much-needed agricultural labourers. This was a shambolic rush to easy riches, the ports filled with tall-masted vessels at anchor, empty, after even the crews abandoned their ships for the diggings.

As there were still many groups who had been saving for years to emigrate, the society continued to send its ships to the colonies. Six ships arrived in 1852; it is not known how many of these families sought help to relocate through the colonial agent or how many headed straight up to the goldfields as soon as they were allowed ashore.

Realising that her work was done in England, Caroline returned to Australia in 1854. Even though she had toiled almost ceaselessly for more than thirty years, and was nearing her fiftieth year, she still felt called to her Christian duty. She decided to tour the diggings and seek information that would help make the journey for the newly arrived as comfortable as possible. Just as she had done in New South Wales many years before, she established shelters along the roads to the diggings for families to take cover at night.

A fuss was made of Caroline Chisholm at each goldfield she visited. At a meeting held in the Hall of Castlemaine in November 1854 one prominent local figure, William Hitchcock, proudly announced that he had enjoyed the pleasure of having Caroline Chisholm staying with him for the past two days and that he wished 'she were to be his guest for two years'. The audience burst into sponta-

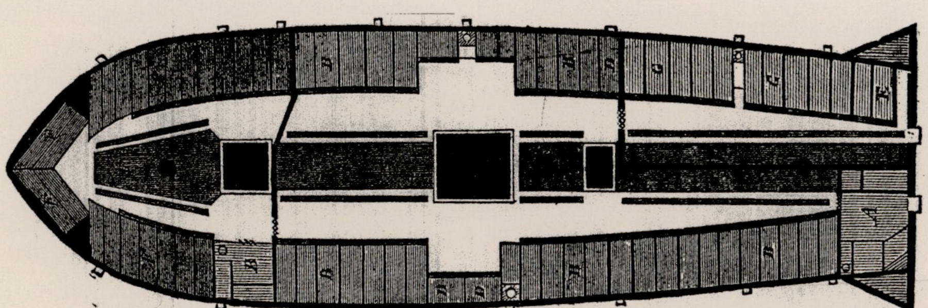

PLAN OF AN EMIGRANT SHIP BETWEEN DECKS.

A. The hospital for females, fitted up with six bed places (one of which is prepared and devoted to accouchments.)
B. The hospital for males, with four bed places.
Between A and B are 48 bed places, each 6 feet by 3 feet, for married people above, and for their children below, every one furnished with bedding, pegs for clothes, and each divided from the adjacent bed place by stout planks.
From the men's hospital (B) a bulkhead goes across the ship to separate that part of the vessel forward, which is appropriated to the single men and youths, whose bed places number 46, and every one sleeps alone in a bed 6 feet by 2 feet.
Between C and D are 24 bed places for married people (as on the opposite side), a bulkhead then goes halfway across the deck, and runs in the amidships to the stern, enclosing the apartment of the single females, and containing 24 bed places, each 6 feet by 3 feet, as two are required to sleep together.
Along the whole of the amidships are tables with fixed seats, and beneath the tables are plate racks and battens to hold small casks containing the daily allowances of fresh water, provisions, etc.

neous applause at Hitchcock's enthusiasm for his guest.

Hitchcock went on to denounce those who were critical of her, condemning those 'persons [who] were blaming her for bringing to the colony a class of persons not sufficiently good'. She replied that there were others who blamed her for carrying to the colonies the 'very cream of the English population'.

Caroline Chisholm was convinced that the rough-and-ready society on the goldfields needed the ministration of 'God's police', a term she had coined to describe the redeeming influence of wives and children, hearth and home, on the wayward, independent and free-wheeling diggers.

Although she had always fought to improve the lot of her needy 'charges', Chisholm was no revolutionary. When disgruntled diggers pressed her to represent their demands for franchise, land reform and release from the onerous licence fees that were creating such unrest on the goldfields — ultimately leading to bloodshed at the Eureka diggings near Ballarat on 3 December 1854 — she was not moved to use her influence, even though she always had the ear of the authorities.

The *Mount Alexander Mail* reported remarks made by her at the meeting in Castlemaine in November, in the issue published on 11 December, just one week after the fall of the Eureka Stockade:

> I do not feel sympathy for any body of men who pay so little respect to their own sex as to live without wives when they can well afford to pay for them ... what a cheer the diggers would give if the houses they go to at night were something better than the blankets which they had to creep like dogs.[13]

BELOW:
Family on deck of migrant ship

The vessels that were commissioned by the Family Colonisation Loan Society were airy and clean. Ample food and clean water were supplied and each family had its own quarters. Although the ships were cramped, the journey was made as safe and healthy as possible.

Single female passengers were quarantined well away from the crew, their virtue protected by the thoughtful planning of Caroline Chisholm.

(National Library of Australia Collection)

Her answer to the diggers' grievances was not the rallying cry of the azure blue standard that fluttered briefly over Ballarat, but to suggest that they would all be better off 'at home with their wives and families, when they live in peace and quietness'.

Caroline Chisholm, who was a friend of emancipist William Wentworth, had sat with governors, chatted with Dickens and had even been blessed by the Pope himself, was never likely to preach sedition or even to side with the 'evil agitator'.

Although she had worked her entire life in the service of those dispossessed by the injustices, inequities and discrimination that flowed from English Imperialism, she accepted rule by those who had inherited their status, and contributed to this 'rule by class', helping to keep the labouring classes in their place by making them happy with their lot.

She did, however, have one reasonable suggestion as to how the digger's lives could be improved — the relief of all taxes on married men and 'a bounty on all women and children introduced into the diggers' districts'.

With Chisholm's help, shiploads of young migrant women made their way to the diggings, dray loads stopping overnight at her shelters and then moving on the next day, carrying future wives for men in the canvas

BELOW:
Portrait of Caroline Chisholm
Lithograph by Thomas Fairland, published in Advance Australia, *London, 1 September 1852*

(Rex Nan Kivell Collection, U6413. By permission, National Library of Australia)

townships on the goldfields. Her policy of 'hearth and home' was well in place as she sought to change social behaviour through 'happy' marriage.

Her own happiness as a child, on the family farm in Northamptonshire—a good, strong and loving man at the head of the family, and a devoted wife and mother—and her meaningful worship of God had laid the foundation for this program she continued to implement wherever she was able to press her influence.

'Unlock the lands!'

Following the battle at Eureka the colony was forced to consider the diggers' grievances. At the forefront was the question of land reform; diggers demanded the opportunity to purchase land on which to build a future. Chisholm also turned her mind to this matter and spearheaded a campaign to 'Unlock the lands!' Just as she believed that men's deliverance was bound to a happy home, she also believed that social order could be advanced if families could stake their future, together, on their own plot of ground.

With the failure of the alluvial goldfields diggers needed the security of land on which to invest in their future and the future of the colony. Caroline Chisholm maintained that it would be impossible to continue to encourage the right sort of emigrant if men were continually denied access to good land.

Reflecting the diggers' frustration, more than 12,000 departed from the Victorian diggings and emigrated to New Zealand, and thousands more left for the west coast of America, and Canada.

Caroline's wishes were thwarted by the squatters who brooked no opposition to the pre-emptive tenure over the properties they had secured with vice-regal patronage before the gold rushes.

Poverty in retirement

Caroline Chisholm left the business of land reform unresolved. Towards the end of 1857 her health failed; she had developed a disease of the kidneys which was to cripple her for the remaining few years of her life.

The family moved to the Central Highlands township of Kyneton, on the road to Mount Alexander, where they had bought a store for two of their sons with part of the money from a testimonial collection of £7500 raised in Melbourne some years earlier.

The extremes of weather felt in the Central Victorian township only added to Caroline's decline and her doctor suggested that returning to Sydney was the only possible chance for her to regain her health.

Mrs Chisholm's sheltersheds

The first track to feature Mrs Chisholm's shelters was the road to Castlemaine, where shelters, one day's march apart, were built at Essendon, Keilor, Aitken's Gap, Gisborne, the Black Forest, Woodend, Carlsruhe, Kyneton, Malmsbury, Taradale and Elphinstone, through Castlemaine to Muckleford and on to Maldon.

The sheds were able to accommodate thirty single men and ten single women, with spaces for married couples. There were cart sheds and stables, cooking houses and other conveniences attached. A hut-keeper's house stood nearby and the keeper was able to provide wood for cooking, candles, water and some stores, at fixed rates. Caroline was keen to ensure that her huts did not interfere with the trade of local stores and hotel keepers; her aim was to provide for the needs and comfort of the travellers, not to profit from it. A bed would cost 1s per adult per night and 6d per child. Tickets could be bought in Melbourne and were even available for purchase in England.

Following Mrs Chisholm's return to Melbourne in 1854, a collection of £7500 was raised by public subscription, in appreciation of her work over the years, to provide for her in her retirement. She spent most of this money on the construction of the shelters.

The winter trip to New South Wales almost killed her and she was bedridden for several weeks after, unable to leave the Post Office Hotel in George Street where she had taken rooms. As a mark of his respect for Caroline, prominent Sydney physician Doctor William Bland, who had stood on a joint ticket with her friend, William Charles Wentworth, in the New South Wales parliamentary elections of 1853, treated her for weeks without fee.

This was just as well, as she was now absolutely impoverished; she and Archy had done all they could to give their boys a financial foothold, but they had done little to prepare for themselves. As ill as she was, she continued to make some money by teaching English to Chinese migrants for 1s 6d a lesson. She even pawned the medal given to her by the Pope, to buy food for the family.

In July 1862, as a last attempt to earn a reliable income, Caroline opened a girls' school at Rathbone House in Newtown. The school probably operated for only a few years, as she seems to have disappeared from public life in around 1864.

Wishing to have their children complete their schooling in England, the Chisholms left Australia for the last time in June 1866. Surprisingly, there was no official farewell; not even the Sydney newspapers carried any comment on the departure of the woman who had played such an important role in the 'settling' of colonial society.

The government did settle an annual pension of £100 on her in the same year, but, with her children still at school in England, Ireland and Belgium, it is hard to imagine how they all managed to survive on such a small income.

Living in a rented house in Highgate in 1871, Caroline again fell ill; she remained bedridden for the last five years of her life. She and Archy moved to another house in Fulham, where her bed could be placed in a bay window at the front of the house so she could watch the world go by.

On Sunday 25 March 1877, she drifted close to death. Just before she passed away she rallied for a brief moment and cried out 'Take me home! Take me home!'

The London *Times* carried a ten-line obituary the following day; months later when the news reached the colony, the Australian papers barely noted her passing. Her body was taken to be buried in Northampton, with the full rites of the Roman Catholic Church. Major Archibald Chisholm died soon after and was buried in the same grave with Caroline. Their headstone bears a simple inscription: 'The Emigrant's Friend'.

'To Mrs Chisholm'

The guardian angel of her helpless sex,
Whom no fatigue could daunt, nor cross vex,
With manly reason and spirit pure,
For them with unrepining love she bore
The boarded cottage and the earthen floor.
The sultry days in tedious labour spent,
The endless tale of whining discontent
Bore noonday's burning sun, and midnight's chill,
The scanty meal, the journey lengthening still;
Lavished her scanty store on their distress,
And sought no other guerdon than success,
Say ye who hold the balance and the sword,
Into your lap the wealth of nation's poured,
What have you done with all your hireling brood,
Compared with her the generous and the good?
Much ye receive and little ye dispense,
Your alms are paltry, and your debts immense;
Your toil's reluctant—freely hers is given;
You toil for earth, she labours still for Heaven.

ROBERT LOWE
Spectator (Sydney), 28 February 1846

Sir Henry Parkes

1815 – 1896

Sir Henry Parkes features on the face of the $5 polymer note, first issued in 2001.

OPPOSITE:
Sir Henry Parkes
Oil on canvas by Tom Roberts, 1894
(Art Gallery of New South Wales Collection)

BELOW:
The young Henry Parkes
(State Library of New South Wales Collection)

The father of Federation

WHEN THE BOUNTY SHIP *STRATHFIELDSAYE* SAILED into Sydney Harbour on 25 July 1839 it brought to Australia's shores a big man who was to be made larger than life in the colonies. Never mind that Henry Parkes was an uncommonly poor businessman who made failure a habit; his power over language, and his reforming ideals, would see him become known as the 'father of Federation'.

After a 109-day journey out from Plymouth, the *Strathfieldsaye* dropped anchor in Neutral Bay; on the deck stood a striking young man, his shock of unruly hair swept back against the breeze. This unusually tall fellow (Parkes stood at over six feet) surveyed the wooded shoreline and envisioned the better life he planned for the young bride he had brought with him to the colony. Below decks, Clarinda Parkes waited; in her arms she cradled the baby born only two days before they first sighted Port Jackson.

Parkes recalled his first sighting of the Australian coastline on the same day that the couple welcomed their daughter into the world. They had woken a few hours after the ship had cleared Bass Strait:

> The sun rose ... to take possession of an almost cloudless sky. The line of coast continued to lengthen till it stretched either way as far as the eye could reach in the bland and beautiful sunlight.[1]

A childhood of constant toil

Henry Parkes was born in the village of Canley Hamlet, near Stoneleigh, in Warwickshire, England, on 27 May 1815. He was the son of a poor tenant farmer, and he was never to know anything but hardship and hard work. As a child he first started work as a rope-walker; all day Henry walked up and down the length of a long, narrow factory, pulling strands of hemp behind him as they were twisted into ropes. He was paid fourpence a day for his efforts. He then worked in a brickyard and, while still a mere lad, broke rocks on the King's highway.

By the time he was in his teens and lucky enough to be apprenticed to a bone and ivory turner in Birmingham, Henry Parkes, who was later described as the greatest democratic, liberal politician in nineteenth-century Australia, had seen so much deprivation and near-slavery that his mind was set towards political activism.

He had just enough schooling to enable him to read and write; in an effort to improve himself he spent his spare moments studying his books, and attended classes at night school. He liked to read the works of the British poets and soon began to write verse of his own. For a young man born to poverty and educated in the workhouses, the way of the poet was obscure, but in Henry Parkes the romantic muse would prevail.

Clarinda had given birth just as the sun came up and as the ship sailed in sight of the Australian coast. Parkes called the baby his 'little blue-eyed ocean child'; baby Clarinda Sarah Parkes was born in Australian waters, a true-blue currency lass.

Henry Parkes descended into the longboat brought alongside the ship to ferry passengers to shore, and headed off, eager to find lodgings for his young family and to look for employment.

The *Strathfieldsaye* was a bounty vessel and the captain had no further responsibility for the welfare of his passengers once they left the ship.Although Clarinda and the baby were able to stay aboard the ship until Clarinda felt stronger, and until suitable lodgings were found, Henry was distressed to discover that all in the colony was not as he had expected. For one thing, the price of nearly all goods was far greater than at home, and he ended up with only three shillings left in his purse with which to embrace his new beginning.

Once ashore, bounty migrants were given no help at all from the colonial government; they were not eligible for accommodation in government-run migrant shelters and were simply left to their own devices. When it became known that few of the passengers from the *Strathfieldsaye* had come ashore for fear that they would not be able to find work or lodgings, the *Sydney Herald* published details of the occupations of these newcomers to the colony.

The *Herald* advised potential employers to make haste in securing the skills brought to Australia's shores by these bounty emigrants, lest they fall into despair and turn to ruinous means of survival as so many had done before them. But there was little call for the unique skills of the bone and ivory turner from Warwickshire.

When the Parkes family eventually took leave of the *Strathfieldsaye*, Clarinda had to carry her newborn infant over a mile through the muddied streets of Sydney to the mean lodgings that Henry had secured at a cost of five shillings per week.

Work was still not easy to find, and Henry had to sell his belongings just to survive. Before long almost all of his treasured books and most of his spare clothing had gone; he was fast reaching a state of desperation. For another two weeks he tramped the Sydney streets, without success.

'Being completely starved out', he took a position as a common labourer for squatter Sir John Jamison at Regentville, a model property at Penrith, for ten shillings a week, a ration-and-a-half of food, and lodgings.

The arrival of the 'pure blood hounds'

The arrival of the *Strathfieldsaye* was announced in the *Sydney Herald* on 26 July 1839. While the vessel had carried 205 bounty migrants, it had also landed on Australia's shores:

> ... a great number of highly respectable cabin passengers, all of whom have arrived in a healthy state ... This vessel has made a fair passage of being about three months on the voyage ... great credit is due to the captain and surgeon for the cleanliness and order of everything on board: only two infants died, and three were born on the voyage. This vessel has brought out some pure blood hounds which will be a great acquisition to the colony.[2]

It is unclear whether bounty migrants such as Henry and Clarinda Parkes were noted as 'pure blood hounds' at that time; however, the colony was sure to see Henry Parkes's blood rise many times over the years to come.

They lost most of their belongings on the 36-mile dray ride into the country and the first few months were spent in poverty. Their accommodation was crude, to say the least:

> For four months [our] only bed was an old door and a sheet of bark laid on two cross pieces of wood, and the hut ... poor shelter for a young mother and child; 'the morning sunshine, the noontide shower, and the white moonlight of midnight, gushed in upon us alike'.[3]

As farm labourers they were not even allowed to grow a plot of their own vegetables, lest they take time away from their labours for the squatter.

Henry Parkes, who had once been a supporter of the ideals of the Chartist movement in England, had migrated before the workers had finally risen up against the merchant class in the mass rallies which swept across the midlands. But he was to see the same rebellious attitude kindled in the squalid labourers' huts of New South Wales.

After six months Parkes headed back to Sydney town. First, he took a job with an ironmonger, then at a brass foundry where he was engaged finishing brass work for five shillings a day. Although this work was hard, and he was in poor health, the pay was at least much better than the farm labourer's pittance. Although he longed to be able to return to his turning lathe, he had no means of providing for his old craft.

Just as he was again about to despair, through the intercession of Sir John Jamison he was offered a job as a tidewaiter with the customs office. The job involved travelling out to meet ships as soon as they were sighted off the Heads, to ensure that none attempted to avoid their customs duty. This gave Henry quite a lot of spare time, and he spent it wisely. He had always been dedicated to his own self-education, and as he had often fancied himself to be a poet, he read the works of the favoured poets of his day and began to put his own pen to paper.

Before long he had amassed quite a collection of works that he had written while on board the customs ship. He wrote to his family in England in 1840:

> I spend most of my time on board ships, where I have a good deal of leisure to write poetry—I have enough already to fill a book, most of which has been published in a Sydney newspaper.[4]

Henry Parkes had in mind to write a series of letters describing Australia, which would later form an anthology of the country. But this never happened. Instead, in 1842 he published his first book of verse, *Stolen Moments*;

Stolen moments

Never one to doubt his own abilities, in 1842 Henry Parkes published *Stolen Moments,* a collection of his own poems, which sold for five shillings.

Few regarded his poetry as anything but romantic doggerel, but this did not dissuade Parkes from continuing to write. Over the years he published six volumes of verse and contributed countless letters and articles to almost every journal and newspaper published in the colony.

He regarded himself as one of the first truly Australian writers; he had not published before he stepped onto Australia's shores and few native-born Australians did so before him.

His poem 'The Song of the Australian Settler' gives some idea of the attachment Parkes was beginning to form with the colony:

> Our home is in the wild bush far,
> Of peaceful spots the boonest;
> Where the kangaroo and emu are,
> Which flee the white man soonest.

While he may have captured the prevailing sentiment about Australia's flora and fauna, it is plain to see that he was no Banjo Paterson.

canvassing for subscribers financed this volume. Among those who subscribed was Parkes's former employer, Sir John Jamison. Even the Governor, Sir George Gipps, was pleased to receive a complimentary copy.

After a disagreement with the administration at the customs office, and disappointed at his lack of advancement in his situation there, Parkes abandoned his job. With the little capital he had saved, he opened his own shop in Hunter Street, Sydney, in 1845, where his shingle announced to the world that:

> Henry Parkes — Ivory, Fancy Hardwood and Bone Turner, was prepared to supply Billiard and bagatelle balls, chessmen, dice, needle cases, stilettos, auctioneer's hammers, ivory and bone dog collars &c.

Now that Henry was his own master at last, his mind again turned to matters political. The colony still had shiploads of transported convicts landed on its shores and free settlers such as Henry Parkes, along with scores of successful emancipists, demanded that the government in England put an end to the policy of transportation altogether.

It seems that the English government's policies regarding both immigration and transportation were entirely inadequate; the vagaries of the colonial economy and the many ad-hoc attempts at assisted migration, the bounty scheme, the Wakefield scheme and the aborted attempt to establish the Swan River settlement in Western Australia, saw thousands of ready and willing emigrant workers abandoned to an uncertain fate in an unforgiving environment.

The Anti-Transportation League of Australasia sought to address these problems by advocating systematic migration through schemes such as those instigated by Caroline Chisholm and her Family Colonisation Loan Society.

The birth of democracy

Henry Parkes next turned his attention to the sphere of political activism. He had been writing political articles for the *Atlas* and the *People's Advocate* and eventually it came his turn to mount the podium. In 1848 he took on the task of committee secretary for lawyer and editor Robert Lowe's tilt at a return to

politics. Lowe, who had once been favoured by Governor Gipps and fought against emancipist William Wentworth at every turn, was elected to the legislative council alongside him. Lowe had become disillusioned with Gipps when he ushered in his new squatting regulations in 1844, which effectively gave squatters the security over their extensive holdings that they had always wanted. Lowe stood for self-government, land reform and the cessation of transportation. He had des-cribed the squatters as having 'sought to confiscate the whole of the lands of the colony for their own use and benefit'.[5] Henry Parkes described Robert Lowe's election to parliament as 'the birthday of Australian democracy'. Although Wentworth shared Lowe's desire for self-government and land reform, he continued to promote transportation as the economic saviour of the old landholder in the colony, of which he was one.

Transportation had ceased in 1853, but unlike the depressed Australia when Parkes landed in 1839, there was a shortage of cheap labour, as most new migrants were fully occupied in the search for gold. Squatters, along with the government, pressed England to resume the practice and send more convicts.

After the failure of the government attempt at free immigration, and following repeated demands from the established settlers for labour, the English government decided to resume transportation to the colony. It planned to send out 'exiles', ex-convicts who had served their terms in British prisons and would be transported to the colonies on probation. They were to be matched in their number by free immigrants and Britain was to bear the entire cost of the exercise.

While there was little resistance to this move from within the colony, this plan of Lord Grey's was altered when the British government ran into unforeseen financial difficulties. Grey decided to rescind the order-in-council that had forbidden further transportation to New South Wales, as the government was then unwilling to commit sufficient funds to that part of the scheme that promised free migration. The government shelved the idea and sent out the transport vessel the *Hashemy* with only exiles on board instead.

The *Hashemy*, the first transport for three years, sailed from England with 200 exiles on board to arrive in Sydney on 11 June 1849. In the months after news of the *Hashemy's* departure had reached the colony Parkes had

OPPOSITE:
Fort Macquarie from Pinchgut Island
Watercolour by Frederick Garling, c. 1840
When the *Strathfieldsaye* dropped anchor in Sydney Harbour in 1839, it was a scene such as this that greeted the young immigrant Henry Parkes.
(State Library of New South Wales Collection)

RIGHT:
The Hon. Henry Parkes,
Premier of New South Wales
Wood engraving, published in The Australian News for Home Readers, *26 February 1867*
(Private Collection)

THE HON. H PARKES, PREMIER OF NEW SOUTH WALES

lobbied hard to raise the voice of protest against the revised scheme. On the grey, wet morning that the ship pulled into Circular Quay, thousands of protesters braved the filthy weather and rallied to the cause.

Shopkeepers put up their shutters and merchants closed their stores to join in the 'Great Protest Meeting', so called by Parkes because the title echoed that given to the great protest meetings of the unions, and the Chartists, that he had encountered in his Birmingham youth.

The leading members of the Anti-Transportation Committee stood upon an omnibus to address the crowd. On the platform alongside Parkes stood prominent landlord Robert Campbell, merchant John Lamb and solicitor Archibald Michie. Lamb, possibly the 'most eminent speaker of the day', read a stirring speech, which Parkes had composed for him:

> We, the free and loyal subjects of Her Gracious majesty, inhabitants of the city of Sydney and its immediate neighbourhood, in public meeting assembled, do hereby enter our most deliberate and solemn protest against the transportation of British criminals to the colony of New south Wales.
>
> Firstly—Because it is in violation of the will of the majority of the colonists, as is clearly evidenced by their expressed opinions on the question at all times.
>
> Secondly—because numbers among us have emigrated on the faith of the British Government that transportation to this colony had ceased forever.
>
> Thirdly—Because it is incompatible with our existence as a free colony, desiring self-government, to be made the receptacle of another country's felons.
>
> Fourthly—Because it is in the highest degree unjust to sacrifice the great social and political interests of the colony at large to the pecuniary profit of a fraction of its inhabitants.
>
> Fifthly—Because, being firmly and devoutly attached to the British Crown, we greatly fear that the perpetration of so stupendous an act of injustice by Her Majesty's Government will go far towards alienating the affections of this colony from the mother-country.
>
> For these and for many kindred reasons—in the exercise of our duty to our country, for the love of our families, in the strength of our loyalty to Great Britain, and from the depth of our reverence to Almighty God—we protest against the landing of British convicts on these shores.[6]

Although the gears of the great machine of democracy were slowly grinding away, it was still many years before its engineers were able to speak plainly without fear of the charge of

The Hashemy *protest*

> The CONVICT SHIP has arrived!
>
> The GREAT MEETING will be held on the CIRCULAR WHARF, TO-DAY, at Noon, to Protest against the Landing of the Convicts.
>
> The Chair will be taken by Robert Lowe, Esq., the Member for the City. Let all places of business be closed! Let every man be at his post![7]

So read the announcement broadcast across Sydney which called more than 5000 people to assemble at Circular Quay, in pouring rain, on 11 June 1849, to protest at the arrival of the 'exile' ship the *Hashemy*. The mob was angered more by the British government's change of mind, without consultation, rather than the fact that convicts were once more being sent to the colonies. Robert Lowe stood alongside Henry Parkes on the back of an omnibus and addressed the mob:

> As in America, oppression was the parent of independence, so would it be in the colony ... it was the degradation of submission to an unrighteous demand. And so sure as the seed will grow into the plant, and the plant to the tree, in all times, and in all nations, so will injustice and tyranny ripen into rebellion, and rebellion into independence.[8]

The *Hashemy* was sent up the coast to land at Moreton Bay, and the exiles landed there, as did many others who followed later.

sedition, and without the need to continue to pledge their undying love for the Crown.

A week later, after some deliberation from Governor Fitzroy, and a few heated discussions with the leaders of the protest, the *Hashemy* was sent north to Moreton Bay. Over seventy per cent of the exiles had already been settled quietly in jobs in the country and the squatters of Moreton Bay eagerly took the rest.

Loss of Empire

In December 1850 Parkes began what was to be one of his most daring business ventures; he founded the newspaper he called the *Empire*. While the paper was to play an important role in the development of political debate in the colony, and certainly in the promotion of those issues so closely identified with Parkes — franchise, suffrage, land reform, anti-transportation, republicanism and self-determination — it was to eventually bring about his financial ruin. The prospectus of the venture proclaimed that: 'The politics of the *Empire* will be best indicated by the word Radical'.

There was another mass influx of free migrants to the colony when gold was discovered in New South Wales in February 1851; but these migrants were not interested in becoming farmhands, sheep herders or fodder for the factory floor. Over 100,000 people migrated into Victoria alone following the discovery of the yellow metal in the creeks across Central Victoria in September that year. The governments in both colonies reacted by imposing heavy taxes on the diggers and set in train the very seeds of revolt that would alter the relationship between the colonial administration, the people and the Crown.

In direct contrast to the mood of the public at the time, William Wentworth proposed the establishment of an upper house for parliament along the lines of the English House of Lords. He proposed a colonial aristocracy, its members drawn from the wealthier sections of society; as one of the wealthier Australasians, he no doubt envisaged himself comfortably ensconced in the house 'for life'. Critics dubbed the scheme a 'bunyip aristocracy'; the Melbourne *Argus* called it the 'Botany Bay Peerage'. Parkes wasted no time in attacking Wentworth; he said that while he could not deny the squatters from having representation in the new parliament, he demanded fair representation 'which made no distinction between the great commercial, the populous city of Sydney, and the sheep-walks of New England'.[9]

The White Australia Policy

For a poor Englishman who had arrived on Australia's shores in desperate circumstances, with only a few shillings in his pocket, Parkes was curiously lacking in generosity to others who followed his path — unless they were English, and white.

Parkes first proposed that the numbers of emigrants from Ireland be restricted, to ensure that the English-born remained dominant in the colony. Then he proposed to deal with 'the Chinese question', the unrestricted migration of Chinese.

Following an attack at Lambing Flat on the New South Wales goldfields on 30 June 1861, where a party of grogged-up diggers marched upon the Chinese camp behind a banner that bore the slogan 'Roll Up! Roll Up! No Chinese', rioting as they went, the government sought to bring an end to Chinese migration.

The solution came in the form of the imposition of a heavy landing tax on every Chinese person who set foot on Australian soil. This tax was to be uniformly applied across all Australian ports. In June 1888 the Chinese Exclusion Bill was passed through the New South Wales parliament in a single sitting. Dubbed 'The White Australia Policy' by socialist William Lane's radical journal *Boomerang*, the ensuing active racial discrimination remained effective policy until 1973.

BELOW:
Attempted assassination of HRH the Duke of Edinburgh at Clontarf NSW
Wood engraving by Samuel Calvert, 1868
(National Library of Australia Collection, S4491)

William Wentworth resigned his seat in 1854 to go to England; Parkes nominated in his place and won the seat on a platform that promised educational reform, the extension of the power of the people and the establishment of a railway system that would open up and unite the whole continent.

The troublesome Irish

One of the lasting legacies of Parkes's time as colonial secretary of New South Wales was the passage of the Public Schools Act of 1866, which ensured that no child, regardless of location or capacity to pay, would be denied an education. No doubt with reference to his own upbringing and subsequent rise to the highest ranks of society, Parkes declared that he wanted to 'make it possible for the child of even the poorest man to attain the highest place [in society]'.

In the colony there were thousands of children under the age of fourteen who received no schooling at all. Parkes asked the parliament: 'Is it any wonder that young men of spirit become bushrangers? We need schools to prevent crime. We want schools not gaols, schoolmasters not gaolers.'

In a move guaranteed to upset the Catholic Church (which provided education to Catholics only), the bill refused to allow any funds to be allocated for new church schools. Although established schools would still receive some government funds, the shift was towards secular education. It was impossible for churches of different denominations to provide for the smaller communities. Parkes wanted to provide a standard level of education for all Australians no matter where they lived, nor what their religion.

It is fair to say that Henry Parkes was not enamoured of the Catholic cause, and the refusal of his government to assist any more than was absolutely necessary in the provision of sectarian education put him at odds with the Catholic Church and the large number of Irish in the community.

His attitude to the Catholic population at large, and the clergy in particular, following the assassination attempt on His Royal Highness the Duke of Edinburgh at Clontarf on

12 March 1868, did not endear him at all to their number. Irishman Henry James O'Farrell had taken a shot at Prince Alfred as the prince enjoyed himself at a picnic held in his honour at the Sailors' Home at Clontarf. O'Farrell's aim was poor and Prince Alfred's rubber braces deflected the bullet from its target, saving the young prince from serious injury.

As O'Farrell was taken away by the police sergeant he shouted: 'I don't care for death ... I'm sorry I missed my aim — I made a bloody mess of it ... God save Ireland'.[10]

O'Farrell claimed that he was a member of the Fenian Brotherhood, a secret society formed in America in 1858 to fight for Irish independence. Parkes seized on this admission; he rushed to Darlinghurst and interviewed O'Farrell himself. He then went to the hotel where O'Farrell had been lodging and carried away the 'tools of revolution' he found there: gunpowder, some shot, a Douay Bible and some letters and papers.

The next day the *Empire* reported the find, and although it would not specify the contents of the papers, it alluded to a seditious plot to reap vengeance for Ireland on the English and their lickspittle apologists. Parkes was convinced that civil war had reached Australia, and that it was the Romish Irish who were its proponents.

This brought howls of protest from the Catholic Church, and Parkes received death threats in the mail daily. But the only sentence of death to be executed was on the hapless O'Farrell; he was hanged in April 1868.

Although the Catholic priest who attended O'Farrell in his last moments said that he had recanted on his association with the Fenian Brotherhood, Parkes would not accept it.

For the first time, Parkes feared for his life. He had raised the animosity of the entire Irish Catholic community against him. He became fearful of walking home through the bush at night, as had been his practice. He wrote at this time: 'If the murderer comes he must be in some open place; and there are not many O'Farrells who will commit murder with their own lives in their hands'.[11] His connection with the Public Schools Act and his dismissal of some public servants who were Irish Catholics, combined with the O'Farrell affair, had almost brought him undone.

Fearing that Parkes was about to embark on yet another of his attacks on the Irish, their clergy and the church, many in his ministry withdrew their support from him. When a trusted friend was dismissed from his position as customs officer over a discrepancy in Parkes's travel claims, Parkes branded the dismissal as retribution by a Catholic in the

The royal, the republican and the revolutionary

When His Royal Highness Prince Alfred, Duke of Edinburgh, visited the colony of New South Wales in 1868 he was the first member of the royal family ever to do so.

He was greeted with unprecedented enthusiasm. One newspaper even depicted him as some kind of 'Cleopatra', sailing into Circular Quay surrounded by exultant mermaids.

Parkes's behaviour after Irishman Henry James O'Farrell's attempted assassination of the Duke, on 12 March 1868, belied the stance he had previously taken on matters concerning the monarchy. While Parkes had long used the pages of the *Empire* to promote the republican cause, the actions of the self-confessed Fenian, failed goldfields investor and bar fly, gave Parkes a stick with which to beat his 'popish' detractors.

The Catholic Church was displeased with Parkes over the withdrawal of funds for sectarian schools; his life was even threatened. Through his paper Parkes demonised the 'seditious' Irish, using O'Farrell as an example. Parkes returned to this theme many times.

Parkes went on to disappoint the leading lights of the Free Australia movement, who had counted on him to lead the colonies into a federated republic, when he accepted Imperial Honours from Queen Victoria in her Jubilee year.

service; by attacking Parkes's friend, he had attacked the man himself. Parkes had never enjoyed comfortable relations with the large community of Irish Catholics in the colony; he was never likely to in the years ahead.

On 28 August 1858 the *Empire* was suspended from operation due to financial difficulties. Although it had proved popular, it was not making money. In an attempt to save the paper, Parkes resigned from parliament to devote all his energies to its survival — but to no avail. Exonerated of any blame for the financial ruin of the newspaper, Parkes again stood for election and was returned as the independent member for East Sydney on 10 June 1859.

Again his platform included his old causes: land and education reform. Suffrage had been won and transportation ended, so he turned his attention to the development of free trade, agriculture and manufacturing, and the immigration of the 'right' kind of workers for the task.

In and out of the house

In September 1870 Parkes resigned once again from the legislative assembly. The member for Kiama quit this time because bankruptcy proceedings had again been issued against him, but his constituents pressed him to reconsider. This time his insolvency was a result of all the years he had spent in public service, for which he never received any stipend. He had always fought against the notion of payment from the public purse for parliamentary members, and only survived by the generosity of his supporters.

However, Parkes did not stay away for long. He was soon back in parliament. In an effort to gain public approval, Parkes, as Premier of New South Wales, granted a pardon to the bushranger Frank 'Darkie' Gardiner in 1874. This was quite a daring move, as his government had been forced to resign over the same issue the year before.

The public had been pressuring the government to relax the harsh sentences passed on the bushrangers during the gold rush of the 1850s. They complained that the sentences passed in Governor Sir Hercules Robinson's day were unnecessarily severe and that some of the daring 'kings of the road' who had served a reasonable time should be pardoned.

While the public may have approved of Parkes's act of clemency, there were plenty of others in the upper echelons of the community who thought otherwise. There was a resurgence of bushranging activity around this time which caused them to fear the release of men such as Gardiner. These

The ladies with the lamps

In 1866 Henry Parkes turned his attention to the reform of the public health system in the colony. He visited hospitals and asylums and was disgusted by the 'prison-like' treatment of the inmates at the Tarban Creek Asylum (Gladesville). He appointed the naval surgeon, Frederick Norton Manning, to undertake sweeping reforms to the asylum system

Parkes next visited Sydney's general infirmary and was completely dissatisfied with the conditions and the administration of this public hospital. He complained of the drunken staff, improper practices between staff and patients, misappropriated stores, inefficient nursing and poor management. He wrote to English nurse Florence Nightingale, asking for her 'benevolent assistance' in the provision of nurses trained by her to help change health care in the colony.

She obliged, and in March 1868 six nursing sisters trained in the Nightingale system arrived in Sydney. Parkes even went aboard ship to welcome them. It was not long before these nurses were able to prove their worth. One of the first patients they had to tend was the Duke of Edinburgh, shot in the back by Irishman Henry James O'Farrell, only a week after they had arrived.

Below:
Departure of Sir Henry Parkes from Sydney
Wood engraving, published in the Daily Telegraph, *14 January 1882*
(State Library of Victoria Collection)

predominantly Irish, Catholic, daring young outlaws were being promoted in the press as some kind of popular heroes. The Englishmen who dominated the governments all around the country were anxious to crush anything that resembled Irish Nationalist sympathy or Fenian insurrection. The fight over the government's right to pardon created a furore and in the end parliament was dissolved.

In December 1878 Parkes was installed as Premier of New South Wales for the third time. Sir John Robertson, a bitter rival of Parkes for many years, had paved the way by allowing himself to be appointed to the upper house. The Governor, Sir Hercules Robinson, had hoped:

> that these gentlemen, who have for nearly a quarter of a century assailed each other with such bitter political hostility, will now work together harmoniously.[12]

By 1880 Parkes had turned against immigration for all and now proposed a system that would restrict the number of Irish emigrants in favour of English. He returned to his prejudice against the Irish by this attempt to ensure that people of English descent remained dominant in the colony.

Now aged sixty-eight, Parkes fell ill; more than four decades in the public eye had taken its toll. He spent a considerable time in recovery at Faulconbridge, the home he had built for himself in the Blue Mountains, and when he recovered he came back with a vengeance. To further aid his recovery he took a long sea voyage, travelling to England by way of America, where he stayed for six weeks and was a guest of the US President at the White House.

While away, Parkes always promoted Australia. He made friends with the poet Tennyson, and was invited by Lord Leigh to visit Stoneleigh Abbey near the village where Parkes had been born. He visited the old farm and reminisced over the hard days of his childhood when he had broken rocks on the King's highway for only a few pence a day.

Parkes returned to Australia in the spring of 1882, landing first at Melbourne, where he was entertained at a public banquet on 15 August. He was back in Sydney two days later. He stood for parliament again, but this

time he was unsuccessful. Another seat was found for him, but he showed little interest in pursuing the old arguments.

Having once inadvertently fanned the flames of Fenian dissent, Parkes offered his conciliatory solutions to the 'Irish question' when two Irish Nationals toured Australia seeking support for home rule. On 6 March 1883, a meeting was held at the Protestant Hall in protest at the arrival of Mr J. E. Redmond MP and Mr W. Redmond in Sydney.

Parkes was the principal speaker at this meeting and warned those who attended that old animosities should be repudiated:

> Let Irishmen cherish the memory of the bright and heroic passages in her history; let them if they will, cherish with a burning indignation the wrongs they have endured. But they come here for a very different purpose, and I at once take my stand on this very simple ground, that when Irishmen, or Englishmen, or Scotchmen, or Germans come to this land, they have no right to revive the animosities of the land from which they have come. Our public life ought not to be disturbed, ought not to have its very heart torn, by the revival of the injuries of other countries.[13]

Feelings ran so hot among the sectarian and politically motivated audience, divided by dogma and idealogy and patriotic fervour, that the meeting soon erupted into riot. Fist fights broke out in the hall, and among the thousands more gathered in the street outside. Parkes had to be escorted to safety by the police.

In November 1884 Parkes once again resigned from his parliamentary seat, this time saying that he lacked 'sufficient strength to confront the gigantic difficulties which must soon come upon us'. He announced that he had decided to retire from the world of politics altogether.

He opened an office in Sydney, and worked on behalf of a firm of financiers, until he was aroused from his 'retirement' in 1885 when the acting premier, W. B. Dalley, decided to send a contingent of troops from New South Wales to assist the British army in the Sudan.

Parkes objected strongly to this proposal. He stood once more and, although he was often at odds with public opinion, was elected as the member for the seat of Argyle.

True to form, Parkes was back on his feet, as vigorous as ever, rising to the position of Premier of New South Wales for the fourth time when parliament was dissolved in 1885. George Dibbs had dissolved parliament for a second time when Parkes stood against him. Parkes accused the former premier of sending

The wives of Henry the first

Henry Parkes married three times and fathered eleven children.

His first marriage, to Clarinda (nee Varney), ended after fifty years when she died on 2 February 1888. Henry and Clarinda had produced five daughters and one son. Clarinda was buried in the graveyard at Faulconbridge near their son Robert, who had died of Bright's disease in 1879.

Parkes then married Miss Eleanor Dixon on 6 February 1889, in St Paul's at Redfern. It had long been rumoured that Eleanor had been his mistress and the marriage threatened to split his family apart. After his happy union with Clarinda for over half a century it was difficult for Parkes's children to accept the need for their father to remarry.

Henry and Eleanor had five sons and a daughter. This second marriage ended when Eleanor died suddenly during Parkes's election campaign of 1895.

Aged eighty, the father of Australia — and the father of several little Australians — once again took a bride, 23-year-old, Irish-born Julia Lynch. Julia had been in his household to care for his children even before Eleanor's death; after Henry's death in 1896 she continued to care for them as if they were her own.

the colony bankrupt (a state of affairs with which he was most familiar), claiming that since he had left office public debt had more than doubled. He claimed that he had left a legacy of £2,000,000 in the treasury, which had been completely eroded, to a deficit of £2,500,000. At the ensuing ballot Parkes defeated Dibbs and was returned with a majority of two to one.

Towards federation

The move towards federation of the colonies was gaining currency. The colonies had started to discuss the possibility of making the postal service cooperative, and also extended their thoughts to the railways. But they stopped short of issues such as free trade and taxation; the colonies were ever jealous of their rights to control such matters and to enjoy certain peculiarities of civil law.

Parkes was called on to form his fifth ministry in March 1889 and it was this, his final term as Premier of New South Wales, that gave him the platform to seriously mount the case for federation of the colonies. The first steps were taken in May 1889 when the rail link that was to unite the four colonies of South Australia, New South Wales, Victoria and Queensland was finally opened. When Parkes opened the Hawkesbury River bridge, the final link in the railway chain that stretched from Adelaide to Brisbane, he declared: 'In this great system of material arteries which we complete today we see a crimson fluid of kinship pulsing through all the iron veins'.

But for the dispute over the gauge of the rail lines the system would have been almost perfect; each colony still wanted to do it their own way, and for more than 100 years passengers, and freight, would have to transfer from train to train at the borders to make the journey from one colony (state) to the next.

In June 1889 Parkes discussed with Governor Carrington the relationship of the colonies to the Crown and the lengthy decision-making process of administering colonial policy across the globe — from New Zealand, to Canada, Australia to South Africa.

LEFT:
[The] Usual Moral
Drawing by Phil May, 1887

Phil May was one of the most prominent cartoonists of his day, and Henry Parkes was one of his favourite 'cartoon characters'. Parkes's distinctive figure, wild mane and exuberant beard gave May plenty to play with.

This cartoon shows Parkes and parliamentarian John Cash Neild. Parkes is offering Neild a gag.

Neild had earned the nickname 'Jawbone' during a parliamentary debate in which he proved his ability to talk, non-stop, for hours on end.

(National Library of Australia Collection)

Carrington said that the idea of 'a huge council representing England and the colonies, debating whether we go to war &c, seems to me absurd'. Parkes replied that that was the way it must be, at least 'until we federate'.

Parkes added, 'I could confederate these colonies in twelve months', to which Carrington replied 'Then why don't you do it ... it would be a glorious finish to your life'.[14] The following day, Parkes wrote to Duncan Gillies, Premier of Victoria, offering to take a 'leading step in the cause of Australian federation'.

The Tenterfield oration

In 1889 Henry Parkes delivered a speech at a meeting of a federal council in Tenterfield, New South Wales. This speech was seen as a turning point in pushing the colonies towards fully accepting the need for federation.

The speech followed a review of the standing colonial armies in which the Imperial general recommended that the Australian colonial forces be united into one army. There were many impediments to this being achieved: one was that there was no federal body that could command such an army, another that the separate colonies would never accept command by the Imperial parliament.

When Parkes declared that 'the time had come for the creation on this Australian continent of an Australian Government' the room burst into spontaneous applause. He continued:

> Australia had now a population of three and a half millions, and the American people numbered only between three and four millions when they formed the great commonwealth of the United States ... surely what the Americans had done by war, the Australians could bring about in peace without breaking the ties that held them to the mother country.[15]

Parkes was sure that the only argument that could be put up against federation was that its time had not yet come. During his impassioned keynote address at Tenterfield he quoted these words from the Queensland poet Brunton Stephens: 'Not yet her day! How long? Not yet!' As far as Parkes was concerned, the time for federation had surely come, and for him there was to be no going back.

Parkes introduced a bill proposing the establishment of a federal council in 1889. This bill passed both houses of the New South Wales parliament but was rejected by the secretary of state for the colonies. Parkes telegraphed the other premiers of the colonies and invited them to join a federal conference, which was held in February 1890. It was the first time they had all sat

LEFT:
Federation Flag, 1867
This flag was first flown at a banquet held by the Federation League to honour Prince Alfred, Australia's first royal visitor, in Melbourne in 1867. Although it was never to become the flag of the new nation, there was a time, even after 1901, when flagmakers in England still received orders for this striking design.
(Private Collection)

down together and seriously considered federation.

While preparing for the federal convention to be held the following year, Parkes fell and broke his leg. This injury, serious for almost all other men of his age, simply slowed him down for two to three months; then he insisted on resuming his duties, and had to be carried to his chair in the house.

The following year he was elected president of the convention, which began its work on 2 May 1891. The convention spent most of its time debating proposals drafted by Sir Henry Parkes and concluded when a draft of the bill to constitute the Commonwealth of Australia had been prepared.

'One people, one destiny'

Lord Carrington, with whom Parkes had a long and intimate friendship, turning to him time and again for the wisdom of his counsel, was recalled to England and replaced by Lord

ABOVE:

Members of the Australasian Federal Conference, Melbourne, 1890

(National Archives of Australia Collection)

All of the parliaments of all colonies were represented at the first Australasian Federation Conference, held in Melbourne in February 1890.

From left to right (standing): the Hon. A. I. Clarke, MP (Victoria); Captain Russell, MP, colonial secretary (New South Wales); Sir Samuel Griffith, KCMG, MP (Queensland); Sir Henry Parkes, KCMG (New South Wales); the Hon. Thomas Playford, MP (South Australia); the Hon. Alfred Deakin, MP, chief secretary (Victoria); the Hon. Stafford Bird, MP, treasurer (Tasmania); Mr. G. H. Jenkins, secretary to the conference.

Seated, left to right: the Hon. William McMillan, colonial treasurer (New South Wales); Sir John Hall, KCMG, MP (New Zealand); the Hon. J. M. Macrossan, MP, colonial secretary (Queensland); the Hon. Duncan Gillies, MP, Premier of Victoria, chairman of the conference; the Hon. Sir John Cockburn, MP (South Australia); Sir James Lee-Steere, MP, speaker (West Australia).

Jersey. Parkes never felt the same intimacy with the new governor, yet he seemed enchanted by the governor's wife, Lady Jersey. At a state banquet held to honour the forty-odd delegates to the National Australasian Convention at the Gaeity Theatre in Sydney in 1891, Lady Jersey, the daughter of Lord Leigh and herself a native of Stoneleigh, Parkes's birthplace, made her first official appearance in the colony. When she entered the banquet hall, the 900 gathered for dinner stood and gave her three hearty cheers. The grand old man of Australia, Sir Henry Parkes, sat at a raised table, Lord Jersey to his right and James Munro, Premier of Victoria, on his left. For that one glorious occasion it was Parkes's prerogative to propose the toast that ignited the torch of federation. As Sir Henry Parkes raised his glass, 900 others joined with him, in a toast to 'A United Australia'. Parkes then addressed the guests:

> There is no other way for true federation of this Australasia than to unite under one great government. It will be a fatal mistake to curtail the power of the government we shall create when we are as an Australian nation, as brave and as powerful as any other nation on the face of the earth, when we shall have become 'one people, with one destiny', and be bound together by the crimson thread of kinship that can never perish.[16]

When Parkes's draft constitution bill was presented to the parliament on 22 October 1891, it hit a snag when G. H. Reid proposed an amendment. In the argument that ensued, Parkes thought he could push the bill through if it was further down the list for debate. Because of this a vote of no confidence in Parkes was moved and carried; he resigned. He never held public office again.

Having set the course for a federated Australia, the time had come for the old man to take his rest. Parkes retired to his country house, but he was again living in straitened circumstances. He had never agreed to the payment of parliamentary members but he still had to support a large family. His business ventures over the years had left him little capital on which to live. He had been living off the interest from a trust fund of £9000

RIGHT:
Federated Australia
Drawn by Herbert Cotton, wood engraving, published in the Daily Telegraph, *9 July 1900*
The text in this illustration reads:
> I do see very clearly that there may come a time and that time not very remote, when the Australian Colonies may be brought more into the position of one great and united people. We should have an outline of empire, such as we could never hope for as isolated colonies, and our place would be admitted in the rank of nations.
> —Sir Henry Parkes, August 1889

(National Library of Australia Collection)

RIGHT:
Sir Henry Parkes
With his distinctive leonine physiognomy, Sir Henry Parkes dominated the political scene leading to Federation. Unfortunately, he never saw his dream realised.
Four years after his death the colonies finally forged themselves into 'one nation'.
The 'old lion' of Australian politics may have never taken the honour of first Prime Minister of Australia, but the legacy of his tireless efforts in bringing the nation together will stand for all time.
(State Library of Victoria Collection)

established by his supporters, but the depression of the 1890s had seen the return from this investment fall to only about £200 per year.

After a lifetime of dedication to the future of his adopted country, Parkes was forced to sell his goods just as he had done when he first arrived in the colony. He began to sell many of his prized possessions: his autographed letters, and books given to him by the great writers and poets of the day.

He fell ill in April 1896 and never recovered. He died on April 27 at Annandale in Sydney's west. He had requested that his be a simple funeral and the state, which had much to honour him for, respected his wishes. He was buried at Faulconbridge in the Blue Mountains, near Clarinda and their son Robert.

Duncan Gillies, MP, a former Premier of Victoria and Chairman of the Federal Conference held in Melbourne in 1890, wrote:

> The universal sentiment throughout the colonies of Australia was that there was no man, so far as they knew, at present living, which could do the work, which that gentleman had begun ... on every occasion there was a necessity, that brought the man. And on this occasion, in their great need they unquestionably had got the man. [17]

Sir Henry Parkes had certainly come a long way, and he had brought Australia along with him. More than any other man, he had recognised the potential of the colonies and had cast the die that would see them forged into one federated nation.

Birth of the nation

Australia celebrated its federation on 1 January 1901 when the first governor-general, Lord Hopetoun, proclaimed the birth of the nation before a crowd of more than a quarter of a million people in Sydney's Centennial Park.

The first parliament assembled in Melbourne's Exhibition Buildings on 9 May 1901. After the ceremony in the Exhibition Buildings the Australian federal parliament sat in Victoria until 1927.

When the Duke of York (later King George V) declared the parliament of the Commonwealth of Australia to be officially opened, he touched an electric button which sent a signal to all state schools across the new nation, and they raised the Union Jack together.

A new glistening, brilliant white Parliament House was officially opened in the 'bush capital' Canberra, by the Duke of York on 9 May 1927. Dame Nellie Melba sang the anthem 'God Save the King' on this occasion.

Australian artist Tom Roberts painted a huge portrait of all who attended the opening of the first temporary parliament in Melbourne. It is sad to reflect that Sir Henry Parkes, the one figure who had set the colonies on the course to nationhood, was never able to take his place among all those remembered in Roberts' grand work. The painting hangs today in the Supreme Court on the shores of Lake Burley Griffin in Canberra, a gift to Australia from the Crown.

Catherine Helen Spence

1825–1910

Catherine Helen Spence is featured on the obverse of the $5 polymer note, first issued in 2001.

OPPOSITE:

Catherine Helen Spence (standing), and her mother Helen Brodie Spence, c. 1880

Photograph by Charles H. Manning

Short, and plump already at twenty, with bright carrot-orange hair and the pale complexion typical of the northern Celt, Catherine Spence was no beauty, and she knew it.

Once, when complaining of not being informed of some meetings of a board to which she had been appointed, she made the remark that she 'didn't just want to be an ornament to the board'. The chairman turned to her and replied 'There is no chance of that Miss Spence'. She threw her head back and roared with laughter before the poor man had even realised his faux pas.

Spence was, however, well aware of the presence she had when she began to speak: her light Scots accent, which stayed with her all her life, always charmed her audience.

(Photograph courtesy of the State Library of South Australia, SLSA: B 7106)

The new woman of Australia

'I AM A NEW WOMAN AND I KNOW IT. I MEAN AN AWAKENED woman ... awakened to a sense of capacity and responsibility, not merely to the family and the household, but to the State; to be wise, not for her own selfish interests, but that the world may be glad that she had been born.'[1] So said Catherine Spence, on the occasion of her eightieth birthday in 1905.

At the beginning of the twentieth century, octogenarian Catherine Helen Spence had lived through a period of great change in the fortunes of women in Australian colonial society. She had spent most of her adult life in pursuit of equal rights for women, and had witnessed a change in attitudes from the patriarchal colonial society into which she had migrated as a young girl, to the modern age of federated Australia, where women not only had the right to vote but had also demanded an equal place in all aspects of social, political and commercial life.

Catherine Helen Spence was born in Melrose, Scotland, on 31 October 1825. She arrived, with her mother and siblings, in the colony of South Australia aboard the passenger ship, *Palmyra*, in November 1939, when she was fourteen years old.

George Fife Angas and his South Australian Company had only just settled on the Gulf of St Vincent in 1836, when Angas, in a joint venture with the British Government, established the free colony of South Australia under the Wakefield scheme of assisted migration.

A radical family tree

Catherine Helen Spence was the fifth of eight children born to Scots Helen Brodie and David Spence. Helen Brodie came from a long line of innovative farmers; David's father was a naval surgeon who had retired from the sea to practise his own brand of 'natural' medicine in Melrose, Scotland.

Spence remembered her mother's family as 'intelligent and respectable people'. One aunt, Margaret, ran the 800-acre family farm for thirty years after a stroke had incapacitated her father. Spence remembered Margaret as a 'vigorous, business-like woman — riding or driving her little gig all over the farm'. Spence's mother wrote letters, under a pseudonym, to the local press, spelling out her ideas for social reform.

Spence's father also wanted to become a farmer, but there was not enough capital on his side to finance his desire. He was apprenticed to a law firm at sixteen, and after a three-year term he moved to Edinburgh, where he earned threepence a page writing letters. He also tried his hand at creative writing and had some personal success until failed investments ruined his fortunes and he left for the colonies.

The only 'conservative' element in the Spences' lives seemed to have been their membership of the Established Church of Scotland. The family attended church twice every Sunday, where all the children studied the catechism and were only allowed to read improving texts on the Sabbath.

RIGHT:
English poster offering free passage to skilled labourers and artisans, to join in the building of the colony of South Australia

He abandoned the scheme two years later, when it proved that commerce and the Crown were not comfortable bedfellows.

Emigration to the colonies offered a popular escape route to a fresh start for those oppressed by theocratic rule and monarchical privilege. Disaffected workers and the intellectual middle class responded to the message proffered by the idealists, socialists, Chartists and reformers who were leading the charge to social change in Britain.

Emigration also provided an effective escape route for those wishing to avoid financial obligations at home. David Spence was one such man; having lost his money, and much of his wife's fortune, through foolish investments in imported wheat shares, he abandoned England, leaving his family to join him when he had become established in the colony.

With £500 advanced by his mother-in-law, Spence purchased an 80-acre portion of land in South Australia. This investment entitled him to bring four adults to the colony free of charge. He was able to bring his wife Helen and their children, William, John, Jessie, Mary and Catherine, to meet him in Adelaide. As two of the children were under-age, he was also able to bring out a servant girl as part of his quota of emigrants.

When the newly arrived emigrants stepped ashore they found not the developed township that they had been led to expect, but a hot and dusty collection of huts, tents and temporary dwellings, most unlike the pleasant and green Lowlands of Scotland's border country that they had left behind.

Catherine Spence wrote in her autobiography, published after her death in 1910, that when the family arrived in Adelaide, her father

Settling South Australia

After the death of his shipbuilding father, Manchester-born George Fife Angas moved to London in 1832, and established a trading bank. Like so many others interested in capital improvement, he was convinced of the opportunities offered by migration to the colonies.

He was impressed by the concept of sponsored migration paid for by successful migrants as proposed by Edward Gibbon Wakefield.

Eager to get into the emigration business, Angas joined with the South Australian Company in 1834 and encouraged shiploads of eager emigrants, also committed to capital success, to venture forth into the new world.

Most of his first emigrants were disaffected Scottish Protestants eager to escape the discriminatory strictures of English monarchical rule and the Anglican Church.

Angas also encouraged German Lutherans, who, similarly, sought refuge from Catholic domination and discrimination. Free of the convict stain, South Australia was the perfect place. It was the first place in Australia where the Protestants were in the majority, until the gold rush of the 1850s and the great influx of Cornish Methodists tipped the balance in favour of Victoria.

met them and ushered them to see their first home: 'We sat down upon a log in Light Square, waiting till my father brought the key of a little house in Gilles Street, in spite of the dignity of my fourteen years, I had a good cry'.[2] Such was her disappointment at the state of the settlement to which the family was now committed.

Catherine Spence had come from a stolid Calvinist background dedicated to self-improvement through scholarship, with a family of strong-minded, independent women, and some degree of middle-class comfort. Her father's failed investments in England was the reason for their present situation; she felt that his failure had cast a pall over her young life. Her strict adherence to the dogma of the Presbyterian Church had convinced her that these failures were God's punishment — that when she stepped ashore into the rough-and-ready colony, it seemed to be the place of her damnation. In her unwavering commitment to improving the lives of others, she would spend her next sixty years in atonement for her 'original sins' — whatever she thought they were.

Spence was also committed to her girlhood dream of being a writer. Walter Scott and the Brontë sisters were the popular writers of her youth; Scott wrote of the country in which she had been born and she was schooled in his words. It was a curious combination of the legends of the Lowlands, the romance of Scott, and Bible-belting Calvinism that blended a girlish romanticism into her ironclad sense of morality and duty.

In her own time Spence saw a world changed from Brontë's repressed nobility and middle-class manners, through the dark alleyways, poverty and pickpockets of Dickens, to Lawrence's thwarted, working-class ambition and social miscegenation and James Joyce's denial of faith and celebration of veniality.

The nineteenth century began in strife and ended in war. The years between saw the flowering of the Victorian age of progress, the

BY ORDER OF THE
Colonization Commissioners
FOR HIS MAJESTY'S PROVINCE OF
South Australia

Notice is hereby given,
that from and after the 15th Day of July next, the Commissioners will
SELL ORDERS
FOR
Town and Country Sections
OF LAND,
Entitling the holders to priority of choice; and will receive applications from such intending Settlers as may wish to have Servants or Labourers conveyed to the Colony Free of Cost by means of the
Emigration Fund.

The GOVERNOR, COLONIAL COMMISSIONER, and other CHIEF OFFICERS, will depart about the beginning of the month of SEPTEMBER next, or as soon as the preliminary arrangements shall be completed.

Copies of the Regulations for the Disposal of Public Land and the Emigration of Labourers, may be obtained at the Office, *No. 61, Lincoln's Inn Fields*, where persons desirous of purchasing Land are requested to apply, & where a Register of such applications will be immediately opened, & continued in the order of application.

By Order of the Board. **ROWLAND HILL,** *Sec.*

MARTIN & CO. Lithographers & Printers, 26, Long Acre.

LEFT:
English poster advertising the sale of land in the colony of South Australia
The signatory to this poster is interesting: Catherine Spence met Rowland Hill at his home when she visited England in 1865.

growth of Empire, the creation of the middle class, the birth of Darwinism and the rise of unified labour — each movement, each rising, born in the blood of men, the sweat of the toiling classes and the tears of their women.

Catherine Spence was committed to staking her claim as one of this class; although she was the product of an educated middle class, she bore the passion of the labourer for the struggle and sought the company of those who had also opened their minds to the possibility of another way to live a good and spiritually enriched life. Catherine Spence was like an open field into which the seeds of ideas and possibilities were to be sown. First, though, she had to plough in the years of Calvinism that were stunting her growth. She determined to become a writer.

Late in 1843 Catherine Spence took employment as governess to the children of three government officials. She taught each family for two hours a day, five days a week and earned sixpence an hour.

At the time, the South Australian School Society could not find parents who could even spare sixpence a week for tuition fees. Before the decade was up, in a period of economic boom, the privately operated schools could set their fees at four shillings a week. In May 1846, when Catherine opened her own school, her father thought that all their money worries would be over at last.

Above:

The Proclamation of South Australia 1836

Oil on canvas by Charles Hill, c. 1856-76

Having no convict labour upon which to draw, the young settlement was in urgent need of the willing labour of free, stout-hearted men and women to ensure its success. Advertisements extolling the opportunities in the new colony appeared across the United Kingdom.

The poster shown at right calls together a group of dissatisfied emigrants unhappy at the treatment they had received at the hands of their emigration agent when migrating to South Australia.

Complaints were common, as shipowners and agents stretched the limits of their vessels to carry as much profitable human cargo to the colony as possible.

(Art Gallery of South Australia, Adelaide. Morgan Thomas Bequest Fund, 1936)

TO THE

EMIGRANTS.

We the undersigned, being EMIGRANTS arrived in the Colony of South Australia, do declare our opinion that the Emigration Agent, and others intrusted by the Honorable Commissioners in England, with a duty of providing for the welfare of the Emigrants, have not performed that duty as we were led to expect, but have neglected their interests in every way. We, therefore, sufferers from their conduct, do request a PUBLIC

MEETING

OF THE EMIGRANTS, AT

MR. COCK'S SALE ROOM,

ON MONDAY NEXT,

At Ten o'clock in the Forenoon, in order to obtain their sentiments on the subject, and on the example set by the Colonial Commissioner, in acting in defiance to the local Government of this Colony.

G. WELLS. W. HUMPHRIES. J. HART.
R. BLACK. W. NASH. G. MANTON.
T. WELBOURN. C. FORBES. W. BACON.

Adelaide, September 13, 1837.

EMIGRATION.

Catherine Spence also began contributing articles to Andrew Murray's (sister Jessie's husband) paper, the *South Australian*, but it is unlikely that she earned much, if anything at all, from this work.

After David Spence died, the family had quite a long period of financial hardship. Although Catherine's brothers were employed, the extended family had grown, and they all lived together in their mother's house. Catherine took a position as a live-in 'nursery governess and house counsellor' in 1850, but it seems that this type of domestic employment restricted her even more than marriage may have done. She must not have lasted long in this position, as later in the same year, 25-year-old Catherine Spence decided to live her dream and finally began to attempt to make her living from her pen.

Four years later she published her first novel, *Clara Morrison: A Tale of South Australia during the Gold Fever.* While over the next twenty years her earnings were both piecemeal and unreliable, she did have some degree of success and her publishing royalties were not insubstantial.

A question of faith

Among the early settlers in South Australia were a number of interesting men and women who had taken up the faith of Unitarianism. These were educated, artistic and literate people, with a passion for life and an enthusiasm for ideas. As a young published writer Catherine Spence was soon drawn into their circle. Before long she threw away the restrictions of the Presbyterian Church and fully embraced the enlightening philosophy of the Unitarians.

She felt that a great weight had been lifted from her shoulders, that she was no longer doomed to an eternity in hellfire:

> The dark pall, which enveloped heaven and earth, was lifted; the confused conscience was made clear and straight; the rebellious heart was made submissive and contented under his ministrations. I have been a very cheerful person ever since, more comfortable in the world.[3]

She now regarded the Calvinist doctrine of innate depravity as 'one of the most paralysing dogmas that human fear invented or priestcraft encouraged'. She now saw God as a deity who had created a world of wonder, and believed that it was the inquiring human intellect and scientific discovery that would bring enlightenment to all humankind.

Spence travelled to America, where she met other prominent Unitarians. Among the American flock were Ralph Waldo Emerson and

A unique concept of God

Martha Turner, the first female pastor of the Unitarian Church in Melbourne, offered Catherine Spence such inspiration when she first heard her in the pulpit in 1873 that she exclaimed:

> [I] was thrilled by her exquisite voice, by her earnestness, and by her reverence ... when I heard a highly intelligent and exceptionally able woman conducting the services all through, and especially reading the Scriptures—with so much intelligence that they seemed to take on new meaning. I felt how much the world had been losing for so many centuries.[4]

When Spence heard Turner preach she was captivated by her and ready to believe also that:

> God speaks by the voice of science today as he spoke to the prophets of old, and it has given us the gospel of natural law, of cause and consequence, of evolution ... and upon these foundations we have to build the temple of the spirit.[5]

This notion of God speaking through science excited the humanist in Spence, who had long held an interest in astronomy and physics. She came to see Christ not 'as an incarnate God, but a more or less Godlike man'.[6]

While the Unitarians accepted the spiritual authority of Christ the man, as the Son of God, he was not deified as God the Son.

Henry Thoreau, whose own ideas were radicalising attitudes to the separation of church and state, and obedience to the state itself.

She preached from the pulpit while in America and on her return was invited to do the same in Australia. She was among the first women ever to preach in Australia and was certainly the first to stand in the pulpit in South Australia. In the beginning she was invited to preach from the sermons of the American church leader James Martineau; while she agreed to read from Martineau's words, she followed this by offering to read from her own. On 24 November 1878 she preached an original sermon for the first time. She knew the power of the pulpit in Victorian society and was well aware of the symbolism of her being the first woman in South Australia to be preaching from it.

Private life, public duty

Unlike the 'popish' Caroline Chisholm, who primarily sought to ensure the morality of the girls she settled into service of the squatting classes — always with a view to marriage as the saving grace of the toiling class — Spence sought to free all humanity from the yoke of servitude and the terrors of an unjust hell on earth as well as in the 'afterlife'. She was convinced that through education, science and a quest for knowledge, the shackles of repression, both social and spiritual, would fall away.

She embraced the ideas of John Stuart Mill. Mill and many other bright minds of his day sought to understand the natural state of man's humanity; in doing so, they were subverting the repressive panoply of centuries of religious, social and monarchical tradition. Like John Stuart Mill, Spence had diverse interests; she took an active interest in matters religious, economic, educational and social. She corresponded with other determined 'feminists' who shared her desire to consummate the era of the 'new woman'. She made friends with Vida Goldstein, the prominent Victorian suffragette. She travelled to England in 1865 and she met leading Unitarians who were at the vanguard of the push for social reform. With introductions from supporters in Australia she met social reformers Florence and Rosamund Davenport Hill; their uncle, British administrator and creator of the postal service, Rowland Hill; and their father, penal reformer Matthew Davenport Hill.

Matthew Davenport Hill was prominent in the campaign for changes to the treatment of juvenile offenders. The Davenport Hill sisters were working on ways to help destitute children and promoted the idea of 'boarding out', a concept that Catherine was to introduce

Calvinism vs Unitarianism

The Presbyterian Church believed that a citizen demonstrated his fitness for salvation through his good deeds, by being law-abiding, industrious, sober and thrifty. Even though the state of original sin made it difficult for Calvinists to enter the kingdom of heaven, they believed that working really hard and saving all their money could put them in a slightly better position for redemption.

It is easy to see where the Protestant work ethic had its foundation. Presbyterianism, and similar Protestant creeds, was the bedrock on which the temple of capitalism was to be built in the industrialised nineteenth century.

The Unitarians believed that reason and conscience are the only guide to spiritual truth. The Unitarians denied the theological construct of the Holy Trinity and believed in one God only.

Unitarians demanded the right to seek a God of their own construct and not one formed by dogma, popishness or the threat of eternal misery. Unlike the traditional church, the Unitarian Church believed in innate human goodness, universal salvation and the final harmony of all souls with God. It is easy to see how the educated middle class of Spence's time was drawn to this radical concept of a contemporary, humanitarian, almost socialist kind of friendly God.

into South Australia with great success. At Rowland Hill's home she met Barbara Leigh Smith, the golden-haired philanthropist, artist and feminist on whom George Eliot's character 'Romola' was based. When Smith wrote in 1849, 'I hope there are some who will brave ridicule for the sake of common justice to half the people in the world', Spence took these words to heart.

Spence's trip abroad convinced her that she was on the right path. By the 1890s her opinions were almost impossible to avoid, in South Australia at least. She wrote regularly for the *Register*, one of South Australia's daily newspapers, and often preached in the Unitarian Christian Church. Although her voice was occasionally heard across south-eastern Australia and even in the United States of America, Spence was ready to really make her presence felt on the global platform.

She began by acting locally. She assisted in the establishment of the State Children's Council in 1871; this saw orphaned children removed from the Destitute Asylum and placed in ordinary homes. The following year she established the Boarding Out Society, which operated until 1886, placing hundreds of neglected children into foster homes.

In 1880 Spence was the first woman to be appointed to a school board, and she contributed to the education of South Australia's children with a small book on the duties of citizenship titled *The Laws We Live Under*. Many school children benefited from her generosity, as she donated monies earned from her efforts in journalism to state education.

Catherine Spence was involved with a wide range of organisations committed to social, educational and political reform. She was elected president of the Girls Literary Society in 1892, and was the first female member of the Hospital Committee in 1895. In 1896 she was instrumental in the establishment of the world's first children's court, in South Australia, and was appointed to the Destitute Board in 1897.

She was also a foundation member of the Criminological Society of Adelaide, which was primarily interested in prison reform. She was made the first president of the South Australia Co-operative Clothing Company in 1901, and established the National Council of Women in South Australia in 1902.

The Co-operative Clothing Company had been established exclusively for women, and was run by women. Its investors were women only; £1 shares were offered and workers and management all held stock. The Blyth Street factory was the first clothing factory in Adelaide to be powered by electricity. The

Vida Goldstein, 1869–1949

A friend of Catherine Spence, Portland-born Vida Goldstein, of Polish, Jewish and Irish heritage, was one of the most prominent leaders of the Victorian suffragette movement.

When she nominated for a seat in the Australian Senate in 1903 she was the first woman ever to stand for election to a national parliament in the British Empire. Although this and four later bids were unsuccessful, Goldstein continued the fight for women's suffrage, women's rights and social justice.

During World War I she became an ardent pacifist, was elected chair of the Peace Alliance and formed the Women's Peace Army. She was possibly the only Australian feminist to achieve an international reputation for her views on disarmament, birth control and naturalisation law.

(National Library of Australia Collection)

co-operative survived until 1913, when competition from larger companies, who had also electrified, forced it into liquidation.

Among those who had invested in the co-operative were Catherine Spence and several supporters of the suffragette movement, including Elizabeth Webb Nicholls, secretary of the Working Women's Trades Union, and Agnes Milne.

Following the publication of her article: 'Mother State and her little ones: Children's Courts of Justice and Infant Life Protection' in *Charity Review* on 2 June 1904, which detailed the work of the court, it became a model for similar courts right across Australia, and was adopted by the British in 1907.

Spence became Vice-President of the Kindergarten Union of South Australia in 1904, and first President of the Social Students' Society in 1905; she revived the Effective Voting League in 1908, and was the first president of the Women's Non-Party Political Association, a group started in 1909 by Vida Goldstein.

Towards the end of her life Spence offered an observation that may shed light on her lifelong pursuit of the equality of opportunity for her gender to contribute to public debate:

> ... law and custom have put a bridle on the tongue of women, and of the innumerable proverbs relating to sex, the most cynical are those relating to her use of language. Her only qualification for public speaking in old days was that she could scold, and our ancestors imposed a salutary check on this by the ducking stool in public, and sticks no thicker than the thumb in private.[7]

While Spence may have avoided the ducking stool, she had also avoided the domination of a husband's thumb. When asked if she ever felt remorse at never having children of her own she replied that while she may envy the happiness a mother finds in her child, she never envied women their husbands. She wrote that while the home should be allowed to remain the centre of a woman's sphere, it should not be her limitation. She observed that 'the larger social life has been ignored, and women have consequently failed to have the effect on public life of which their political privilege is capable'.

Her attitude to most members of the male sex seemed almost one of disinterest. In her own novels she rarely created a male figure of any great depth, as she considered that Australian writing was too committed to the representation of failed men:

> ... the 'deadbeat'—the remittance man, the gaunt shepherd with his starving flocks and herds, the free selector on an arid patch, the

A closed book

Catherine Spence's personal affairs remain a mystery. It is known that as a young woman she had refused two offers of marriage: once when she was still quite young, a second when she was twenty-five. In the first instance she refused a 'clever young man', with whom 'she would argue on many points'. She was 17, had just begun to earn her own money and decided to remain independent. Within six weeks he was engaged to another woman.

The second offer came from a widower, and father of three, 57-year-old artist John Gilfillan. It is not known why she refused him, but a clue is given in her fourth book, *The Author's Daughter*, where three of the characters are horrified at the suggestion that the heroine marry such an 'old man'.

Spence was prepared to face the world alone; she had decided that she would discipline her mind 'to manly values, to manly strength, and to manly studies, that [she] may learn to live without leaning on anyone'.[8]

She was eager to 'place the garret steadily before [her] and endeavour to train [her] mind so as to be a useful and amiable member of society, no man's wife, no one's mother'.

There was only one relationship that she allowed to enter into her private household and it

RIGHT:
Catherine Helen Spence, c. 1900
(Photograph courtesy of the State Library of South Australia, SLSA: B36575)

drink shanty where the rouseabouts and shearers knock down their cheques, the race meeting where high and low, rich and poor, are filled with the gambler's ill luck ...[9]

Hers was a different world of political discourse, and she was committed to not leave the world as she found it but to make a difference for the advancement of all humanity.

Single for all her life, Spence often wrote of women's experience from her imagination, but her works were at the beginning of the genre of Australian realist fiction. She wrote:

> The domestic life represented ... is the sort of life I have led—the people are such as I have come in contact with—the politics are what I hear talked of—the opinions I give are what are floating about among Australian Society ...[10]

One vote for all

Catherine Spence conducted a tireless campaign for voting rights for women. She was a persistent pamphleteer on the topic of proportional representation, and in 1894, as vice-president of the Women's Suffrage Movement, she was successful in gaining the right for women in South Australia to vote, before any other colony.

She became the first female political candidate in Australia when she attempted to be elected to the 1897 Australian federal convention. She had stood on the single issue of proportional representation, which some, fearful of too much change too fast, had described as 'Too damned fair' to be even considered. One organisation even put her name on a ticket headed '10 BEST MEN' and she was awarded the accolade of the 'best man of the lot'.[11] However, she was not elected.

She was a strong and energetic woman right up to her last years. Not long before she died she declared that 'no woman in Australia has been richer in friends'. She died at her home in Norwood, Adelaide, on 3 April 1910, aged eighty. The uncorrected proofs of her autobiography lay beside her bed. *C. H. Spence: An Autobiography* was published by her friends later that year.

was with Ellen Louisa Gregory, a lass she had met in England in 1865, at the home of relatives of her brother-in-law William Wren. She encouraged Ellen to migrate to South Australia to care for an aunt living out in the country.

The aunt didn't take to the girl at all and, almost as an apology for making the mistake of encouraging her, Catherine took Ellen Gregory in. While the rest of Spence's family may have resented the intrusion of an outsider into their tight family unit, Catherine appeared to treat Ellen as an equal, over the years suggesting an intimacy that went far beyond the relationship of domestic servant or secretary.

Ellen Gregory stayed with Spence for forty years, even after Spence had given up her own house and had gone to live with the McQuilty family. Mrs McQuilty had once been a maid to the Spence household; Spence and Gregory shared two rooms—a study and a bedroom—in the McQuilty house.

When Spence died she left all her household furniture, her china, linen, and even her best brooch to her companion of forty years.

John Tebbutt

1834–1916

Star gazer of the Hawkesbury

THE HAWKESBURY RIVER DISTRICT FROM SYDNEY TO Windsor played a most important role in the development of the colony of New South Wales. John and Elizabeth Macarthur began their fortune there; Governor Macquarie established the town of Windsor, giving Francis Greenway the commission to build St Matthew's Church on a rise overlooking the river in whose grounds lay buried some passengers of the First Fleet; and amateur astronomer John Tebbutt, aged only nineteen, first gazed at the heavens through the lens of an old marine telescope in an observatory he had built for himself in the yard of his father's farm. It was not long before Tebbutt made the startling discoveries that would ensure his name sparkled forever among the stars.

In 1857 John Tebbutt predicted a solar eclipse that would black out the skies over Sydney. The colonial society of New South Wales had only just shaken off the shackles of the penal settlement and was ready to embrace any new science that would lift New South Wales from its bloody past into an enlightened future. When Tebbutt's prediction came to pass, and the skies over Sydney darkened as if on cue, the townsfolk and government alike marvelled at the seemingly prophetic power of their home-grown 'man of science'.

When Tebbutt predicted next that a great comet would pass between the sun and the earth, beginning its trajectory in May 1861, the whole world took notice. Tebbutt had been studying the skies when on 13 May he noticed a faint hazy object that he had not seen

John Tebbutt is featured on the obverse of the $100 paper note, first issued in 1996.

OPPOSITE:
Astronomer John Tebbutt

John Tebbutt's keen eye coupled with a natural inclination towards complex mathematics made him unusual among astronomers. His work was so accurate that even seventy years after his death in 1916 his calculations were used in the rendezvous of the space probe *Giotto* with Halley's comet in 1986.

(Courtesy Hawkesbury Regional Library Collection)

ABOVE & RIGHT:
Tebbutt's observatory, Windsor

John Tebbutt built several observatories in the backyard of Peninsula House, his father's farming property overlooking the Hawkesbury River at Windsor, where he lived for his entire life.

The first timber one was replaced in 1863, another was constructed in 1874, and a second dome added in 1879. The buildings shown at right are still owned by descendants of John Tebbutt today.

Although he was technically an 'amateur', Tebbutt's observatory at Windsor was listed alongside all the best public-funded observatories working around the world.

(Author's photographs)

before. Night after night he fixed his attention on the heavenly object and determined that it was moving slowly across the sky.

On 25 May he announced the discovery of his comet in the *Sydney Morning Herald.* The discovery of the 'great comet', which had become so bright by the middle of that year that it was visible in daylight, was the most spectacular astronomical event of all seen in the nineteenth century. It lasted in the sky for several months, the earth passing through its tail, just as Tebbutt had predicted, on 30 June 1861. As it passed between the earth and the sun it caused the daytime sky to darken considerably. People crowded onto rooftops to observe this phenomenon.

ABOVE:
Tebbutt by the timber observatory, c. 1863
(Courtesy Hawkesbury Regional Library Collection)

The comet passed within 14,900,000 km of the earth, at its closest in June 1861; its tail covered 120 degrees, or two-thirds of the sky.

Following this initial success, and the world-wide recognition that it brought him, in 1863 Tebbutt decided to build a new observatory adjacent to his earlier timber building, which was by now being destroyed by termites. This was only one of several built over the next few years; he added another in 1874, a second dome in 1879, and an adjoining library in the same year. Tebbutt had established an astronomical observatory that posed a serious

A 'star' is born

John Tebbutt was born in 1834, the son of free settlers who had emigrated to the colony of New South Wales in 1801.

Tebbutt's own birthdate was somewhat serendipitous. He was born in the very year that the great English astronomer Edmund Halley had predicted the return of the comet that today bears his name. Although Tebbutt was too young to recall the proof of Halley's calculations, he lived long enough to see the comet's return when it flashed through the skies again in 1910.

John Tebbutt died six years later in 1916 and is buried in the family vault in St Matthew's churchyard, Windsor.

(Author's photograph)

BELOW:

The Tail of the Comet of 1853

Although this illustration is not Tebbutt's comet, it is indicative of the intense public interest in the unusual display of such astronomical phenomena.

The appearance of a comet was once seen as a harbinger of bad fortune and thought to bring ill health, pestilence and even death to those who observed them. The accurate mathematical predictions of scientists such as Halley and Tebbutt demystified what had previously been seen as unpredictable portents of bad luck.

This engraved cartoon by George Cruikshank was published as the frontispiece to the first issue of his magazine in London in 1853.

(Rex Nan Kivell Collection, NK11149. By permission, National Library of Australia)

challenge to the various state-run establishments. Between the years 1880 and 1889 he recorded more than twice the number of cometary deter-minations as the Sydney, Melbourne and Adelaide observatories combined. He had made 700 determinations; they had recorded only 289 between them.

Tebbutt now scanned the heavens with a 20 cm 'Grubb of Ireland' refractor that he had bought from the estate of the late Victorian astronomer Dr William Bone. With his 'Grubb' he discovered his second comet in December 1881. The newspapers eagerly announced this sighting to a public fascinated by the discovery of scientific phenomena:

> A great comet has been discovered by the internationally recognised Australian, Astronomer, John Tebbutt.
>
> Mr Tebbutt saw the comet from the private observatory he has established on his property at Peninsula Farm on the Hawkesbury. This is the second sighting for Mr Tebbutt. The first was in May 1861, and the great comet he observed then has since been known as 'Tebbutt's Comet'.
>
> At one stage it had a tail that could be traced for over 110 degrees.[1]

Over his lifetime John Tebbutt published more than 370 scientific papers, of which 150 concerned the phenomena of comets. He was awarded the silver medal at the Paris exhibition in 1867, for his work titled 'On the Present Progress and Present State of Astronomical Science in New South Wales'. In 1873 he was made a Fellow of the Royal Astronomical Society in London and received the Hannah Jackson Gift and Medal of the Royal Astronomical Society in 1905.

Tebbutt's calculations were so accurate that even in the 1980s, seventy years after his death in 1916, his calculations were used to guide the space probe *Giotto* to its rendezvous with Halley's comet.

Tebbutt had once served as president of the Astronomical Society of Sydney and, in 1973, was recognised by the International Astronomical Union when a crater on the moon was renamed 'Tebbutt Crater'. On the face of the moon the name of John Tebbutt, the 'stargazer of the Hawkesbury', is forever commemorated — in good company, alongside Plato, Copernicus and Pythagoras.

William James Farrer

1845–1906

William James Farrer is featured on the obverse of the $2 paper note, first issued in 1966.

BELOW:
William James Farrer as a boy
(State Library of New South Wales Collection)

The saviour of the Australian wheat industry

WILLIAM JAMES FARRER WAS A GIFTED STUDENT. When he was only eight years old he won a scholarship that took him from his home in Westmoreland to Christ's Hospital School in London. The school had the sobriquet 'Blue-coats' because of the long blue coats, adorned in the front with two rows of silver buttons, that were worn by all of the students.

He excelled at 'Blue-coats', winning gold and silver medals for mathematics and attaining the status of a 'Grecian', a cohort of talented high achievers who were regarded by the other pupils as the 'lords of the school'. 'Blue-coats' had among its alumni the noted men of letters Samuel Taylor Coleridge, Charles Lamb and Leigh Hunt — it is not known whether the school ever expected young Bill Farrer to achieve the notoriety to challenge these great names.

Farrer won a scholarship to Pembroke College, Cambridge, going down in 1864. He read for a degree in Arts and graduated with distinction in 1868. While at Pembroke he enlisted in the Cambridge University Rifle Volunteers and won cups for his expert skill as a marksman. Farrer was a talented, young, academic gentleman who, like the other young gentlemen from similar yeoman stock, made the most of the privileges that his birthright would afford — and he was enjoying his advantages.

LEFT:
William James Farrer at school in London

William was the son of yeoman farmer Thomas Farrer, whose family had been farmers and landowners in Westmoreland and Cumberland for generations, and Sarah (nee Brunskill), the daughter of farmer John Brunskill of the neighbouring farm, Lambrigg.

When William James Farrer was born on 3 April 1845, in a farmhouse at Docker, near Kendal, his mother Sarah was already showing the symptoms of consumption.

Following his mother's early death when he was only eight years old, William was sent on scholarship to attend Christ's Hospital School in London.
(State Library of New South Wales Collection)

OPPOSITE:
William James Farrer, c. 1887
(State Library of New South Wales Collection)

BELOW:
Lambrigg foote, Kendal, Westmoreland, England
William Farrer's home in England, c.1930
(National Library of Australia Collection)

After completing his bachelor's degree, Farrer began to study medicine but fell ill and was forced to abandon the course. A fellow student, Australian Frank Betts from Parramatta, suggested that Farrer should join him on his return voyage to the colony.

On their arrival in Sydney in 1870 Farrer first went to stay with Betts's family at Parramatta, while Frank went on to New Zealand to try his luck. Unfortunately, Frank Betts was drowned there.

William Farrer stayed in Parramatta until he had decided his future. His intention on leaving England was to buy a sheep station somewhere in New South Wales, so, to get himself acclimatised to the country life he took a pos-ition as tutor to the children of gentleman farmer George Campbell on his station Duntroon in the southern tablelands.

Farrer settled into his 'colonial experience' with ease and the enthusiasm typical of his character. He made himself aware of all that was going on around him; he talked to farmers about their work, their crops and the weather; he developed a love of horses and spent hours in the saddle. He loved to take long walks all over the countryside and would stride out purposefully, always shod in the large boots he preferred to wear. Mrs Campbell good-humouredly complained that she could tell when William was in the house by the big, muddied (often manured) footprints he left in his wake.

In these latter years of the nineteenth century, little had been done to improve farming practices nor to secure sustainability since the arrival of the First Fleet. Farmers complained of the poor returns they were getting from the tired soils that they had been planting over and over again, year after year. They complained of the cycle of disease inflicted on the grains they struggled to grow — rust, bunt and smut were the bane of the wheat grower and returns were so poor that Australia was even

forced to import grain for milling in the years before the turn of the century.

The academic in William Farrer was soon at work. In 1873, following another season of poor soils, diseased grain and dying stock, he wrote his first published thesis, 'Grass and Sheep Farming, a paper Speculative and Suggestive, by William Farrer, B.A., Pembroke College, Cambridge'.

This paper proposed the need for a serious study of husbandry in the colony and an investigation into the value and possible use of native plants for the feeding of stock. Farrer had seen sheep dying, affected by the parasitic diseases he could only speculate were in the grasses on which they were feeding. He wrote:

> The sheep were then dying in the Southern tablelands district of the colony in which I was then wandering, I then began to make enquiries in order to see if anything could be done to stop or trace the real cause of the parasitic diseases which were causing the sheep to die: of course, it was the wet weather that we had long been having that was the immediate cause. But I thought that if we could find out why it was that wet weather produced such disastrous results, we might be in a position to prevent an occurrence of the disasters that arise in such seasons.[1]

In his paper he was critical of the lack of the study of pastoral science in the colony, where farmers and graziers were simply repeating the farming methods of Britain without making any concessions for the climate and conditions of the new world. He continued to admonish the lack of foresight of the leaders of agriculture in Australia:

> I am afraid the charge of excessive slowness, and the character of the colony has earned for itself of being behindhand in every

BELOW:
Cuppacumbalong Station, New South Wales central tablelands, 1952

Farrer moved into the central tablelands sheep-grazing and wheat-growing district of New South Wales soon after his arrival in Australia in 1870, where he stayed at Duntroon station.

A number of years after he had married, he moved on to Cuppacumbalong station on the banks of the Murrumbidgee River. Cuppacumbalong can be seen on the left in the distance, with the Murrumbidgee at the right of this photograph.

(National Archives of Australia Collection)

BELOW:
Farrer's laboratory in 1929
Farrer took over this property five miles from Cuppacumbalong Station, naming it Lambrigg after his maternal grandfather's farm in England.
(State Library of New South Wales Collection)

> advance that the world makes, has some truth in it. America has colleges in almost every state in which not only agricultural chemistry is taught, but at many of her colleges practical instruction is also given.[2]

He concluded with a broad swipe at the farming community in general and the government in particular:

> In this way America has made immense strides since the Civil War. This institution [agricultural research] is largely supported by Government, but out here a morbid, overstrained, and generally misguided policy of economy seems to be paralysing all progress.[3]

Farrer was way ahead of the conservative thinking of his day. Australia was still stuck contentedly in the malaise of a 'cargo cult' economy; while funds, foods and goods still flooded in from the old country to support the needs of the colony, what need had the governments to really try to effect change?

While Australia was content to be tied to Great Britain and reliant on 'home' as its reason for being, what need was there for an independent mind who sought to make the colony independent of its 'Imperial mother'?

But times were certainly changing, and Australian farmers had to change with them. The push towards federation, the end of the mad scramble for gold and the growing sense of a character that was peculiarly Australian, all had an impact on the national psyche.

Farrer was one man among many who saw the potential for the colony to become a leader in the world in all kinds of ways; and especially in the production of food and fibre, able to feed itself while it fed the world.

After making some poor investments in mining ventures, which diminished the funds left to him for his intended pastoral property, Farrer had to find some kind of employment to help him restore his capital.

Being of a mathematical inclination, he took a position as assistant to licensed surveyor George Commins. This life was perfect for him: he was outdoors, which was good for his persistent lung complaint; he was in the bush, which he loved; and he was able to pursue his interest in agricultural matters as he travelled

across the southern tablelands with his surveying chains in his hands.

On 3 August 1876 William Farrer was officially licensed and took a contract with the Lands Department of New South Wales to undertake surveys of the Dubbo district.

He was a meticulous worker whose methods became the hallmark by which all others were judged. When some of the men who assisted him in his work were unable to reach a conclusion on a particularly difficult mathematical problem, they telegraphed Farrer to seek his advice; from miles away he replied, suggesting the correct method of computing the answer to their problems. His reply remained stuck to the wall of the Wagga survey office for years to come as an example of the Farrer method of solving problems.

A fall from a horse

On a visit to the Betts family in Parramatta in 1878, William Farrer was thrown from his horse. He was severely concussed and taken to the nearby Woolpack Inn, where he lay until he had recovered sufficiently and was able to be moved. For a time it was thought that he would not recover, and when he did he was left with his eyesight damaged and one shoulder permanently stooped a little lower than the other.

After he had fully recovered he took a voyage back to England and visited his family, returning to Dubbo to resume his duties in July 1879.

While the accident had damaged him physically, the trip away seemed to have put his thoughts into focus. On his return to New South Wales he married Nina Fane de Salis of Cuppacumbalong station on 11 September 1882; as Nina's father, Leopold Fane de Salis, was widowed and Nina was his only daughter, the couple agreed to stay with him for as long as he lived. This was a most satisfactory arrangement for all of them, as William was away on the Nyngan and Cobar stock routes, and later around Cooma and Forbes, returning to Cuppacumbalong at irregular intervals.

William and Nina continued to reside with Leopold even after Cuppacumbalong was sold and they all went to live at Lambrigg, the nearby property where Farrer had begun his research years earlier.

A crazy, faddish, woolly headed crank

At Lambrigg, Farrer planted his garden alongside his acreage of experimental pasture. He built a long rose walk, and planted vines but, although he dabbled in the crossbreeding of

From Cuppacumbalong to Lambrigg

Before Cuppacumbalong was sold Farrer rode the five miles out to Lambrigg each day. He occasionally slept in the laboratory, where a bed was always kept made, just in case. This three-roomed pisé building with its iron roof and flag-stoned floors looks more like a stable than a laboratory, but within these walls the direction of the Australian wheat industry was changed.

Farrer kept his hundreds of little bags of labelled grains stored here, his milling wheel among his notebooks. He could locate a sample stored years before and accurately recall its characteristics from his carefully kept records.

It is not known whether the property was a wedding gift from Nina's father or if it was left to her by her late brother Rudolph, but it was only after he had been appointed as 'wheat experimentalist' to the Agriculture Department of New South Wales that Farrer, his wife Nina, and her father Leopold, sold Cuppacumbalong and moved in permanently.

Before that Farrer had been able to live off his work as a surveyor, and an allowance that came from his family in England. After his father died, an uncle contacted him and requested that he return to England; his failure to do so would guarantee the loss of his allowance. Farrer decided to remain in Australia.

roses, his real interest was in his plots of billowing grains. Other farmers saw him as a very strange fellow indeed. He didn't plant broad acreage as they did; he simply planted long strips of wheat, separated by long strips of barley.

They watched him on his hands and knees moving among the stalks of grains, tying strips of coloured cloth to those he had selected, all the while making copious notes: eventually hundreds of little pocketbooks filled his shelves. He worked from first to last light, returning to his laboratory only when it was too dark for him to see any more. His fields of grains separated into types, each line labelled, numbered and adorned with hundreds of tiny coloured flags, convinced the neighbouring farmers that he was a 'crazy, faddish, woolly headed crank'.

As a student William Farrer had taken a great interest in Charles Darwin's theory of evolution and he was keen to test these ideas in the wheat fields of the southern tablelands. In an address to the Australasian Association for the Advancement of Science in 1898 he stated:

> The idea of making improvements in the wheat plant was taken hold of as early as 1882, when I had a controversy with *The Australasian* newspaper on the possibility and best manner of securing varieties of wheat which would satisfactorily resist rust.[4]

He had pitted his intellect against the problems of the wheat industry and in 1882 proposed through the *Australasian* that by importing varieties of wheat known to resist rust, the fortunes of the wheat industry could be changed. He also proposed that:

> ... farmers should gather seeds from 'individual plants that were free of the parasite, and thus secure for themselves seed for planting that would prove rust-resistant'.[5]

For Farrer these suggestions were simply the beginning of a decade of experimental work, much of it unsatisfactory, and it wasn't for several years that he made his first attempts at crossbreeding.

He began to correspond with scientists from all around the globe who were interested in similar research; from them he received samples of all kinds of grains for his experimentation. At the beginning of his work there were no agricultural colleges at all in Australia and the notion of research into centuries-old farming practices was all but vilified. America had a college in almost every state and Farrer received a lot of encouragement, as well as some excellent samples of crossbred grains, from Professor A. E. Blount of the Colorado Agricultural Experiment Station.

The very image of the English country gentleman

William Farrer was a familiar yet peculiar sight to his neighbours at Lambrigg. Dressed in his long grey linen or silk coat, a large handkerchief tucked under his brown felt hat to protect his neck from the sun, he looked the part of the bumbling, rambling village curate.

On his knees he wore leather kneeling pads, and his coats were adorned with multiple pockets all bulging with scissors, coloured tapes, notebooks, forceps and the little calico bags he needed for his samples.

He always wore large boots with extra-heavy soles and was notorious for tracking mud all over the house.

On his rare trips to town Farrer wore a finely checked woollen suit. His tie seemed always to be askew—the mark of a man who, once dressed, was unaware of his appearance, his mind set on matters of far greater importance.

Lambrigg was a two-storeyed pisé-and-sandstone structure designed by Farrer himself. It had a large verandah at the first-floor level which overlooked the three acres of experimental plots in front, between the house and the laboratory. The balcony was completely covered with a climbing rose that bore three kinds of flowers which bloomed in succession, a testament to Farrer's skill as a horticulturalist.

BELOW:
Farrer's house in 1929
(State Library of New South Wales Collection)

Blount was keen for Farrer to attempt the American experiments with his crossbreeds in Australia, and Farrer sent some of Blount's samples to others within Australia who could assist in breeding for application in different regions, climates and conditions.

Blount wrote to Farrer in February 1885:

> I have become very much interested in your account of the rust, etc. I am quite sure there is a way to prevent its ravages on the coast in good milling wheats ... I wish I could visit you. I think a 4 to 6 years breeding of your standard wheats would almost entirely revolutionise them so that rust, smut, mildew and blight would be unknown ... I will send you several kinds of my crosses to test.[6]

Later the following year Farrer sent samples of the wheats from Colorado to Professor Lowrie of Roseworthy College in South Australia, who had also been sending Farrer some of his wheats:

> By this mail I am sending you some small (ridiculously small) samples of eighteen different wheats I have lately received from my friend, Professor Blount, of Colorado ... these wheats are quite untried except perhaps it be the Egyptian, identical with an Egyptian wheat I have already in Australia. Some may possibly be of value and I hope will ... I shall be delighted and interested if you will furnish me reports of the different wheats I send ... I am distributing wheats as widely as I can for trial in different parts of Australia ...[7]

These men of science, although thousands of miles apart, were all cooperating in the creation of new grain species that could be suitable for different physical environments and help to develop an environment of sustainability in local agricultural production.

In his letter to Lowrie, Farrer described his attempts to acclimatise strains for different environments. He had already discovered what sort of grain survived best in Queensland, and it was not the same as what was best at Lambrigg, which was 2000 feet above sea level and freezing in winter. He had also noted

BELOW:
Grain variety trials, Cowra, 1921
(State Library of New South Wales Collection)

that the grains that did well on the Queensland coast did not do so well inland.

While Farrer and his colleagues across the country, and across the globe, were making slow but steady strides, few in Australia were even aware of Farrer's work, nor of the importance being placed on agricultural research internationally.

When the first Inter-Colonial Agricultural Conference was held in 1890, Farrer was not even invited to attend. It was not until the following year that he was finally able to place his ideas before his contemporaries when he delivered his paper on wheat breeding at the conference held in South Australia in 1891. It was only then that the New South Wales Department of Agriculture took any notice at all of the 'woolly headed crank' from Cuppacumbalong.

In 1898 Farrer was offered a position with the New South Wales Department of Agriculture as 'wheat experimentalist', on a salary of £350 per year. He was able to continue with his work on his own farm and added to this was the opportunity to conduct comparative experimentation on the government farms throughout New South Wales. By expanding the number of regions in which his experiments were conducted, he was able to collect valuable data which explored not only grain characteristics but soil and climatic conditions as well.

Once Farrer was on the government payroll, the department expected to see quick results for their investment. However, nature didn't work as fast as the government demanded. Farrer had spent years working at his own pace, allowing nature to take its own evolutionary course. Crossbreeding could take three to four years to establish a 'type', and then testing for milling quality could take another twelve months. After the results of his lengthy experimentation proved satisfactory it would take another two years before

enough grain could be produced to make it available for distribution to farmers.

All through the six or seven years' of experimentation with one type alone, Farrer was making hundreds of other experiments at a time, making careful records of every attempt in scores of notebooks kept in his 'laboratory' at Lambrigg. He was a meticulous worker; his impeccable records kept track of every single experiment at all of the farms engaged in his research.

When he was finally able to produce a variety of wheat almost one hundred per cent resistant to smut-ball or 'bunt', the government was delighted that at last it had a result. A two-hundred-acre farm was established at Cooma. Farrer discovered that wheat under Australian conditions was best left to ripen on the stalk; he then spent hours crawling along on his hands and knees among his rows of wheat looking for the plant that would best hold its head to the stalk right up to the end of the ripening stage.

By the turn of the century Farrer had created what was to become his most famous variety. He named the strain 'Federation' in honour of the newly federated Australian nation. By 1903 there were sufficient quantities of this new drought-resistant strain for it to be made available to any farmer who wanted to plant Farrer's new wheat for a new nation.

He created a large number of wheat types all with characteristics of their own that made them suitable for milling, or for stockfeed, or for both. The most commonly planted types were named — Bobs, Bowen, Bunyip, Canberra, Cleveland, Cowbar, Firbank, Rymer — and, of course, Federation.

As well as his experimentation with, and the subsequent creation of, the large variety of wheat strains which revived the moribund Australian wheat industry, William Farrer was also interested in the types of soil he had to contend with and in finding methods of improving soil conditions. He had been a lifelong proponent of the benefits of green manuring (turning in paddock growth and stubble prior to planting) and had conducted many experiments with lupins; he promoted these as the most efficient way of introducing nitrogen to the soil.

In 1904 Farrer was thrown from a buggy and severely dislocated his shoulder. It took him months before he was fully recovered and able to write again without pain. Although it was around this time that he wrote that he was finally in the throes of mastering Mendel's laws, the years of hard, physical labour, the days spent in all weathers

Bobs, Bunyip and Federation

Each of the wheat strains bred by Farrer had their own characteristics. Florence and Firbank were early-maturing; Bowen came on in mid-season; and Cleveland and Rymer matured late in the season. Federation and Bunyip were of the 'soft white' type, while Bobs and Cowbar were 'hard'.

While most were grown for both grain and hay, Firbank was the best for hay and green fodder. Federation and Bunyip produced little hay and were grown almost entirely for grain.

Farrer never really succeeded in creating a strain that was wholly resistant to rust or smut, and he never really popularised the strains of durum wheats for Australian growers.

It was his methodology, his dedication and his belief in his ideas that created an environment of research that had been unknown in Australia when he arrived from England for the sake of his health in 1870.

RIGHT:
'Gresley' (left) and 'Hard Federation' (right) ears and grains

This grain sample was photographed by the New South Wales Department of Agriculture in 1926

(State Library of New South Wales Collection)

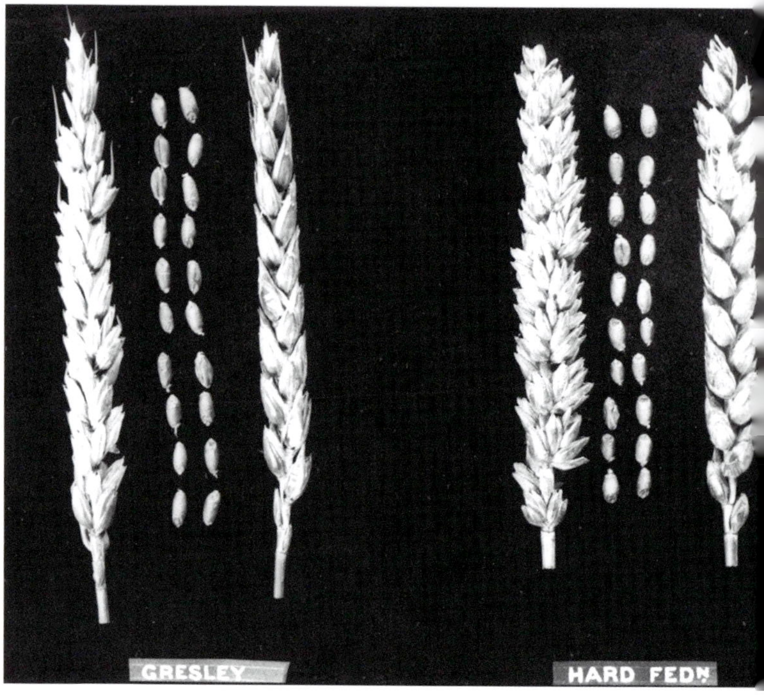

in concentrated effort in the field, and the endless nights spent in the laboratory, were all beginning to take their toll.

Two years after this accident William Farrer was reclining on his couch making some notes when Nina Farrer noticed that her husband was having difficulty breathing. His niece was also in the house; all of the others who were staying at Lambrigg for the Easter holidays were away in Tuggeranong at a picnic. His wife called out to her niece, but by the time she ran into the room Farrer was dead. He died, not of a failure of his lungs from the tuberculosis that had prompted his migration thirty-six years earlier, but of a massive heart attack.

In respect to his wishes to be buried on the property at the top of a hill in the back paddock, his family and friends prepared to dig his grave. At two feet they hit solid rock and could not dig any further. As it was at the end of the day when they began to dig, and owing to the failing of the light, they decided to postpone their efforts until the following morning and to obtain the services of Dan Harris, an old miner who lived nearby, and make the most of his expert knowledge in blasting.

The funeral was set for midday on 18 April 1906, but again was postponed as it took until almost sunset to get the grave down to four-and-a-half feet. As the light faded and dusk fell, William Farrer was finally laid to rest, on the tree-topped hillside overlooking his beloved Lambrigg. It was dark when the private service ended, flowers were placed upon the coffin as a strong wind blew up, and rain began to fall as the mourners picked their way back to the homestead by lantern light.

At the time of William Farrer's death more than one and a half million acres of wheat were under crop across the continent, yielding a harvest totalling more than sixteen million bushels. By 1920 this number increased to more than three million acres, yielding

Mendelism

Gregor Johann Mendel was a member of a religious order from Bino in the (now) Czech Republic, who alongside the theories of Charles Darwin, changed the way thinkers of their time saw the natural world.

William Farrer was still a student when the bold new ideas of evolutionary theory were propounded in the middle of the nineteenth century, shocking a reactionary world.

Mendel's theory proposed the law of heredity; that it was possible to predict the character or characters of offspring by studying the character of the parent and their lineage. This idea was first canvassed by Mendel in 1866, just four years before Farrer arrived in Australia. Farrer could not have been aware of Mendel's 'theory of heredity' before he began his own experimentation. While Charles Darwin was a great influence on scholars such as Farrer, he was, later on, also aware that his work was 'Mendelian'.

Mendel's ideas gave Farrer a sense of direction in the knowledge that he was not working alone — that others also saw the science in what he was doing.

fifty-three million bushels. Farrer's legacy was to increase the yield per acre by two to three bushels, adding £750,000 to £1,5000,000 per year to the farmers' pockets.

But incredibly, in the years that followed his death, Farrer was not honoured as might be expected. When it was proposed that a fitting memorial to the 'saviour of Australia's wheat industry' be constructed, only £1030 was subscribed. It was not until almost thirty years later that a memorial was eventually unveiled, in Queanbeyan near Canberra.

The Farrer Memorial Scholarship also commemorates him. The first recipient of the Farrer Memorial Medal (inset) was W. L. Waterhouse, whose research into the effect of superphosphate on Australian wheat growing was a fitting project to honour the man who had spent his life promoting grain and the benefits of manure.

INSET:
Farrer Memorial Medal

(State Library of New South Wales Collection. Courtesy, Farrer Memorial Trust)

BELOW:
Federation celebrations, Sydney 1901

This arch constructed over Bridge Street in Sydney for the Federation celebrations of 1901 features sheaves of wheat of the new strain — Federation.

(State Library of New South Wales Collection)

Lawrence Hargrave

1850–1915

Lawrence Hargrave is featured on the obverse of the $20 paper note, first issued in 1966.

OPPOSITE:
Aeronautical inventor, Lawrence Hargrave

Lawrence Hargrave was born in Greenwich, England. When his parents migrated to Australia in 1857, he stayed on until he had completed his schooling, joining them in 1866 at their 'charming' home, named Cliff House, at Stanwell Park on Sydney's south.

It was at Cliff House that Hargrave first became enthralled by the flight of seabirds as they hovered in the air rising up from the sea, and glided, soaring across the ocean with effortless grace.

The inquisitive Hargrave set himself on a course of experimentation with kites that before long saw him soaring 'like a bird' out across the sea.

It was his designs for box kites that inspired the Wright brothers in America, who are today credited with being the first to achieve manned flight.

(National Archives of Australia Collection)

The first man to fly

THE LIFE OF LAWRENCE HARGRAVE SPANNED TWO defining events in Australia's history. He was born one year before the discovery of gold in the colonies of New South Wales and Victoria, and died one year after the outbreak of World War I. In his sixty-five-year lifespan Hargrave saw Australia emerge from being an embattled and bickering group of colonies into a proud and prosperous unified nation.

He witnessed the federated nation's 'blooding' at Gallipoli, but his heart was broken as he watched nation set against nation, battling each other in the skies over the Western Front in flying machines powered by the fruits of his imagination.

Lawrence Hargrave was born in the age of horse-drawn carriages and bullock drays, an age of steam and steel, and lived to see his obsession with manned flight of machines heavier than air become an everyday occurrence.

He never attempted to profit from the results of his experimentation with flight that consumed his every waking hour for the better part of thirty years. Lawrence Hargrave was a real pioneer of aviation; he discovered the principles of wing design and propulsion and shared his discoveries with the world — for no personal gain. He was the epitome of the eccentric nineteenth-century dilettante, the 'crazy' inventor the world preferred to mock, yet ultimately the new world of aviation benefited from his unparalleled generosity.

Lawrence Hargrave was born in Greenwich, England. His parents migrated to Australia in 1857, leaving him at Queen Elizabeth's Grammar School in Kirby, Westmoreland. After he completed his schooling in 1866, he joined his parents at Stanwell Park, south of Sydney. He was then sixteen years old.

His father, John Fletcher Hargrave, rose rapidly through the ranks of the legal profession following his arrival in the colony of New South Wales. He had been made a district judge on his arrival, had resigned two years later and won a seat in parliament in 1859. He served as solicitor-general in Cowper's ministry, and later as attorney-general with Robertson. He was next appointed to the position of high court judge.

Although father and son had a reasonable relationship, Lawrence saw little of the important, busy and often irritable gentleman and was left to his own devices. When his mother died Lawrence was effectively on his own, but this did not seem to bother him at all; he was used to making his own amusement, and often turned his attention to the flight of the seabirds who soared and dipped into the waves off the cliffs near his home. He spent many hours observing the graceful flight of seabirds as they hung in the air currents rising up over the water by the cliff face.

It was not long before Lawrence himself was to be seen 'flying' above the same cliffs held aloft by the wind.

In the meantime, he had other trails to follow and a whole world to experience. His father would have preferred Lawrence to go to the bar, but he failed to matriculate. Although he had a brilliant mind, Lawrence Hargrave preferred to confine his scholarship to mathematics; the rest was of little interest to him. His was a mind of abstraction, inventiveness and inquiry.

Not prepared for university, Hargrave left school and took a position in the drafting office of the Australian Steamship Navigation Company. The office desk didn't suit him at all, so as soon as he was twenty-one years old and able to make his own decisions, he resigned and set on a life of exploration. He boarded a ship bound for the wilds of New Guinea. The vessel was wrecked off the Queensland coast, and as the survivors struggled to reach the safety of the shore, hostile Aborigines attacked them. Hargrave was lucky to escape with his life.

He returned to Cliff House, but coastal New South Wales offered little adventure for the young man at this time in his life. He joined an expedition to New Guinea being mounted by Luigi Maria D'Albertis and with this party ventured far into the dense jungles of the Fly River. With D'Albertis, Hargrave travelled up the river for more than four hundred miles; they were the first Europeans to go so far into the hostile jungle. Hargrave was responsible for drafting the first maps of both the Fly and Sepik Rivers.

After his return to Stanwell Park in 1877 Hargrave became a member of the Royal Society of New South Wales.The tropical heat, mosquitoes and hostile natives of the Fly must have been enough to satisfy his hunger for adventure abroad; he married Margaret Preston Johnson the following year and settled down quite happily into domestic life.

He took a position as astronomical observer at the Sydney Observatory, and although during his time there he assisted in remeasuring Herschel's double stars and in the discovery of 480 new stars, the monotony of the work began to bore him.

RIGHT:

Model of Flying Machines, c. 1884-85

This flapping-winged machine was powered with a rubber band pulled into tension, not twisted, as one would expect. There was no screw-type propeller; Hargrave believed at this time that it was the flapping up and down of the wings that provided lift, not the shape of the wing as was later discovered.

OPPOSITE, LEFT:

Model of three-cylinder rotary engine, 1889

OPPOSITE, RIGHT:

Model of curve-winged, rigid box kite

The curved surface of the wing allowed for greater lifting power. This discovery by Hargrave revolutionised the way people thought about designs for flight.

(National Archives of Australia Collection)

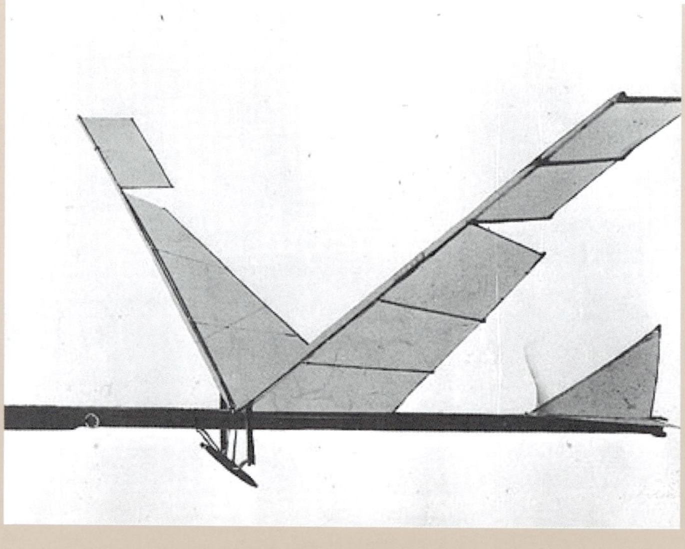

At the age of thirty-three, he quit his job and devoted his life to research into his all-consuming interest: manned flight. He had private means of support and was therefore able to provide for his wife, their four daughters and one son, enabling him to spend his days playing with his kites.

Hargrave had long been a part of the world-wide scientific community and had contributed papers and corresponded with others of a similar mind across the globe. His ideas were to play a vital part in the research and success of others from as far away as the United States of America and Europe.

He was considered a true eccentric when he advanced his theory of 'trichoidal propulsion' in 1884. While he had been experimenting with flapping-winged devices, which had propelled themselves along in a satisfying horizontal movement, there was no vertical movement at all. He was searching for the clue to natural movement that his study of birds was not giving him. He turned his attention away from the skies to the world underground. He observed the sliding movement of snakes and the curious means by which the common earthworm squeezes itself along the ground. He made a model with a series of radial wires that replicated the worm's method of self-propulsion. He recorded the curves that were made as the machine moved forward; the records proved to him how propulsion was achieved. He was convinced that his 'trichoidal' motion device would be able to propel a heavier-than-air flying machine. When he presented a paper showing a series of clockwork 'snake' models demonstrating mechanical simulation of snake movement, members of the Royal Society thought he had lost his marbles.

A year later, in 1885, Hargrave achieved flight with a small model paper-and-wood monoplane he powered with a stretched rubber band. The 'flying worm' gained the speed of fourteen miles per hour, its oar-like wings flapping in the breeze.

He next experimented with screw-type propellers driven by rubber bands, then with compressed air and next with steam. Although he got greater forward propulsion with each higher-powered device, he saw no greater vertical lift. Reasoning that if more and more power couldn't achieve lift, maybe moveable wings were not the answer, Hargrave next experimented with fixed wings set at different angles and discovered that wings set at a dihedral angle (sloping upwards) gave a greater stability in flight.

In November 1889 Hargrave invented a rotary engine. His tiny engine only weighed

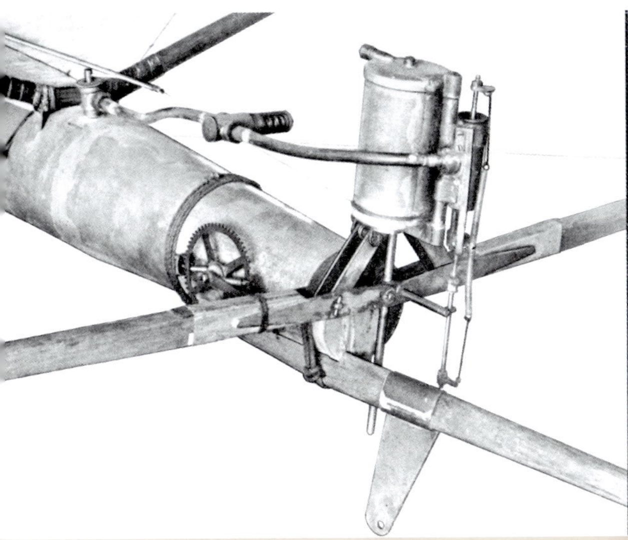

seven-and-a-half ounces and turned at 456 revolutions per minute. The motor was driven by compressed air and was powered by three rotating cylinders. As he had not yet fully developed a suitable craft to be powered by his engine, he continued to construct his monoplane models.

This invention alone should have made Hargrave both wealthy and famous, but in 1889, the golden age of steam, locomotives and great steel ships, no one seemed at all interested in the tiny copper-and-brass 'toy' motor.

He continued to experiment with wing shape and when he fitted curved wings to his models he was thrilled to see them lift off the ground. One model, fitted with his new motor, took off into the air and turned a few loops before it crashed back into the ground. At least Hargrave had proven his ability to achieve aerial movement both up and down.

Hargrave applied these observations to some structures of his own that he had been experimenting with. In 1893 he invented a revolutionary form of aerial device he named the box kite. Unlike traditional kites, which replicated the sails of a ship, capturing the breeze behind a flat mass and gaining lift from an anchored point, the box kite allowed for movement of air across its surface to gain its propulsion.

On 15 November 1894 Hargrave at last experienced the unique sensation of being airborne. He took a contraption made of four box kites strapped together; a type of cradle was hanging below the two top canvas boxes and above the lower pair. Hargrave sat upon the cradle and launched himself off the cliff face at Stanwell Park into the air. The wind was blowing at 19 mph, and as it gusted to 21 mph Hargreaves was lifted sixteen feet into the air above the cliff. He had proven that curved wing surfaces provided more lift than flat ones and offered greater stability once in the air.

On another occasion he was carried out over the ocean and was only saved by the mast of a wrecked boat that was left in the bay. He grabbed the mast and clung there until he was rescued.

By 1895 Hargrave had demonstrated the power of his invention when he lifted from the ground a payload of 241 pounds with a wind velocity of 21 mph.

He wrote to the Royal Society:

> The particular steps gained are the demonstration that an extremely simple apparatus can be made, carried about, and flown by one man, and that a safe means of making an ascent with a flying machine, or trying the same without any risk of accident, and

The quest for the air

Across the globe there were many other minds set upon a quest for achieving manned flight in heavier-than-air vehicles. The Montgolfier brothers had pioneered aerial flights in inflated balloons as far back as 1783.

Even Leonardo da Vinci had sketched plans for flying machines based upon screws and centrifuges, and bird-like machines whose movement relied upon flapping wings for propulsion. None had ever understood the form of the wing structure that allowed for aerial lift and control of movement through the air; all had believed that to fly like a bird one must first look like one.

Although he had constructed flapping machines as well, Hargrave followed a different path. He observed the unique structure of birds' feathers and the structure of wings; he watched birds in the air and observed the manner in which their wings moved and captured the currents, seemingly without any effort.

His experiments with curved surfaces set a new direction for all attempting to get up into the air.

BELOW:

Lawrence Hargrave astride his man-carrying box kite at Stanwell Park, 15 November 1894

(National Archives of Australia Collection)

RIGHT:

The Wright brothers' first flight at Kittyhawk, North Carolina, 17 December 1903

Orville and Wilbur Wright's engine-powered biplane was based directly on Hargrave's designs for box kites.

Wilbur had written to Hargrave in 1900 asking for permission to use his designs, if patents had not been taken out on them.

Wary of potential difficulties with the American patent office, the Wright brothers never publicly acknowledged their debt to Hargrave after their historic first flight that lasted just twelve seconds.

(National Library of Congress, Washington)

descending, is now at the service of any experimenter who wishes to use it.[1]

Hargrave had no intention of keeping his discoveries to himself, and didn't patent any of his designs. He believed that what he had discovered belonged to the world, and hoped that a fresh and fertile mind somewhere else across the globe would make the breakthrough that had been eluding him for years.

That breakthrough came in 1903 when the Wright brothers took the first powered, manned flight across the sands at Kittyhawk, North Carolina. Wilbur Wright had written to Hargrave in 1900 requesting permission to use the results of his experiments, if he had not already patented them. Hargrave replied that there were no patents and that the Americans could take what he had learned and apply his findings to their own ideas as they wished. When the Wright biplane ascended into the air on 17 December 1903 its design was essentially based on Hargrave's experiments with box kites.

In 1906 another plane that made history was also based on Hargrave's box kite design. Piloted by Santos Dumont, the short flight was the first public aeroplane flight in the world, winning its pilot 1500 francs for being the first to fly 100 metres. Again, in 1909, a 'French Gnome' engine, a three-cylinder rotary engine similar to Hargrave's engine of 1889, powered Bleriot's monoplane, the first to fly across the English Channel. Hargrave had originally conceived this engine, describing it in his own words as:

> A three-cylinder screw engine could be made by turning the boss of the propeller into an engine, thus allowing the cylinders to revolve on the camshaft, the shank and crankpin being stationary, and the thrust coming on the valve face.[2]

Even in the United States the weather bureau adapted Hargrave's kite designs for meteorological observations; the devices known as the Marvin-Hargrave apparatus were also adapted later for military use. Baden-Powell had also used his box kites in the Boer War for the same purpose. Hargrave was never pleased by the adoption of his inventions for military use. He believed that mastery of the air would '... not make war more terrible, but absolutely impossible', and that the flying machine would be instrumental in 'bringing peace and goodwill to all ... it will throw light on the few unexplored corners of the earth and herald the downfall of all restrictions to the free intercourse of nations'.[3]

Hargrave was bitterly disappointed that no one in Australia had taken up his legacy and

Recognition

The American inventor Octave Chanute, with whom Hargrave had often corresponded, was in no doubt as to who was the true father of aeronautical flight. In his book, *Progress in Flying Machines,* published in 1894, Chanute wrote:

> If there be one man, more than any other, who deserves to succeed in flying through the air, that man is Lawrence Hargrave, of Sydney, New South Wales. He has [now] constructed with his own hands no less than eighteen flying machines of increasing size, all of which fly.

Hargrave wrote in a private letter to Chanute:

> The people of Sydney who can speak of my work without a smile are very scarce; it is doubtless the same for the American workers, I know that success is dead sure to come, and therefore do not waste time and words trying to convince unbelievers.

Success did come to many of those who had shared the generosity of Hargrave's work.

that all the glory was being taken by the Americans and the French. He had presented his last paper to the Royal Society in the year that Bleriot had proven the possibilities that had arisen from his three decades of selfless research and was saddened that there had been so little interest among Australian inventors to take up the exciting challenge into the skies.

When fellow inventor George A. Taylor suggested that Hargrave should offer his papers and models to the state of New South Wales, he willingly agreed. His only request was that the collection should remain available to inventors and engineers for future research. But the short-sighted government showed no interest in accepting his extensive research collection for posterity.

George Taylor next sought a home for the collection in Melbourne; by the time the Premier finally agreed, it was too late. Believing that the Victorians were not interested either, Hargrave had given his life's work to the new Deutsches Museum of Technology in Munich which had opened in 1903. The Germans travelled all the way to Australia to meet Hargrave and pay their respects to the great inventor.

It is a sad twist of fate that Hargave's only son, Geoffrey, was killed at Gallipoli in May 1915. The Germans had studied the machines that Hargrave had sent to the Deutsches Museum and the fighter planes that had great success for them against the Allies in World War I were based on their studies of Hargrave's models. A quarter of a century earlier Hargrave had protested 'against the repeated connection of the flying machine with dynamic missiles' and, unknowingly, he had delivered into the hands of his country's enemy the precise means to make his fears become a reality.

His wish that his work not be adapted for hostile purposes was not granted; many of the planes that fought over the Flanders battlefields were powered almost exclusively by the rotating radial engine developed from his ideas. Two months after his son was killed, he too died, apparently of a broken heart.

Repeated Allied bombing of Germany during World War II destroyed much of the Deutsches Museum, and 176 working models of Hargrave's designs were destroyed with it. Twenty-five models were saved, restored and returned to Australia in the 1960s.

Today the models are housed in the Powerhouse Museum in Sydney's Darling Harbour, very close to where Lawrence Hargrave sat, in the office of the Australian Steamship Navigation Company, more than a century ago.

RIGHT:

1910-type Bleriot monoplane takes off from the Melbourne Cricket Ground

A plane similar to this was the first to cross the English Channel in 1909. The Bleriot was used in World War I for reconnaissance, and later for balloon attacks and strafing the enemy on the ground.

The three-cylinder rotary engine that powered the Bleriot aeroplanes was a French 'Gnome' based upon Hargrave's earlier design of 1889.

(National Library of Australia Collection)

MELBA AS "AÏDA"

MELBA AS "ELAINE"

Dame Nellie Melba

1861–1931

Dame Nellie Melba is featured on the face of the $100 polymer note, first issued in 1996.

'The most glorious voice God ever put into the throat of a woman' — Sir Landon Ronald, 1931

Opposite:
Top Row, Left:
Melba as Violetta in La Traviata
Top Row, Centre:
Manon
Top Row, Right:
As Nedda in Pagliacci, *with Tonio*
Centre Row, Left:
As Marguerite in Gounod's Faust
Centre Row, Centre & Right:
As Ophelia, as Aïda
Bottom Row, Left to Right:
As Helene, Elaine and Marguerite

Nellie Melba was an operatic tour de force, with complete command over the most popular of all soprano roles, which she made her own, and jealously guarded her dominance over the operatic stage for over forty years.

(All photographs courtesy of Melba Museum Lillydale, State Library of Victoria, National Library of Australia)

When Scottish stonemason David Mitchell left his home of Forfar, near Dundee in the highlands of his native Scotland in April 1852, bound for the Victorian goldfields in Australia, he would have had no inkling of the legacy he and his family were to leave for the Australian nation. A theft of his money pouch on the journey out left Mitchell almost penniless on his arrival in the colony; but when he died just over half a century later he left an estate worth more than £1,500,000, and a musical legacy that has never been surpassed.

Mitchell headed for the diggings at Ballarat, but he did not take to the life of the itinerant miner. He was soon back at his trade, and left the diggings after a short time, not with nuggets, but pound notes earned by contracting on building constructions. After settling back into Melbourne he began work as a mason and building contractor; carefully saving his money, he soon had enough to purchase some land at Richmond, where he built the mansion 'Doonside'. He lived at Doonside for the rest of his life.

Although Mitchell demanded every bit of value from every shilling he spent, he was a fair and honest man who asked no more of his employees than he was prepared to give of himself. It was these

A poor start for David Mitchell

On the journey out to the diggings, aboard the sailing vessel *Anna*, some of the sailors attempted a mutiny, and, in reply to the captain's call for assistance from the passengers, Mitchell rushed to his aid. With his help, and that of several other passengers, the mutiny was crushed.

When Mitchell returned to his cabin he was dismayed to discover that his money pouch had been stolen from where he had secreted it beneath his pillow. Although David Mitchell had set out from Scotland in 1852 cashed up for his arrival in Australia, when he stepped ashore in Melbourne he had only one gold sovereign left in his pockets. Thirty years later David Mitchell was one of the most influential men in the colony; his daughter Nellie endowed the world with her golden voice.

Left:
David Mitchell, father of Nellie Melba
(National Archives of Australia Collection)

qualities of character that he endowed on his third child, daughter Nellie, who was born at Doonside on 19 May 1861. In 1857 David Mitchell had married Isabella Dow, the daughter of a fellow Forfar man, foundry engineer James Dow, whom he had visited in Melbourne shortly after his arrival in the colony. It was on this first visit that nineteen-year-old Isabella had caught the eye of the young Scot.

The first two of the couple's babies died, both aged eleven months. Fearful that the same fate might befall baby Nellie, the couple watched over her very carefully for the first year. But Nellie was made of stern stuff, a fact she was to prove over and over again throughout her long life. Nellie was followed by seven more siblings, one every year or two: Annie and Belle; then Frank and Charlie; another girl, Dora; then Ernest; and, last of all, Vere.

Nellie proved to be the most determined of the Mitchell offspring. She was strong-minded, wilful, independent, even tomboyish; right from the start, she took it upon herself to monitor the lives of her siblings. Her proprietorship over the family continued unchallenged for the rest of her days: none of her brothers and sisters, or indeed their children, seemed to resent the manner in which Nellie sought to include herself in all of their affairs.

The Mitchell household was in many ways a privileged one, though it was never a household given to flights of excess or wastefulness; the spectre of the conservative, often dour, Scots Presbyterian work ethic, and a distaste for frippery or wanton display, were ever-present.

It is hard to reconcile the grandiose theatrical demeanour that was the signature of Nellie Melba's professional life with the modest ways in which the parsimonious Scot guided her early days. However, Mitchell was able to provide all the best opportunities in life for his family.

Isabella Dow had come from a background of privilege, by colonial standards. She was well-educated, and possessed considerable musical talent and instrumental skills.

Her sister Lizzie, Nellie's aunt, 'possessed a fine soprano of extraordinary beauty', and Isabella was an accomplished pianist, organist and harpist, who sang quite competently herself. It may be surmised that Nellie got her talent from the Dow side of the family, but David Mitchell was known to have possessed a fine bass voice and he was a self-taught violinist. As all of the Mitchell children had fine voices, it appears that the marriage between David Mitchell and Isabella Dow had given rise to an extraordinary musical legacy.

LEFT:
Doonside, Melba's birthplace in the Melbourne suburb of Richmond

(National Archives of Australia Collection)

Ernest is said to have developed a timbre and trill that equalled his older sister Nellie's, and Nellie remarked that Ernest had 'the sweetest, most divine tenor voice that ever came from mortal lips'.[1] Little Vere was also showing to have a prodigious young talent before she died, at only four and a half years of age.

Yet it was Nellie alone who had been blessed by the muse. She jumped at every opportunity to perform for family or friends. As a young girl she was constantly humming. She learnt the piano and would accompany herself in performance of her early repertoire which included 'Comin' thro' the Rye' and 'Shells of Ocean'. 'Comin' thro' the Rye' remained with her for the rest of her performing life and was her father's favourite.

Nellie, Belle and Ernest were all accomplished in the 'common' art of whistling, much to the dismay of their mother, who considered it to be 'vulgar and unladylike, a pastime for butcher boys'.[2]

Nellie Mitchell adopted many other 'bad' habits when she was a wild young girl: swimming naked in the Yarra River, chewing gum and swearing. She continued to whistle, swear and chew gum for the rest of her days.

Nellie Mitchell was self-willed, obstinate, demanding, irreverent and strong-minded. But it was these traits that cemented the foundations of her greatness. It was also these same qualities that frustrated many who tried in vain to compete with her, destroyed many who railed against her, and often distressed those who loved and supported her.

While still a student at Presbyterian Ladies College in Melbourne, she took singing lessons with the Italian tenor Petro Cecchi, and from this time on Nellie set her heart on becoming a great singer, determined to conquer the world.

However, Nellie's plans were upset when her mother died in October 1881; shortly after, little Vere followed Isabella into an early grave. These events cast a pall of gloom over

LEFT:
Nellie Mitchell as a little girl
(Melba Museum of Lillydale Collection)

the usually effervescent Mitchell household. David Mitchell decided to leave Melbourne for a while to seek restoration in warmer climes. He arranged to undertake the building of a sugar mill in Marian, twelve miles inland from the port of Mackay in North Queensland. And so it was that early in 1882 David Mitchell, accompanied by his two girls Nellie and Annie, embarked on the journey that was to change their fortunes forever.

The colonial outpost of Mackay was eager to welcome the handsome young girls from the south, and Nellie and Annie soon found themselves at the centre of 'polite' Mackay society — as it was at the time. Nellie began to appear in public concerts, but usually performed the role of piano accompanist to one of the local girls who had already made a name for herself on the local stage. It was considered almost impossible for the newcomer to topple any local lass from her position as the 'prima donna' of Mackay.

But Melba was determined to win the applause of the Mackay audiences. She wrote to Cecchi and requested that he send 'some pretty English songs', as the Queenslanders

Mud and muck!

David Mitchell established quarrying operations at Lilydale in the Dandenong Ranges some 25 kilometres north-east of Melbourne.

From these quarries Mitchell was able to supply his own contractors with lime for mortar, and soon began to supply others as well.

He built a very profitable enterprise out of his Lilydale quarries, and in later years Melba was often heard to say that her father had made his fortune out of 'mud and muck'.

She built her own home, Coombe Cottage, in the Coldstream Hills just further out on the Lilydale road, and was able to survey the source of her own financial independence as she motored out along towards Coldstream, passing David Mitchell's quarries as she descended the winding hill passing through the leafy township of Lilydale.

ABOVE:
'Castle Hill' Lilydale Quarries
Oil on canvas by Arthur Streeton
(Melba Museum of Lillydale Collection)

didn't understand the Italian songs she had been trained to sing. She was preparing to take her place on the boards; she was determined to prevail — and she did. She wrote to Cecchi again after the concerts:

> I had great success at the two concerts I sang at, so much so that all the ladies up here are jealous of me. I was encored twice for each song, and they hurrahed and threw me no end of bouquets. [3]

Nellie ended her letter by informing Cecchi that she would be back in Melbourne by the following January, ready to conquer that city — but it was not to be. Her conquest of Melbourne was many years away, and much was to happen to delay the career of 'Melba' before her time was come.

She was swept off her feet, fell head-over-heels in love and married English-born sugar plantation manager Charles Armstrong in Brisbane on 22 December 1882. This marriage was to prove to be the most difficult and distracting contract Nellie ever committed to. Charles and Nellie honeymooned at Doonside in Melbourne for three months, then returned to Marian, where Charles took over as manager of a sugar mill and plantation.

The manager's house was not ready for the newlyweds and they spent their first few months together in a leaky canvas-roofed hut. Nellie complained of the heat and the humidity of the far north: she complained that everything inside the hut was damp — her clothes, her music, even her piano, suffered from the effects of the tropical climate. When she discovered that she was six months pregnant Nellie decided to return to Melbourne for the birth of George, the couple's first and only child. She never returned to Queensland to live with her husband.

Once in Melbourne and again under Petro Cecchi's guidance, she began to perform on the Melbourne stage. She made her professional debut in a concert at the Melbourne town hall on 17 May 1884, where she was simply billed as 'Mrs Armstrong'. The *Australasian* wrote of her debut performance:

> [The concert] will never be forgotten on account of the delightful surprise afforded by Mrs. Armstrong's singing, and everybody who heard her will desire to hear her again and everybody who did not hear her is at this moment consumed with regrets at having not been present.[4]

LEFT:

Nellie Armstrong (née Mitchell) on her wedding day, 22 December 1882

Nellie married Charles Frederick Nesbitt Armstrong at St Anne's Presbyterian Church in Brisbane.

Where Nellie was ambitious and favoured the life of the aesthete, Charles was a man's man. The son of an English baronet, he was a man of independent means who loved the rough life of the Australian bush and the challenges offered by life in the colonies.

Their match was doomed from the start; it was never to be a happy one.

(Melba Museum of Lillydale Collection)

Following the success of this performance she was engaged to sing, and paid to sing, on many more occasions; she was at last able to call herself a professional. Once she had conquered the Australian concert stage she set her sights on London, and the world. Fortuitously, just as she wrote to a friend that 'she would give up ten years of [her] life to be able to get to Europe to have a trial', her father was appointed commissioner to the Indian and Colonial Exhibition in London. He decided to take Nellie, her husband Charles, two-year-old George, and sisters Annie and Belle to England with him.

Off to the world of opera

The family group set sail aboard the *Bengal* on 11 March 1886. Before they had even passed through the heads of Port Phillip Bay Nellie had organised a choir of the passengers, under the approving eye of Bishop James Moorhouse, the unorthodox Bishop of Melbourne, who was returning to England to take up the bishopric of Manchester.

They arrived in London in May 1886 and immediately settled into a comfortable home in Sloane Square. Nellie had not come to London as a poor, struggling artist desperate to eke out a living as she sought to break onto the concert stage. She was supported by a wealthy and influential father, she had the company of her husband and little George, the support of her sisters and introductions to some of the most influential names in the English theatre.

She was at last exposed to the greatest theatre in the world. It seemed that all the great singers were in London for the opera season; the billboards announced their names in bold black type on hoardings across the city.

Nellie dreamed that one day she too would see her name printed on posters all around London. She joined the audience when the great Swedish soprano Christina Nilsson sang 'I Dream I Dwelt'; Nellie thought to herself, 'I think I can do better than that'. She listened as the Canadian prima donna Emma Albani sang; she again mused 'I think I can do as well as that'. When she was finally able to hear the voice of the great Adelina Patti, who was at that time at the height of her powers, she thought to herself, in a rare moment of humility, 'I shall try to do as well as that'.[5]

LEFT:

Nellie Armstrong with her son George Photographed in Paris c. 1889

Mrs Nellie Armstrong had certainly taken a great chance on her future when as a married woman, and a mother, she made her first attempt to conquer the European stage.

Regardless of a performer's talent, opera-goers sought a diva who would excite them, tantalise and seduce them into a world of fantasy and desire, who would play at life just like the characters she portrayed on the stage.

It is proof of her determination that the mannish and encumbered colonial mother made her mark among greats such as Adelina Patti and Christina Nilsson, and the other great beauties of the world of nineteenth-century European opera.

(State Library of Victoria Collection)

Nellie set out with her letters of introduction; they did not get her very far, as there were hundreds of colonial and American singers desperate for a trial on the greatest concert stage of the world. She auditioned for the famous composer of popular comic opera, Arthur Sullivan, who after hearing her sing 'Ah! fors'è lui' from *La Traviata*, simply remarked, in a tone that expressed his apparent boredom with the tedium of auditioning a seemingly endless parade of colonial hopefuls: 'Yes, Mrs Armstrong. That is all right. If you study for another year you can come back—I might give you a small part in *The Mikado*'.[6]

Crestfallen at Sullivan's rebuttal, she presented herself to conductor Wilhelm Ganz, who was enchanted by her voice. He arranged for her debut in a charity concert held in the Princes Hall in Piccadilly. On a cold and foggy day in June 1886 Nellie Armstrong sang before a sad little audience who rewarded her with a few half-hearted handclaps then went home.

Nellie was heartbroken. It seemed that she was not going to make her way onto the world stage after all. She begged her father to allow her one more attempt. She had a letter of recommendation to singing teacher Madame Mathilde Marchesi in Paris; she told her father that 'If Marchesi does not like me, I promise you faithfully that I shall return to Australia and try to be happy'.[7] The relationship between Charles and Nellie had deteriorated to the point where they no longer wanted to be together; as she determined to follow her muse, he decided to stay in England, where he went back to the land.

With enough money in the bank to last twelve months in Paris, Nellie and George settled into a modest *pension*. While she had been used to the finer things in life, her strong Scottish Presbyterian background had taught her to be frugal when times demanded it.

Only two months after she had arrived in Europe, Nellie Armstrong knocked on the door of the Marchesi residence on Rue Jouffroy in Paris. She offered her letter of introduction from Madame Wiedermann-Pinschof, the wife of the Austro-Hungarian consul in Melbourne, who was a friend of the Mitchells and a former pupil of Madame Marchesi.

Nellie was ushered in to sit among several other nervous girls who were also waiting to audition. When it was her turn to perform she was invited into a heavily decorated and forbidding classroom, which was dominated by a magnificent glass chandelier. Nellie mounted the small dais at one end of the room and began to sing to Madame Marchesi's accompaniment. She had again chosen 'Ah! fors'è lui', the song that had left Sullivan so

Cartoon published in London Punch *magazine, 1890*

(La Trobe University, Bendigo Library Collection)

Not in her usual good voice!

The critics were often dismissive of Melba's earlier performances; to them she was just another colonial hopeful trying to make a name for herself on the European circuit.

Once, when a gala performance at Covent Garden was cancelled, the critic of a London magazine published a review of her performance that was obviously printed before the concert was to be held. Melba was dismissed as not being in 'her usual good voice'.

Melba sued the magazine and was awarded £100 damages. She soon packed her bags and headed back to Belgium once again, where even the critics loved her.

unimpressed, and as she could not gain any impression at all from the countenance of the rather severe Marchesi she began to fear that Marchesi was of the same mind.

At one point Madame Marchesi stopped suddenly and swung around on her piano stool to face Nellie demanding 'Why do you screech your top notes? Can't you sing them piano?' Nellie was terrified by this time but knew it was her last chance to grasp her dream. She sang on as softly as she could; she hit a top 'B', and Marchesi demanded,'Higher'. Singing as gently as possible, Nellie hit 'C'. 'Higher' demanded Marchesi again. Nellie reached top 'E' almost exhausted by this most demanding performance.

Once again Madame Marchesi stopped playing and rushed from the room. Minutes later she returned and asked Nellie to repeat her performance. When Nellie had finished, Marchesi asked her if she was serious about a singing career. She replied, 'Yes'. Madame Marchesi then told her that,'If you are serious, and if you study with me for one year, I will make something extraordinary of you'.

It was only some years later that Madame Marchesi told Nellie why she had darted from the piano in such a strange manner. She had rushed upstairs to find her husband, snatched the newspaper he was reading from his grasp and yelled into his ear,'Salvatore, j'ai enfin une étoile!'('Salvatore, I finally have a star!').[8]

Madame Marchesi saw immediately that Nellie did not need to waste her year with the repetitive vocal exercises usually demanded of beginners, so her new 'star' pupil began learning the operatic repertoire straight away.

It was usual for promising students to perform in charity concerts and at unpaid society recitals, and for this Mrs Armstrong needed a name fitting for the operatic stage. She chose to call herself Melba, in honour of the city of her birth; she also thought it sounded quite Italian, and therefore most suitable for an aspiring opera star.

On 13 October 1887 Melba made her debut as Gilda, in Verdi's *Rigoletto*, in the Théatre de la Monnaie in Brussels.

Even for her debut Melba was not prepared to be pushed around; as nervous as she was, about to perform professionally in Europe for the first time, she still wanted her own way. She refused to wear the blonde wig typically worn by 'Gilda' and walked on stage with her dark hair flowing over her shoulders.

Although it was usual for performances in Belgium to be sung in French, Melba performed in Italian, so that her Australian accent would not detract from her performance. Her European debut was a triumph. She recalled

Caruso — the hot sausage!

Melba sang Mimi to scores of Rodolfos. Her favourite was Enrico Caruso, who she felt was the only tenor of his day who could match her vocal splendour. She once said: 'In the third act of *Bohème* I always feel as if our two voices had merged into one'.

Caruso was a prankster; once while Melba was singing '*Che gelida manina*' ('Your tiny hand is frozen'), he pressed a hot sausage into her hand. She yelped and flung the offending object across the stage. Caruso continued with the romantic aria and then whispered to her:'English lady, you like sausage?' Her reply is not recorded.

On one other occasion Caruso substituted the gum Melba always chewed before, during and after her performances. She had developed the unladylike habit of chewing gum early in her life; she persisted with this 'bad' habit, claiming that it was excellent exercise for her jaw.

Caruso roared laughing in the wings when Melba picked up the piece of gum she had left on a shelf only to discover that her 'Rodolfo' had put a plug of chewing tobacco in its place.The reigning queen of opera was not amused as she spat the foul mess onto the floor in disgust.

the moment when she sang her first note at the beginning of the second act:

> ... there was a hush that hardly seemed human, a hush in which I heard my voice floating out into the distance as though it were the voice of someone other than myself. Nor shall I forget the thunders of applause, which broke in after the end of the Second Act. I said to myself: 'This cannot be for me. They are clapping and cheering for somebody else'.[9]

She was summoned to meet the Belgian queen, who had watched the dazzling performance from her royal box. The next morning Melba awoke to discover that she was famous all over Europe.

The return of the husband

Charles Armstrong had been trying to make a go of farming in the south of England, when he decided to visit Nellie and four-year-old George in Brussels. He was concerned that her fame and commitment to the stage left little time for her to care for their son, and that, worst of all, the boy was being brought up in France, and with French manners.

One day Charles appeared at Melba's door unannounced, and found her taking tea with the well-known Belgian portrait painter Emile Wauters. Ever the traditional Victorian husband, Charles was furious to find his wife in company with another man, and a Continental male at that; he made such a scene that Melba was almost at her wits' end. Charles threatened that he would disrupt her performance that evening, and Melba had to beg the directors of the opera to find some way to rid their star of her noisome husband.

Charles was persuaded to leave Brussels and never bothered Melba again. It appears that she may have paid him an allowance in return for leaving her and George alone.

Uncrowned prima donna

In May 1888 Melba returned for a second attempt at the English stage. This time she had her Continental success to open doors for her, but England would still be a tough nut for her to crack.

She was invited to appear at Covent Garden, but the reigning prima donna was Emma Albani, who had reserved the plum role of Gilda in *Rigoletto*, the role that Melba wanted to sing. She was stuck with playing *Lucia di Lammermoor*. There was little publicity for her season, and when the opera opened after just one rehearsal the hall was almost empty. Not one of the important critics was there, and the whole show was a disaster. Melba left England disappointed again, but her spirit was

Let them say ... !

Nellie Melba was always good press; for her any news was good news, no matter how bad it was. She was rarely out of the public eye, and if she was she didn't hold back from reminding newspaper editors that she was still alive — and kicking.

While *Truth* publisher John Norton railed against her for her 'alleged' excessive drinking, and linked her name with many and varied lovers, she refused to allow him to drag her through the courts, even when there was no question that she would have won her case.

Once when she had not seen her name in the press for several weeks Melba confronted Edward Cunningham, the editor of the Melbourne *Argus*: 'Edward, I haven't seen any reference to my presence in Australia in the last week or two', to which he replied, 'Oh, there's been a good deal in the *Argus*'. Melba reprimanded him, 'Not enough. Not enough! I don't care what you say, for me or against me, but for heaven's sake say something about me.'

Rumours of scandalous liaisons followed her everywhere she went; she was unmoved by such stories. She once wrote the following words, in large letters that filled the page in a friend's autograph book: 'They say. What say they? Let them say.' This note to her friend just about summed up Melba's attitude to scandal.

not broken, her desire to succeed never diminished.

She next stepped onto the stage in Paris. This time she had spent months in preparation for her role as Ophelia in Ambroise Thomas's *Hamlet*. She took acting lessons from Sarah Bernhardt, the most famous actor of her day, and took tuition in French.

When she made her Paris debut on 8 May 1889 it was a triumph. The Parisian audience loved her, she made three curtain calls and received rave reviews in the newspapers next morning. *Le Figaro* reported that three curtain calls in Paris was the equivalent of seventy-five in Italy and then added:

> We might explain this evening, parodying two lines from Voltaire: 'Each people in its turn has reigned upon the scene; Australia's hour has come, as ours has been'.[10]

The reign of the 'prima donna' — the first lady — of Australian opera was just beginning. Melba returned to London for another attempt to win over the English audience. This time she was supported by Lady Gladys de Grey, whose husband was a member of the committee that had first proposed that grand opera should be staged at Covent Garden. Lady de Grey was a fine judge of singers and after hearing Melba in Brussels insisted that she be invited to perform in London. She had been disappointed when Melba first bid a hasty retreat to Paris after the earlier concerts but persisted in encouraging her to come back to England.

Melba sang again at Covent Garden; this time she was declared a great success. She was invited to a royal command performance but was unable to perform due to illness. However, she did sing for the Prince of Wales and later for the Shah of Persia. She was invited to sing for Queen Victoria at Windsor Castle and was kept there so long that she almost didn't make it back to London in time for her evening performance; as it was, she took to the boards with an empty stomach that night.

She became at ease with the crowned heads of Europe, but this familiarity almost brought her career to an untimely end. She received an invitation to sing for Tsar Alexander III in St Petersburg in 1891 and he gave her a splendid gold-and-platinum bracelet encrusted with natural pearls and engraved diamond cubes in appreciation of her performance. She travelled to Russia with Jean and Edouard de Reszké, her partners over many years, and throughout her performance as Juliette an elegant young aristocrat applauded vigorously from his box. As nobody was permitted to applaud before the Tsar, the young man was

RIGHT:

The Opera-Goer's Diary

Cartoon published in London Punch *magazine, 1890*

The article describes Melba and de Reszké's private command peformance at Windsor Castle, where the performers were delayed so long at the queen's pleasure that they almost missed the curtain call back on the London stage that evening.

(La Trobe University, Bendigo Library Collection)

THE OPERA-GOER'S DIARY.

NOTHING particular this week. Mlle. MELBA, the two DE RESZKÉS, and M. LASSALLE sang, by Royal command, in the afternoon at Windsor Castle. "Wasn't that a dainty dish to set before the QUEEN?" Rather. We meant to wind up the week with *Le Prophète*, but JEAN DE RESZKÉ had caught cold,—perhaps on the return journey from Windsor,—and so *Faust* was substituted, with MELBA as *Marguerite*, and RAVELLI the Reliable as *Faust*. We are looking forward to *Hamlet*. "*To be or not to be*"? Probably "to be." Highly successful Season gradually drawing to a close. Where's *Masaniello*? Not heard it for years. It would

come out as quite a novelty. Let the Sheriff-elect look to it. If not for this Season, let it mark the year of office of DRURIOLANUS OPERATICUS.

RIGHT:
Louis Philippe, the Duc d'Orléans
The duke followed Melba across Europe, the flames of their passion burning brightly, until Melba's estranged husband Charles learned of their affair.
(Melba Museum of Lillydale Collection)

asked to leave the theatre; he was Louis Philippe, the Duc d'Orléans, pretender to the French throne. He was so smitten by the greatest opera singer in the world that he had followed her to Russia.

A romantic relationship developed between Melba and the duke; their affair could not be kept a secret: they were seen together all over Europe, and were not at all discreet about where they went. After they were seen together in public, brazenly cooing like doves in a box at the Vienna opera, the newspaper presses ran hot, feeding the Austrian hunger for gossip and intrigue.

A lasting union between Melba and Louis Philippe was impossible. She was a married woman, an Australian commoner; he, a nobleman, an aristocrat with pretensions to the throne, and a Catholic to boot. When Charles Armstrong was made aware of the public affair of his estranged wife and the amorous young Frenchman he challenged him to a duel. Luckily for Louis, protocol forbade him to duel with a commoner — Charles Armstrong was a man of action and could no doubt have acquitted himself well whatever weapons were chosen.

Charles then decided to file for divorce on the grounds of adultery, citing the young duke as co-respondent. But Louis Philippe had no intention of ever being dragged into the divorce courts. Rumours were damaging enough to his cause, but the divorce court would have been simply one embarrassment too many. He went on an extended tour of Europe, surrounded by minders, ever one step ahead of the process servers, until one day a gentleman in evening dress approached him in Vienna. The well-dressed man proffered some papers and the duke, thinking them to be a petition or address of some kind, took them from him. When he saw that they were divorce papers he threw them to the ground;

The end of the affair

The marriage of Charles and Nellie Armstrong was finally destroyed in the early 1890s when Nellie enjoyed an unfortunately public affair with twenty-year-old Louis Philippe, Duc d'Orléans, pretender to the throne of France.

Charles was obviously hurt by the failure of his marriage and rarely spoke of his relationship with the most famous diva of his day. Although he was very much the typically elegant, reserved English gentleman, he was known to have got up and left the house when a host once placed a Melba recording on the gramophone.

Yet it seems that he was not so embittered that he never acknowledged the years he spent with Melba. On one occasion he spoke nostalgically of his former wife when a waitress offered him Melba Toast and Peach Melba in the dining room of the exclusive Union Club in Victoria, Canada.

In 1890 Charles was eventually granted a divorce, on the grounds of desertion. He lived out his life in a cabin on the shore of Shawnigan Lake, on Vancouver Island in Canada.

Charles had regular visits from family and friends. His son George and his wife Evie Armstrong visited often. Their daughter Pamela married Lord Vestey's only son, William, in Oak Bay, Victoria, not far from Shawnigan Lake.

DAME NELLIE MELBA
by Rupert Bunny

OPPOSITE:
Madame Melba
Oil on canvas by Rupert Bunny, c. 1902
(National Gallery of Victoria Collection)

RIGHT:
Melba's travelling make-up case
(Courtesy Melba Museum of Lillydale Collection)

but once the papers had been served, Charles Armstrong's lawyers could proceed.

The duke used all the intricacies of the legal process to grind proceedings to a halt; it looked as if this case would never have its day in court. Then all of a sudden Armstrong withdrew; the case dropped from the divorce lists. But it was already over for Nellie and her duke; Louis departed for a two-year safari in Africa. His time in the wilderness apparently dampened his passion for opera stars, as upon his return he married the Archduchess Maria Dorothea, granddaughter of the last palatine of Hungary.

Both Nellie and Charles agreed that George should be sent to England for his education, so at the age of ten George was sent to boarding school in Littlehampton, Sussex. One day his father Charles arrived unannounced at the school, packed up George's clothes and told the lad that he was going away on a long journey. He took George to live with him in Texas. It was almost a decade before George saw his mother again.

Melba was always protective of her position as the leading soprano of the world's operatic stage. She did her utmost to outdo her opposition and continued to test herself against all comers.

She did, however, make some serious mistakes in her choice of repertoire. At the very time that Covent Garden was ringing to the voice of a new star, Emma Calvé, Melba chose to perform in a rather dull opera, *Elaine*, written by one of her friends. *Elaine* was a flop, whereas Calvé's debut as Santuzza in *Cavalleria Rusticana* was an outstanding success.

Melba needed the approval of the Italian opera audiences to ensure her domination of the stage. If she was successful in Italy she might even topple the ageing queen of opera, Adelina Patti, from her throne. Melba made

Melba's Order of Knighthood

Melba enjoyed the power and position that her fame allowed. The 'queen' of the operatic stage held certain 'regal' pretensions of her own.

She issued her own 'royal' warrants to tradespeople and retailers who had served her well. One Melbourne fishmonger still proudly displayed a framed, signed Melba warrant on the wall of his shop many years after she had passed away. Melba also created her own special honours, which her friends called 'Melba's Order of Knighthood'. She had a London jeweller make a series of tie pins to her own specific design, with a decorative head that bore the capital letter 'M'.

Plain gold pins were of the lowest order, they bore a head of enamel into which a small diamond was set. The next bore ruby chips, and the highest were platinum, with the 'M' made entirely of diamonds. She gave them away sparingly and those who were awarded a Melba pin felt especially honoured. Once, a conductor of the Melbourne to Sydney train who went out of his way to make her journey a comfortable one was awarded a pin of the third order.

One young tenor who had quarrelled with Melba tossed his pin into the Atlantic. When Melba heard of this petulant act she never forgave him or spoke to him again.

her debut at La Scala in Milan, the most prestigious Opera House in the world, on 16 March 1893, singing the role of Lucia in Donizetti's *Lucia di Lammermoor.*

Before she even stood upon the Italian stage she was again the subject of malicious rumour and her life was even threatened. It took all her secretary's powers of persuasion to get her to perform. When the curtains finally drew back on the evening of 16 March Melba was horrified to see that half of the audience was standing by their seats with their backs to the stage. As they slowly turned towards her a heavy silence fell on the theatre. Melba began to sing. Once again she held her audience spellbound by the power and purity of her voice. Cries of *'Brava!'* punctuated her performance and at the conclusion of the famous 'mad scene' the crowd went wild. Melba received a ten-minute ovation from the most difficult opera audience in the world. She would keep her competitors at bay for a little while at least. Melba followed her Italian success with a tour of Sweden, where she so impressed King Oscar that he awarded her a special Order.

The last stage to conquer was the Metropolitan in New York. The American audiences did not take to the Australian diva immediately, but she gradually won them over, touring the country back and forth, visiting and revisiting America year after year.

It was at the Met that she made the biggest mistake of her career. The taste of the opera-going audience was changing: a fashionable preference for the Germanic style of Richard Wagner was superseding the lighter, more frivolous style of the French and Italian composers. Melba decided that to remain on top she should master Wagnerian roles. But although she had some success singing Wagner's earlier works, her Brünnhilde was a disaster.

She was neither at ease with the music nor comfortable singing in German; fashion then dictated that opera should be performed in the language in which it was composed. Worse still, she strained her voice with the demanding role of Brünnhilde, and had to leave the stage for several months; it was uncertain whether she would ever sing again.

It was not long after this that Melba decided it was time for her Australian public to hear their own 'diva' for the first time since she had achieved international success.

Melba 'at home'

Returning to Australia in 1902, Melba toured extensively. Wherever she went she was given the welcome of a hero's return. But there

Her mistress's voice

Although Melba resisted the temptation to record her voice on the new-fangled recording apparatus developed for the amusement of the general public by American inventor Thomas Edison in 1890, by 1904 she was convinced that she should leave her voice behind for future generations to marvel at the purity of her trills.

She made quite a lot of money from the sale of her recordings and then took to the machine like a duck to water. Melba could not resist two things: the opportunity to prove her superiority over her competitors, and the opportunity to make buckets of money.

LEFT:
Dame Nellie Melba at the recording machine, 1920
(Melba Museum Lillydale Collection)

BELOW:
Dame Nellie Melba and her dog Din on the verandah of her home, Coombe Cottage
Photograph attributed to Pamela Armstrong, Melba's grand-daughter, c. 1910–20
(State Library of Victoria Collection)

were those who were ever ready to cut her down to size, whose long memories recalled the scandals, and rumours of scandals, of her past; they saw Melba as 'good copy' for Australian readers eager for gossip.

After a particularly rough crossing of Bass Strait, Melba arrived in Tasmania for her concert tour of Launceston and Hobart, her throat bleeding from violent seasickness. She was hardly able to speak, and the concerts were cancelled.

John Norton, publisher of the ironically named *Truth* newspaper, told his readers that the real reason the concerts were cancelled was that Melba had been drunk. The *Truth* published an open letter to Melba on 28 March 1903 headed: 'Concerning our Champagne Capers, Breaches of Public Faith, Outrages Against Good Manners, and Insults to Australian Citizens'. The letter accused her of habitual drunkenness, among other dissolute behaviour. She determined to sue Norton for libel, but eventually decided against this course of action; she did not want to waste both time and money dragging her past through the courts, just to outdo the publisher of a Victorian scandal sheet. Nor did she want to give Norton any opportunity to air any 'dirty linen', whether fictitious or factual. Nellie had already suffered too much pain before the divorce courts.

No matter how hard the scandalmongers tried, Melba's tour of Australia was an unequivocal success; the whole country loved the internationally acclaimed diva. She also performed in country towns, including the Victorian goldfields town of Bendigo, where the chimes of the impressive Italianate post office clock were silenced after midnight to allow Melba to get a good night's sleep.

Melba was in Australia at the outbreak of World War I and threw all her efforts into raising funds to help the troops defend her beloved Belgium and France. She was astonished that Germany could be at war with her own country. Germany had given her so much music and many of her friends, musicians,

Sing 'em muck

English opera singer Dame Clara Butt recalled in her autobiography, published not long after Melba's own *Melodies and Memories* first hit the bookstands in 1925, that she had asked Melba what she should sing if ever she toured Australia. The great diva replied: 'Sing 'em muck—it's all they can understand'.

Melba was horrified at seeing these words in print. She denied ever having uttered the damning phrase and demanded an apology. Although alleged witnesses had heard Melba dismiss her countrymen in such a cavalier fashion, Dame Clara apologised, blaming the unfortunate indiscretion on her proofreader.

RIGHT:
David Mitchell Esq.
Oil on canvas by Hugh Ramsay, 1903
(Castlemaine Art Gallery & Historical Museum Collection)

singers, composers, and conductors were of German birth.

Yet she did recall her distaste for Kaiser Wilhelm II, who had once dared to be critical of her rendition of the Jewel Song in Gounod's *Faust*. After he had made the mistake of suggesting she had sung the aria too quickly, Melba turned to the German king and replied, 'I sang the part of Marguerite according to the instructions of the composer himself, Monsieur Charles Gounod, who was pleased to express his entire satisfaction with my interpretation and to compliment me on it'.[11] She was convinced that any man who could dare to instruct the reigning 'queen' of opera was just a 'power-drunk madman to suppose he could conquer the world by force of arms'.[12]

She toured Europe during the war (wherever she was able to go), Canada and the United States, giving charity concerts, and raised £100,000 for the war effort. There is no doubt that the money she raised was well used, but Melba insisted on knitting socks for 'her soldiers' as well. One of her friends was given the unpleasant task of requesting that the great Melba give up her knitting, as she seemed to put more effort than skill into her socks: she told Melba 'that if she sang as badly as she knitted she would be arrested for causing a public nuisance'.[13]

This did not stop Melba from bullying her friends into working for the war effort. As her friends knitted she wrote messages to soldiers she would never meet, pinning her encouraging notes to socks and home-sewn flannel shirts which were sent to the men on the front line. Her notes bore such remarks as 'Show the Germans how the Australians can fight', which was typical of the way Melba felt

In support of needy artists

Melba liked to spend time with other artists, and she supported many struggling young Australian painters who were studying abroad.

She had little time for other singers, but doted on composers, pianists, writers, sculptors and painters. She made friends with Paderewski, Gounod and Saint Saens, among many others, and disported herself among the Hollywood elite. But she reserved a special place for her young Australians.

She supported the young painter Ambrose Patterson, brother of her sister Belle's husband, Tom Patterson, until he made the fatal mistake of marrying an English girl while studying in Paris, without first informing her. She may have feared that his impetuous affair and hasty marriage would lead him on the same destructive path as her own, taken many years before in the tropical heat of Mackay. She cut Patterson off without a word.

Patterson introduced Melba to painter Hugh Ramsay in Paris. Impressed by the hard-working, dedicated Scots-born Australian, she invited him to visit her in London. Ramsay suffered from tuberculosis, the nemesis of many an artist; Melba offered him £100 to help him get back to Australia and restore his health in its sunny clime. When she returned to Australia in 1902 she was dismayed that his health had barely improved and he had been unable to do much new work at all.

about herself, often fighting her lone battle for recognition on the European stage.

After the war Melba was recognised by the English Crown and made Dame Commander of the British Empire (DBE) in 1918. Nellie Mitchell, the whistling sharp-tongued tomboy from Richmond, could at last stand tall among all the titled ladies and gentlemen, her loyal and ardent supporters, who had been such an important part of her life for so long.

Melba searched for many years for a young Australian girl to whom she could pass her mantle. Although there were many bright young singers who burst onto the scene, few had that inner fire that had burned so fiercely in the heart of Dame Nellie. She gave her name to the Albert Street Conservatorium in Melbourne and endowed the school with a generous scholarship. But no singer ever replaced her.

She was pressed to retire from the stage in her sixties; although she was still performing, her voice was not quite up to the constant strain and her friends did not want to see her decline in public. While the world still loved her, it was time for her to go. But for Dame Nellie Melba, leaving the stage took almost as long as getting there in the first place.

She embarked on a comprehensive tour of farewell concerts, playing in almost every theatre that she had appeared in over the course of her forty-year career. She didn't want any of her fans to miss the opportunity of seeing one of her farewell performances.

Between the years 1926 and 1929 she played out her long farewell; the saying 'to do a Melba' entered the Australian lexicon, and came to represent any process that never seemed to end.

She retired to Coombe Cottage, the house that she had had designed for her by Melbourne architect John Grainger, father of Percy Grainger, the famed pianist and composer whom Melba had helped to establish in Europe. Coombe Cottage was built on a property at Coldstream in the Dandenong Ranges, not far from her father's Lilydale quarries. The house was an elegant building reminiscent of one she had once rented from Admiral Beresford in Kingston Hill, Surrey, twelve miles from London.

The last farewell

One of Dame Nellie Melba's last public performances was in the national capital; she sang the Australian national anthem on the steps of the new parliament in Canberra when it was opened by the Duke of York in May 1927. A crowd of more than 30,000

Just as she did for so many others who lived in her shadow, she took over. She decided to have an exhibition of his work in the house she had rented in Melbourne's most prestigious suburb, Toorak. Melba organised a three-day exhibition and almost all of Ramsay's pictures were sold. The young painter was able to get back to work without the constant fear of debt and hunger that pervaded the lives of most artists before they found fame.

Melba commissioned him to paint a picture of her father, David Mitchell, which was completed in 1903. In his seventy-fifth year, Mitchell had suffered a stroke and was almost unable to stay awake while sitting for Ramsay.

Upon completion of the painting Melba told Ramsay that she didn't like the portrait at all, and that he had made her father's hands look too rough. He replied that he considered Mitchell's hardworking, builder's hands to be well drawn, painted just 'the way they look to me, and I am not going to alter them. I'll paint gloves on them if you like'. She told him not to bother.

Melba never liked the painting and gave it to the Castlemaine Art Gallery in 1924. The broadly drawn hands are considered to be among the painting's finest points.

BELOW, LEFT:
Melba's bedroom at Coombe Cottage
Photograph by Fritz Kricheldorff, c. 1910–20
(State Library of Victoria Collection)

BELOW, RIGHT:
The gates at Coombe Cottage
Photograph by Spencer Shier, 1927
(State Library of Victoria Collection)

thronged around the gleaming white building, which had cost £7,000,000 to construct.

This was not the first time that Melba had sung for English royalty, or for a duke for that matter, but certainly the first time she had sung before such a large and enthusiastic crowd, and on such a momentous occasion.

Melba did not have long to enjoy her retirement, or to miss the theatre. She fell ill on a trip back to London and Paris in 1930. No one could understand why she would choose to travel to Europe at the beginning of winter, but it appears that she felt she had been away from the world of European opera for just too long. She came down with pneumonia as the snow began to fall in London.

Melba rallied before the summer opera season was about to begin. She believed that she could still sing better than the new young girls on stage, and she gave some charity concerts, but her time had passed. She went back to Paris. As the snows fell there she went in search of the sun; to warm her 'thinning blood' she decided to see Egypt for the first time 'as a tourist'.

When she returned to Paris two months later she again fell ill, of an infection that had entered through a rash on her shoulder. It seemed that doctors could do little to ease her discomfort; she went to Baden to see a doctor there, but he was not able to help her. She decided to return to home to Australia.

When the ship docked in Melbourne, the infection had taken over Melba's whole system, and she had to be carried from the boat. A specialist from Sydney was called, but as he was unable to treat her in Melbourne, she was transferred interstate to St Vincent's Hospital in Darlinghurst.

She was suffering from paratyphoid (blood poisoning), before the age of antibiotics, and nothing could be done for her. Aware that she was dying, Melba sang a few faint bars of Gounod's 'Ave Maria' to herself, before lapsing into unconsciousness. She died in St Vincent's on 23 February 1931.

The whole country went into mourning, and as Melba's body was brought down to Melbourne in a special funeral train provided by the Victorian government, country stations were crowded with thousands of admirers giving 'Australia's favourite daughter' one last round of applause.

Her simple headstone in the Lilydale cemetery, where she is buried next to her father, bears the words of Mimi, from Act III of Puccini's *La Bohème*: 'Addio, senza rancore' ('Farewell, without regrets').

LEFT:
Petro Cecchi
(Melba Museum of Lillydale Collection)
BELOW:
Madame Marchesi and her star pupil Mrs Nellie Armstrong, c. 1886
(National Archives of Australia Collection)

Cecchi vs Marchesi

Italian tenor Petro Cecchi travelled to Australia in 1871, touring with the Lyster Opera Company. After the tour had finished he stayed in Melbourne and earned his living as a singing teacher. Nellie Armstrong was one of his star pupils, and in her early years she was devoted to him.

In a letter written to Cecchi after the success of her Mackay concerts Nellie wrote:

> Everyone asks me who my master is, and when I say Signor Cecchi, they all say, 'When I go to Melbourne he shall be my master, too!'[14]

However, her devotion to the Italian singing teacher was short-lived. Shortly before she first departed for England, in 1886, a dispute over tuition fees ended their successful relationship abruptly.

Although Nellie was earning little on the Australian stage, Cecchi had benefited from her success and enjoyed recognition as the tutor of the rising young star. As she prepared to sail away to tread the world's stage, he must have known that he was about to lose his young 'star' forever.

Just before she left, Cecchi proffered a bill of £80 for his years of tuition. Nellie was distraught: she had little money of her own and dared not ask her father for assistance. David Mitchell had only just recovered from scandalous rumours about the nocturnal behaviour of his headstrong daughter, Mrs Charles Armstrong; Nellie had been noticed in an oyster bar with a 'strange gentleman' late one night after she had been to the theatre with friends. As a consequence, Mitchell decided not to take his 'wayward' daughter to England with him.

It was only after those responsible for the malicious rumour came clean that Mitchell apologised to Nellie and her travel plans were back on track.

Without asking her father for assistance, Nellie raised the not inconsiderable sum from friends. Although she claimed to have burst into Cecchi's office, flinging her purse before him and exclaiming 'I shall never mention your name as having been a teacher of mine. I shall never refer to you in any way whatever. So good-bye, Signor Cecchi, and may this gain bring you happiness',[15] it would appear that Nellie's recollection may be based more in operatic grand gesture than fact. She wrote a friendly letter to Cecchi from London soon after she arrived there in May 1886, and the tone of this letter does not indicate that she held any heartfelt resentment for her old tutor.

Melba never did, however, give Cecchi any credit at all for her early training; it was on the German-born Parisian singing teacher Madame Mathilde Marchesi that all honour was bestowed.

> I realise that he [Cecchi] was not a good teacher, for all that he taught me I had to unlearn when I was privileged to study under Madame Mathilde Marchesi.[16]

Dame Edith Cowan

1861–1932

Dame Edith Cowan is featured on the obverse of the $50 polymer note, first issued in 1995.

First woman of the west

Opposite & Below:
Dame Edith Cowan OBE JP, c. 1921

From her countenance in these photographs Dame Edith Cowan looks like the sort of woman not to be taken for granted. Her childhood was filled with trauma, from the day her mother died in childbirth when Edith was only seven, to the time that her father shot and killed his second wife in a drunken rage and was sentenced to be hanged.

These events were the beginning of her journey along a path from which she never wavered throughout her entire life, as she constantly sought to improve the status of women, regardless of their class or circumstance. Edith Cowan had an extraordinary life and had an extraordinary degree of success in her work.

(State Library of Western Australia Collection)

EDITH DIRCKSEY BROWN EXPERIENCED THE DISTRESS OF trauma in family life while an adolescent, and the course was set for her life to be one committed to social justice, the improvement of the status of women and the dignity of motherhood.

Born at Glengarry, near Geraldton in Western Australia on 2 August 1861, Edith was the second child of Kenneth Brown and his first wife Mary Elizabeth Dircksey Wittenoom.

The marriage must have seemed a match made in colonial heaven: he was the son of early York settlers Thomas and Eliza Brown; she was the daughter of the colonial chaplain J. B. Wittenoom. However, Mary Elizabeth died in childbirth in 1868, when Edith was only seven. After her mother's death Edith was sent away to boarding school in Perth. The school was operated by the Misses Cowan, sisters of James Cowan, the man she later married.

While Edith was away at school her father, one night enraged with drink, murdered his second wife. He was charged, convicted and hanged for his crime in 1876. Following this terrible and public event Edith withdrew into herself; from this time on she was seen as a solitary figure. It seems that the childhood experience of these dramatic events were the reference points from which she began to commit her life to social reform.

Edith married James Cowan on 12 November 1879, when she was not much more than a girl. At that time James was registrar and master of the Supreme Court of Western Australia, and his subsequent appointment to the position of Police Magistrate of Perth in 1890 gave Edith financial security and a deeper insight into the plight of so many unfortunate women battling against society's ills, as her murdered stepmother had done.

Edith Cowan was a passionate advocate of free education and sat for several years on the North Fremantle Education Board, which was one of the few public offices open to women at the time. She advocated state schooling, free education and even the inclusion of sex education on the curriculum. She was well aware of the need to arm women with enough knowledge, and the desire to learn, to lift them from the gutter, as well as offering them an equal place in society alongside men, rather than being dominated by them.

BELOW:
Dame Edith Cowan is seated second from the end in the third row from the left at this civic reception for aviator Amy Johnson held at His Majesty's Theatre, Perth, in 1930.

(State Library of Western Australia Collection)

Cowan was all too aware of the evils of strong drink and the crimes against the family that resulted. When she began to work for the betterment of her sex it was common for the police to simply turn a blind eye when women were at the wrong end of a drunken husband's fist. They were not going to interfere in a 'domestic' dispute; that was a man's domain, and a woman's place was in the home, no matter how battered, bruised and beaten she might be.

Cowan soon gained a position of influence in the community; her husband was a man of position and she was financially comfortable.

Edith gave birth to four girls and a boy between 1880 and 1891, and soon after her family was complete she became involved in community organisations. In 1891 Edith Cowan began to work for the Ministering Children's League, and from 1894 she also worked with the House of Mercy for Unmarried Mothers, later known as the Alexandra Home for Women.

Three years later, Edith Cowan was appointed Secretary of the Karrakatta Women's Club, a Perth-based club that encouraged the town's leading women to master public speaking and share their knowledge on health matters, literature and women's issues. Detractors thought it was simply a social club for middle-class matrons, but nothing could have been further from the truth.

It was at the Karrakatta Women's Club that Perth's leading women were prepared to argue for reform on a wide range of issues important in developing the status of women. None of this happened in isolation; even though Perth was at the farthest west of the country, with thousands of miles of sea in one direction and sand in the other, isolated from the rest of the world, ideas still travelled.

The concerns of the Western Australian women were the same as those taken up around the globe by suffragette Emmeline Pankhurst in England, feminist Catherine Helen Spence in South Australia, and socialist Vida Goldstein in Victoria. Towards the end of the nineteenth century, wherever discrimination flourished there seemed to be a women's movement challenging the status quo.

At this time it was difficult for any woman to gain a position of influence; the corridors of real political power were definitely out of bounds to them. The only platform for affirmative action where a woman could make her mark was with one of the many charities that always seemed to need help.

In 1906 Edith Cowan became a foundation member of the Children's Protection Society, responsible for the establishment of the

LEFT:
Dame Edith and Mr James Cowan, c. 1921
(State Library of Western Australia Collection)

Children's Court (1907), and she was a foundation member of the Women's Service Guild (1909). In 1915 Edith was the first woman to be appointed to the bench of the children's court. The Women's Service Guild worked to represent the concerns of women to government; it arranged public meetings and did fundraising, leading to the opening of the King Edward Memorial Hospital for Women in 1916.

Edith was a tireless worker for the rights of women. She advocated equal citizenship for both sexes and fought to establish children's day centres for working mothers. Although she was secure in her middle-class home and had a supportive family behind her, she never shied away from the harsh realities of the lives led by ordinary women without her opportunities or advantages.

At times some considered her to be quite an 'indecent' woman, as she was prepared to speak with any woman regardless of status or circumstance — even chatting with street prostitutes to make herself familiar with their concerns and to find ways that she could help make their lives a little better.

Her ability to meet with all comers and to get involved at every level that concerned women may have been the cause of the division in the women's movement which saw the National Council of Women, which supported Cowan, split irrevocably from the more radical Women's Service Guild, of which she had once been vice-president. The dispute centred on Cowan's determination to retain an amendment to the Health Act of 1915, which required mandatory notification of venereal disease. It is hard to see why one half of the Western Australian women's movement would have baulked at the inclusion of this

LEFT:
Parliament House, Perth, Western Australia
Photograph by Frank Hurley, date unknown

Edith Cowan stormed this hallowed bastion of male privilege when she defeated Nationalist MLA and attorney-general J. P. Draper by forty-seven votes in the 1921 state general election.

Few of the members had any real idea of the changes that would be made when women were given a voice. Although she only survived one term in the seat of West Perth, Cowan left behind a legacy of reform that changed the lives of the 'women of the west' forever.

(National Library of Australia Collection)

amendment, but for some it may have seemed that discussion of sexual matters meant that they were descending into the gutter rather than elevating the status of women.

Edith Cowan became president of the National Council of Women and sat in the chair for eight years from 1913 to 1921; she remained vice-president until her death in 1932. The council formed an umbrella organisation that sought to represent the interests of all women, their children and the family.

During the years of World War I, Cowan worked with the Red Cross, and, although she was already heavily involved in social welfare, she threw herself into 'war work' as well. She collected food, clothing and various goods that could be a comfort to the men at the front. For her tireless efforts during these difficult years she was awarded the Order of the British Empire (OBE) in 1920.

The doors finally open

After the war the women of Western Australia redoubled their efforts in demanding change to the status of women. In 1920 legislation was finally passed to remove any legal impediment to a woman standing for parliament. The following year five women, including Cowan, contested seats in the Western Australian elections for the first time.

No one was probably more surprised than sixty-year-old Edith Cowan when she won the seat of West Perth with a slim majority of forty-seven votes after preferences were allocated. West Perth was a comparatively wealthy electorate, with a majority of women and few Labor voters. She had stood as an endorsed Nationalist (a non-party organisation) and deposed sitting Nationalist attorney-general J. P. Draper in Premier James Mitchell's cabinet. Having defeated Draper, she became the first woman member of any Australian parliament and only the second in any parliament in the British Empire.

Order in the house

Crowds of curious onlookers packed into the public gallery to hear the formal induction of the first woman in parliament. Newspaper editors joked that Cowan was about to put an end to male domination of the house. Cartoons appeared showing her in parliament with a feather duster or broom, chiding male members with the words, 'There now, don't let me have to speak to you again, I'll not have your litter on my clean floors!' Most were literally afraid that she had come to clean up parliament with 'a clean sweep'.

Her performance in parliament was quite remarkable; within a short time she had

RIGHT:
'Possibly the house-wifely instincts of the female member will survive'

This contemporary newspaper cartoon shows 'the new member' Mrs Cowan, about to make a clean sweep of the Western Australian parliament.

Few of the sitting members were pleased to see a woman enter the political chamber, yet they had little to fear if they did the right thing by her and agreed to her demands.

Although she was elected as an endorsed Nationalist candidate, Cowan didn't always vote with the government; depending on the issue she would vote with the opposition as well. This endeared her to neither side.

pressed the issues of migrant welfare, infant health centres, and the necessity for motherhood endowment onto the front pages of the newspapers. She introduced, and saw passed into law, two private members' bills, which was quite an extraordinary achievement in itself. The first successfully moved an amendment to the Administration Act, which gave equal inheritance rights to mothers when their offspring died intestate or without issue. The second, *The Women's Legal Status Act of 1923*, opened the way for women to enter the legal profession.

Rumours spread that Cowan's now-retired husband had been virtually 'evicted' from his home due to the neglect of his wife, but he remained a staunch supporter of her in her work. In parliament Cowan stood as her own woman, sometimes voting with the Nationalist government, at other times voting with the opposition; neither side was impressed by her refusal to accept a 'party line'. In the 1924 election a strong candidate representing Perth's business interests defeated her.

The rift between the various women's organisations, which began over the issue of venereal disease, remained unhealed and Cowan's support from the organisations that she had had a long association with evaporated. She never sat in parliament again.

Busy in retirement

In 1925 Cowan travelled to the United States of America as an Australian delegate to the Seventh International Conference of Women.

Never one to stand idle, she was also a founding member of the Royal Western Australian Historical Society; her daughter Dircksey was its first keeper of records. Dame Edith Cowan was also appointed to the planning committee for Western Australia's centenary celebrations held in 1929.

Ill health over her last few years forced Cowan to withdraw from public life. She died on 9 June 1932 and is buried in the Anglican section of the Karrakatta cemetery. After a lifetime of toil for the benefit of countless thousands of women in Western Australia, she left behind an estate valued at just £161, but the value of the contribution she made to the elevation of the status of women is inestimable.

In 1934 'those who admired her many good deeds for humanity' erected a memorial clock tower near the entrance gates to King's Park in Perth. The naming of Western Australia's Edith Cowan University in Perth is a more recent honour, recognising the influential role she played as a remarkable woman of the twentieth century.

LEFT:

Members of the Western Australian Secession movement, 1930

Mrs Edith Cowan MLA stands prominently in the centre of this group of politicians and lobbyists who joined together to seek secession from the Federated Commonwealth of Australia.

The case for secession was put to the vote on 8 April 1933, and, while Western Australians voted overwhelmingly in favour of going it alone (138,653 for, 70,706 against), they also voted out most of the politicians who were about to make it happen. The federal parliament was never likely to take any notice of the 'rebels' from the west, so they intended to appeal directly to Westminster.

In spite of all this effort, Western Australia still remains within the Commonwealth today.

(State Library of Western Australia Collection)

A. B. Paterson

Banjo Pa

1864–19

'You'll co
Matilda

Banjo Paterson is featured on the face of the $10 polymer note, first issued in 1993.

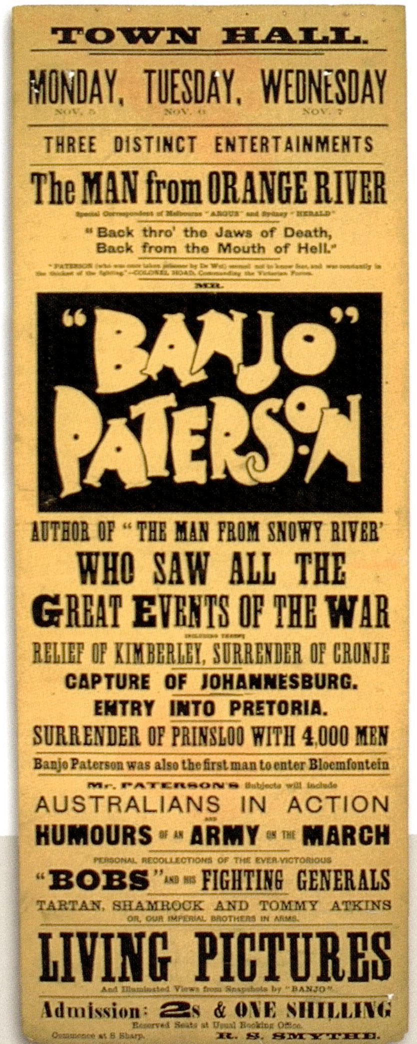

ABOVE:
Poster advertising a lecture by the 'Banjo'—The Man from Orange River, accompanied by 'living pictures', 5 November 1900, Hobart Town Hall, Tasmania
(State Library of Tasmania Collection)

OPPOSITE:
Andrew Barton Paterson in 1900
(National Library of Australia Collection)

BANJO PATERSON HAD A 'VISION SPLENDID' OF THE Australian bush. Unlike fellow author Henry Lawson, his poetic sparring partner at the *Bulletin*, Paterson saw the unique beauty and pleasures of colonial life. Lawson saw only the battle, the bottle and defeat. In describing the difference between the vision of the two most popular writers of the day Paterson said:

> We were both looking for the same reef, if you get what I mean; but I had done my prospecting on horseback with my meals cooked for me, while Lawson has done his prospecting on foot and had to cook for himself.[1]

Although both men loved the Australian bush, and shared a respect for the characters who brought the scrub alive, they were poles apart: one a squatter's son, the other a product of slab-hut poverty and the unlucky digger's disappointment.

Birth of 'The Banjo'

Born on 17 February 1864 in Narrambla in the west of New South Wales, Andrew Barton Paterson was the son of Andrew Bogle Paterson, a Scottish immigrant from Lanarkshire who had sailed to the colony in the 1850s around the time of the gold rush. The Patersons were no diggers; in the family tradition that went back over the generations, they were graziers. Andrew Bogle Paterson's many attempts

The Paterson clan

Young Andrew Barton Paterson spent most of his time around horses, and was such a natural rider it seemed as though horses ran in his veins.

One of his forebears, John Paterson, was responsible for the establishment of the 'Clydesdale' breed in Britain; for many years the breed was known as 'Paterson's'. Another relative, William Paterson, was responsible for the establishment of the Bank of England; unfortunately for 'The Banjo', this aspect of the family heritage seems to have eluded him.

His father's father had been a roughrider in the Indian army, and was given a commission for his command of the 'wild' horses.

'The Banjo' rode all his life: he rode to hounds with the Sydney Hunt Club, regularly played polo and was a successful amateur steeplechase 'jockey' over the hurdles at Randwick and Rosehill in Sydney.

to make a good living from the land saw the family move from place to place. While Andrew was still a boy they moved to Buckenbah, then to Illalong, close to the Lambing Flat gold-diggings and Binalong, where the flash young bushranger Johnny Gilbert now lies buried in the police horse paddock.

Paterson the younger grew up in the bush watching the bullock teams slowly pull their heavily laden drays, groaning, along the dusty roads. He watched the gold escort take its weekly trip from the diggings to the treasury; mounted troopers rode guard over the gold, and each time they passed, Paterson may have imagined that a dashing bushranger would leap from the bushes shouting 'Bail up!' — but the bad old days of Ben Hall and Gardiner's gang were long gone.

Paterson's father and his uncle John were away in Queensland for most of his early years, but trouble with the natives, and devastating droughts followed by torrential tropical floods, forced them to abandon their hopes for the north. They next moved to Illalong, but *The Free Selectors Act of 1861* almost put an end to their hopes, as selectors came in and helped themselves to bits of their run. Paterson later remembered: 'they all seemed to pick on us, as there were creeks everywhere'.

Paterson was first schooled at home by a governess, and then in Binalong. Although it was a four-mile bareback ride to school every day, Paterson loved mixing with the kids from the neighbouring selections: the rowdy Irish Micks, Paddys and Sheelaghs, and the rough-and-tumble sons and daughters of the itinerant railway workers.

Years later these same kids became the characters who peppered his verse in 'Illalong Kids', and Johnny Gilbert lived once more to be shot down again in the sad ballad of the bushranger's betrayal in 'How Gilbert Died', published in the *Bulletin* on 2 June 1894, which ended with the verse:

There's never a stone at the sleeper's head
There's never a fence beside,
And the wandering stock on the grave
may tread
Unnoticed and undenied,
But the smallest child on the watershed
Can tell you how Gilbert died.

Young Paterson was fortunate that his maternal grandmother was quite well off; when he was ten years old she helped finish his education by paying for him to attend Sydney Grammar School. She was a well-educated woman who wrote poetry herself and had lived on the land for twenty-five years. Paterson lived with her in the suburb of

A saddle for Pardon

One New Year's Day, when he was eight years old, and his father was way up country, young Andrew Paterson went with the station rouseabout to the Bogolong races. Bogolong was a town consisting of only two pubs set half a mile apart. When Andrew asked where the rest of the town was he was told: 'This is all they is. One pub to ketch the coves coming from Yass and the other to ketch the coves from Jugiong'.

Hundreds of horses were tethered to the scrappy stringy-barks at the racetrack half a mile out of town. Rough mountain men, Aboriginal lads and 'sporting gentlemen' all gathered for a big, boozy day at the races:

I had ridden over on a pony with a child's saddle; glancing at the pony to see that he was all right, I saw a Murrumbidgee mountaineer about seven feet high taking the saddle off my pony and putting it on a racehorse ... I managed to gasp out: 'That's my saddle.'

'Right-oh, son' he said 'I won't hurt it ... It's ketch weights, and this is the lightest saddle here, so I took it before anybody else got it. This is Pardon,' he went on 'and after he wins his heat you come to me and I'll stand you a bottle of ginger beer'.[2]

The horse duly won and Andrew earned his ottle of lukewarm ginger beer; he recalled this grand day at the Bogolong races years later in the ballad 'Old Pardon, the Son of Reprieve'.

Gladesville and went back home, 'up the bush', for his holidays.

Paterson didn't gain a scholarship to attend university as he had hoped, so at the age of sixteen, he went to work in a lawyer's office. After gaining his qualification as a solicitor he became the managing clerk of a large Sydney law firm. Much of the work of the office was to 'screw money out of people who had not got it'; he resented having to put the screws on the poor farmers and selectors who always seemed to be at the mercy of the banks or government officials.

His first published piece was a political pamphlet called 'Australia for the Australians', which put the case for land reform and protection for small farmers against the large land-holder. The essence of his later, and most enduring work, 'Waltzing Matilda', is evident in this nascent work.

He began to turn his pen to more fanciful words and submitted his first effort in verse to the *Bulletin*; 'The Bush Fire, an Allegory' appeared in print in June 1886. His first poems, including 'Old Pardon, the Son of Reprieve' (1888) were all published under the nom de plume 'The Banjo'. Paterson was cautious about using his own name; the political views he had expressed in 'Australia for the Australians' may well have put J. F. Archibald, the editor of the *Bulletin*, off his work. Archibald was a dictatorial editor who told his writers what to write, and his artists what to draw. He wanted his paper to 'howl for the undermost dog — all the rest of the press are generally sooling on the pup that's got the grip'; he wanted his writers to 'print all the awkward things procurable'.[3]

Although 'The Banjo' was pleased that public response to his verse was so favourable, he didn't become a regular contributor under this nom de plume until 1889. When asked why he chose the name, his answer was that it came from the name of a racehorse owned by his family at Illalong — he had never actually played a banjo in his life.

In 1895, after a decade of seeing his words in the papers, Paterson approached George Robertson of Angus and Robertson, with the idea of publishing a collection of his poems. Not long after the first volume, *The Man from Snowy River and Other Verses,* was released to immediate popular success, the publisher wrote to Paterson, saying 'You will be glad to hear that *Snowy River* has beaten the record in Australian publishing ... we intend going on with a second edition at once'. The first book also attracted favourable reviews in the United Kingdom. Rudyard Kipling, to whose work Paterson's verse had been compared,

The bushman's bible

The *Bulletin* was a weekly illustrated journal first published in Sydney in 1880. It had a huge readership and its influence over political, social and cultural matters was enormous.

Fiercely nationalistic, the dictatorial editor of the 'Bully', J. F. Archibald told his writers what he wanted them to write. When Paterson first went to see him, hoping to get some of his stories published, Archibald asked if he knew anything about the bush. Paterson replied that he had been born there. Archibald suggested that he 'should have a go at the bush ... don't write anything like other people if you can help it'.

The best writers and artists of the day all worked for the 'Bully' — Miles Franklin, Mary Gilmore, John Shaw Neilson, Barcroft Boake and 'Breaker' Morant, Lionel and Norman Lindsay, Phil May, George Lambert, Will Dyson, David Low, Percy Leason — and Henry Lawson of course!

LEFT:
Banjo Paterson, War Correspondent and Lecturer
Paterson toured eastern Australia after the Boer War, giving lectures on his experiences on the front line.
(Australian War Memorial Collection)

even wrote a warm letter of congratulations to Angus and Robertson.

First trip to war

After both Paterson's mother and father had passed away, he felt free of his family obligations. For the first time he felt that he was able to fulfil his boyhood dream of seeing the world, living by his pen, so in 1899 he decided to cast his fate to the winds.

He knew the Fairfax family, owners of the *Sydney Morning Herald,* and one day marched boldly into the *Herald* office and offered to go to South Africa and 'write them letters, descriptive letters' about the Boer War. He was quite prepared to go for a month, but he had very little money; Sir James Fairfax gave him £100, friends gave him two horses, and within a week, after all arrangements had been made, he sailed for South Africa. On board the ship he was handed a copy of the Melbourne *Argus* and was surprised to see a masthead announcing that 'Our Special Correspondent, Mr A. B. Paterson, will write letters to the *Argus* dealing with the life of Australian troops'. He had no idea before he left that he was the war correspondent for two leading newspapers at once.

Paterson didn't sit back away from the front line; he pushed himself right into the thick of the fighting and was often called upon to run dispatches through enemy lines. He wrote honestly, with great passion, understanding and authority. After hostilities ceased and he had returned home, he was considered to be an expert on the Boer War and toured throughout eastern Australia lecturing on his wartime experiences.

The travel bug had bitten the young correspondent. Next, he decided to go to China to report on the Boxer Rebellion, but it was almost over before he even got started. He decided to go anyway; on 29 July 1901 he set

Bloemfontein — March 1900

'The Banjo' was no ordinary observer of the Boer War; he wanted to be right in the thick of it. In fact, he was the first man into Bloemfontein and negotiated the surrender of the town with the mayor, saving hundreds of lives on both sides from senseless slaughter.

He describes his gallop on the town:

> ... when we three correspondents decided to go into town there was considerable risk of capture, but we were so anxious to be the first in that we raced with whips going for at least three-quarters of a mile, and my black horse landed me first in Bloemfontein, a distinction to be proud of ... we guided the mayor out to see Lord Roberts and surrender the town.[4]

While the Australian contingent was resting up in Bloemfontein, Paterson met English writer Rudyard Kipling. Paterson was surprised that the great man, who had given the world *The Jungle Book,* had so readily put down his pen and was now playing the politician.

Paterson cherished their friendship all his life; one souvenir that he treasured most from his time in South Africa was an autographed dinner menu from the Bloemfontein Club signed by Kipling on 28 March 1900.

BELOW:
Banjo Paterson at Jindabyne, c. 1910
Paterson is standing at the far right with his ubiquitous pipe smoking in his hand; his chauffeur Jack Arnott is in front of the tent; the other man is unidentified.
(National Library of Australia Collection)

sail for China with the intention of travelling across Siberia to see what the Russians were up to. He wanted to observe, at first hand, 'where the "Great Game"' is being played, where Empires are being juggled about, and where the fate of nations are likely to be decided in short order'.[5] When he got to China he discovered that the Siberian route was closed. Undaunted, he decided to go on to England via the Suez Canal, and pay a visit to an old acquaintance from Bloemfontein, Rudyard Kipling. He stayed with Kipling in his home in Sussex, but, failing to gain any position as a journalist with an English paper, sailed back to Australia in 1902.

In November that year he finally decided to make a break from the law and put all of his hopes on his pen. Then he could at last truly call himself a journalist.

Paterson was appointed editor of the *Evening News* shortly before he was to wed Alice Emily Walker, of Tenterfield Station in northern New South Wales, on 8 April 1903. He and his bride moved to Sydney and lived at West Hall in Queen Street, Woollahra, where their two children, Grace and Hugh Barton, were born, in 1904 and 1906 respectively.

The pressure of editing the newspaper proved to be too great for Paterson, who would have much preferred to have been a contributor rather than its editor. He resigned from the paper on 6 January 1908 and moved back up country to Coodra, a property near Yass. While he never seemed to make a go of the farming life, the inspiration it gave him was what he had longed for.

Fighting for France

With the outbreak of World War I, Paterson saw another opportunity for his pen. He sailed to England in November 1914 but was again unable to get an appointment as war correspondent. Instead he went to France as an ambulance driver, where he learned that a remount division was being sent to Egypt. He rushed back to Australia, where he gained a

commission as lieutenant in the Australian Imperial Force, and was sent back to the Middle East, where he spent the rest of the war.

Paterson was in his element. He was made major in the First Australian Remount Unit, which was made up of roughriding bushmen like himself, training mounts for the Light Horse. He wrote:

> Being an Australian, a steeplechase rider and polo player, I had a (possibly fictitious) reputation as a judge of a horse, and was constantly asked to go and pick horses for officers out of the remount depots.[6]

It was through the Remount Unit that he resumed his acquaintance with Lord Roberts, General Haig, Rudyard Kipling and Winston Churchill. In 1917 Emily joined him in Ismailia, where she was a volunteer in the hospital.

His third collection of verse, *Saltbush Bill, J.P., and Other Verses,* was published in 1917, and after the war he returned to Sydney and worked as a freelance journalist. He first wrote for *Smith's Weekly* and in 1922 was appointed editor of the *Sydney Sportsman,* a weekly sporting paper that became very popular under his guidance. In 1930 he retired from full-time journalism but continued to write freelance. In 1933 he published *The Animals That Noah Forgot*, a collection of poems for children, illustrated by Norman Lindsay. *Happy Dispatches*, a collection of wartime memories was published in 1934 and the novel *The Shearer's Colt* in 1936.

In 1939 Paterson was made a Commander of the British Empire (CBE) for his services to Australian literature.

Paterson had long suffered from heart trouble and was advised to take things quietly, but he took ill and died in hospital on 5 February 1941, just a few weeks short of his seventy-seventh birthday. In his seventy-six years he had given Australia some of its most memorable verse, which has persisted in its popularity over time. The opening line of 'The Man From Snowy River' is etched on the Australian consciousness:

> There was movement at the station, for the word had passed around
> That the colt from old Regret had got away ...

The last verse of 'Clancy of the Overflow' resonates through to the high-rise, glass towers of today:

> And I somehow rather fancy that I'd like to change with Clancy, Like to take a turn at droving where the seasons come and go,
> While he faced the round eternal of the cashbook and the journal —
> But I doubt he'd suit the office, Clancy, of The Overflow.

Waltzing Australia Fair

A plebiscite was held in 1977 to decide on a new national anthem for Australia. Four songs were placed on the ballot: 'Advance Australia Fair', 'Waltzing Matilda', 'God Save the Queen' and 'Song of Australia'. Around 43% of Australians voted for 'Advance Australia Fair', with only 28% of the votes for 'Waltzing Matilda'.

Conservative prime minister Malcolm Fraser went against the decision of the people and reinstated 'God Save the Queen' as the national anthem, declaring 'Advance Australia Fair' to be the national song. Curiously, though, he approved the use of 'Waltzing Matilda' as the official Australian song for the 1976 Montreal Olympic Games.

Labor prime minister Bob Hawke reversed Fraser's decision when he came to power in 1984, with 'Advance Australia Fair' becoming the official national anthem.

Regardless of the polls, the story of the squatter and the swaggie remains the most popular song of them all.

The story of 'Waltzing Matilda'— Australia's unofficial national anthem

Oh! there once was a swagman camped in a Billabong
Under the shade of a Coolabah tree;
And he sang as he looked at his old billy boiling
"Who'll come a-waltzing Matilda with me?"

Who'll come a-waltzing Matilda, my darling?
Who'll come a-waltzing Matilda with me?
Waltzing Matilda and leading a water-bag—
Who'll come a-waltzing Matilda with me?

Down came a jumbuck to drink at the water-hole,
Up jumped the swagman and grabbed him with glee;
And he sang as he stowed him away in his tucker-bag,
"You'll come a-waltzing Matilda with me."

Down came the Squatter a-riding his thoroughbred;
Down came Policemen—one, two and three.
"Whose is the jumbuck you've got in the tucker-bag?
You'll come a-waltzing Matilda with me!"

But the swagman he up and he jumped in the water-hole,
Drowning himself by the Coolabah tree;
And his ghost may be heard as it sings in the Billabong
"Who'll come a-waltzing Matilda with me?"

PUBLISHED AS SHEET MUSIC IN 1903 — SALTBUSH BILL, J.P., AND OTHER VERSES, 1917

THE WORDS TO 'WALTZING MATILDA' were written by Banjo Paterson in 1895. He wrote the lyrics to accompany the melody of *The Graigalee March*, an old Scottish folk-tune which a friend, Miss Christina Macpherson, had first heard played at the Warrnambool races.

'The Banjo' was engaged to Sarah Riley of Winton for eight years and went with his fiancée and her old school friend Miss Macpherson to spend Christmas 1894 at Dagworth Station on the Diamantina. It was there that Paterson first heard Macpherson play the tune on a zither.

In 1894 the shearers of Queensland went on strike for better pay and conditions, and fought a long, hard and bitter battle against the squatters and the police.

At Dagworth Station Paterson observed the strife brought about by the shearers' strike and the attitude of the squatters to the shearers. This 'war of the classes' is central to the theme of 'Waltzing Matilda', which tells the story of an itinerant worker 'on the wallaby track'. It reflects upon the Australian national tradition of resistance to authority when the 'swagman' prefers to drown himself rather than submit to the squatter and to the law.

The term 'matilda' actually has a German origin, meaning 'mighty battle maiden', and 'matilda' was a name given to the women who followed soldiers on the battlefields of the European Thirty Years War. These 'matildas' kept their soldiers warm at night and the name was eventually bestowed upon their greatcoats and the blankets that effectively fulfilled the same role.

'Waltz' is also a German word: '*auf der walz*' means 'to go on the tramp', a term applied to apprentices, or *zimmermen*, who once tramped from place to place in search of employment with master tradesmen. So, to go *auf der walz* with your matilda was to take to the road with your bed-roll on your back. During the depression of the 1890s thousands of men wandered across the country with their swags across their backs—'waltzing with matilda'.

In an interview on ABC Radio in the 1930s Paterson commented on the birth of his most famous song:

> The shearers staged a strike by way of expressing themselves and Macpherson's woolshed at Dagworth was burnt down, and a man was picked up dead ... Miss Macpherson used to play a little Scottish tune on a zither and I put words to it and called it 'Waltzing Matilda'.

'Frenchy' Hoffmeister, a German shearer who had taken part in the affray, was the man found dead the morning after the conflagration in the woolshed at Dagworth Station.

The song was heard in public for the first time when it was performed at the North Gregory Hotel in Winton, central Queensland, on 6 April 1895, published first as sheet music by tea importer James Inglis, who had acquired the rights from Angus and Robertson in 1902.

James Inglis & Co. published the words to 'Waltzing Matilda' in 1903, with musical arrangement by Marie Cowan, wife of a J. Inglis & Co. director, and an advertisement for Billy Tea on the back cover.

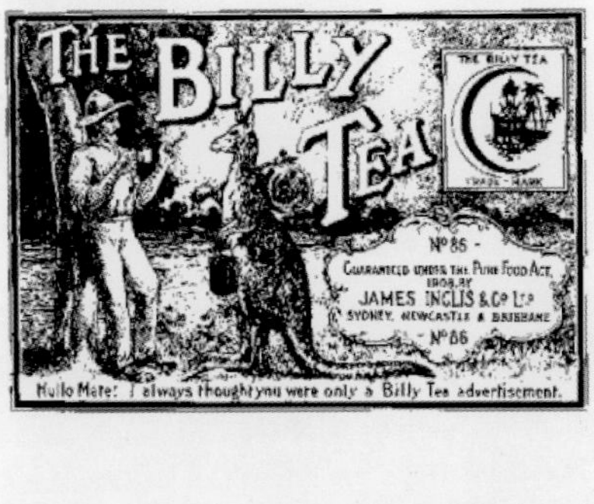

Sir John Monash

1865–1931

Sir John Monash is featured on the obverse of the $100 polymer note, first issued in 1996.

'I would name Sir John Monash as the best general on the western front in Europe.' — Field Marshal Montgomery

ABOVE:
John Monash at nine years old, 1874
(State Electricity Commission of Victoria Collection)

BY THE TIME OF HIS DEATH IN 1931 SIR JOHN MONASH had established such a solid reputation as both soldier and nation builder that it seems incredible that he had achieved so much in his sixty short years.

John Monash was born on 27 June 1865 in Dudley Street, West Melbourne, the first child of Prussian emigrants, merchant and storekeepers, Louis and Berthe Monasch, who had emigrated in 1853. John was born into a prosperous society still enjoying the boom generated by the Australian gold rush and the rush to immigrate that followed. The colonial world at the time was dominated by a fervent love of Empire and the seemingly unending reign of Queen Victoria.

The family moved to Jerilderie in 1874, where John went to the local primary school. He learned to ride, and just like all young lads at that time, spent most of his spare days exploring the bush. His teacher soon recognised the rare qualities in the young boy and encouraged his parents to take him back to the city for further schooling. In 1877 his mother returned to Melbourne with her three children. John was enrolled at Scotch College and it was there that he proved his country schoolmaster to have been correct. He was joint dux of the school and dux in mathematics and modern

RIGHT:
John Monash, 1881, aged sixteen
Monash (circled) gained acceptance into the Arts Faculty at the University of Melbourne in 1881. Over the next forty years he had a distinguished and varied academic career.
(State Electricity Commission of Victoria Collection)

OPPOSITE:
Lieutenant General Sir John Monash
Oil on canvas by John Longstaff, 1919
(Australian War Memorial Negative Number, ART02986)

languages. In 1881, when he was still only sixteen years of age, he was accepted into the Arts faculty at the University of Melbourne.

Young John Monash was seemingly tireless; he engaged in debating, playing chess and piano (sometimes performing in public); he studied the arts of 'legerdemain' (sleight of hand) and enjoyed drawing and painting; he took an interest in student politics and was co-founder of the Melbourne University Union. With friends from the university he often visited Mount Buffalo, where they took to walking through the bush. It seems amazing that Monash found time to attend to his studies at all. At times he could be seen at the Supreme Court listening to legal argument, and then at Parliament House taking in the thrust and parry of political debate. He wandered all over Melbourne watching buildings being erected, dredges at work and the hurly-burly of the score of construction sites throwing up the metropolis then dubbed 'Marvellous Melbourne'. Monash wrote articles and letters to the newspapers, he penned essays on all kinds of varied subjects — and occasionally attended his university lectures.

But things did not always go to plan for the young student. Times were tight for the family and by his third year John could no longer afford to keep himself at university. Although for a while he tutored other students to help him pay his way, it was not enough; in the end he had to get a job.

Before he had completed his engineering degree he took a position with David Munro & Co. on the construction of the new Princes Bridge being built across the Yarra River, joining Swanston Street and St Kilda Road. He also assisted in the building of other bridges around Footscray, Moonee Ponds and Coburg in Melbourne's western suburbs.

Just like so many other fervent and patriotic young men, Monash combined his military

BELOW:

The Old Camp, Mount Buffalo

While at university in Melbourne, Monash and friends developed a love of the outdoors, often journeying to the mountains of the Great Dividing Range and camping out under the stars, climbing and walking across the ranges. Monash is seen seated at the right of the photograph.

(State Library of Victoria Collection)

interests with his civilian career. He joined the newly formed University Company of the Victorian Rifles in 1884, after the Victorian Militia was created to replace the former Volunteer Rifle Corps, which had been a part of the life of most settled communities throughout the state. He continued in his employment with Munro & Co., studying part time, and rising through the ranks of the militia until he was made colour sergeant in 1886. The following year the University Rifles was disbanded and he applied for and gained a commission in the Militia Garrison Artillery.

Around this time he wrote in his diary:

The undercurrent of my thoughts has been strongly on military matters. Yesterday things came to a finality. I have been attached to Major Goldstein's battery with the prospect of appointment before Easter; a combination of military and engineering professions is a possibility that is before me.[1]

By 1887 he had left Munro & Co. and taken a job with another engineering contractor, where he was appointed in charge of construction of the Outer Circle railway works. After this project was completed in early

ABOVE:

Fort Queenscliff, Victoria, c. 1895

Photograph by Nicholas Caire

Monash was promoted to captain of the metropolitan Brigade of the Garrison Artillery in 1895 and took command of the battery at Queenscliff in 1897. The Queenscliff battery protected the heads of Port Phillip Bay, its guns pointing out over the water ready to ward off any hostile invader.

Monash is at the left of the two men examining a chart leaning on the forward railing.

(Australian War Memorial Negative Number, A05326)

LEFT:

University Company, Victorian Rifles 1885

Back left: Colour Sgt. John Monash, Sgt. Farlow, Cpl. McWilliams, Cpl. T. Hodgson, Sgt. Major Sullivan; front left: Cpl. Pringle, Cpl. McCay, Sgt. Chase, 1885.

(Monash University Archives, IN.1416)

RIGHT:
Family portrait of John Monash, wife Victoria and daughter Bertha, photographed in London, 1910

Monash married Hannah Victoria Moss, the daughter of early colonist Morton Moss, in 1891. Bertha was the couple's only child.

(Monash University Archives, IN 1414)

1891 he went on to gain the position of assistant engineer and chief draftsman with the Melbourne Harbour Trust, and remained in this post throughout the worst of the depression years.

In 1891 John Monash married Victoria Moss, daughter of well-known early colonist Morton Moss. The marriage lasted until 1920, when Victoria passed away. They had only one child, daughter Bertha.

John Monash continued to add to his qualifications. While he was with the Harbour Trust he qualified as municipal surveyor, engineer for water supply and patent attorney.

He considered that the combination of engineering with a solid understanding of the principles of law would be a good thing, so he studied for and completed a law degree in 1895; this was added to his masters degree in civil engineering, which he had received from the University of Melbourne two years earlier.

In 1894, towards the end of the depression, Monash had to step down from his position at the Harbour Trust. Monash was never dismayed by any turn of events and simply established himself as a consulting engineer and patent attorney.

This singularly talented and well-qualified young man was soon in demand right across the nation. He assisted in the construction of railways from Queensland to Tasmania; he also designed the King River Bridge in the northwest of the island state.

In 1896 he took an interest in design and construction using reinforced concrete. His firm, Monash and Anderson, designed and built the Anderson Street Bridge, known as a 'Monier Arch' bridge. The technique of reinforcing compacted concrete with steel was developed by the Parisian Joseph Monier; his reinforced garden pots were displayed in the Paris Exhibition in 1876. Monash claimed that

LEFT:
Monier Bridge (Anderson's Street Bridge) under construction, 1899

Photograph by Mark Daniel

The completed bridge with its three graceful 100-ft arches spans the Yarra River at South Yarra.

(State Library of Victoria Collection)

he was perfecting this technique in Melbourne before any one else around the globe had even begun to consider its application to modern architecture.

The Anderson Street Bridge remains today, an elegant structure with three gently arched 100-foot-long spans, gracefully straddling the Yarra River near the Royal Botanic Gardens in Melbourne.

In 1900 Monash created a propriety company, with David Mitchell, the father of Dame Nellie Melba, as chairman of directors; this partnership began a period of real prosperity for Monash. He was soon able to move into a mansion in St George's Road, in Melbourne's most exclusive suburb, Toorak.

From his struggling university days, Monash had seen an enormous turnabout in his fortunes, but every success was earned through hard work, meticulous planning and the sheer effort of a powerful will. His extensive record of experience and achievements continued to grow for all those years leading up to the outbreak of World War I.

On the King's service

At the time that war against Germany was declared in 1914, Monash had been appointed colonel of a citizen force unit (militia). Since his days at university he had considered that he might be suited to the military life, and had always played a commanding role in various citizen militia units, from the University Rifles to the Queenscliff Battery.

With the outbreak of war, the time had come for John Monash the civilian to become Monash the soldier. The cultured and distinguished gentleman of Toorak who had never even heard a shot fired in anger left Australia in command of the 4th Infantry Brigade, bound for Egypt to prepare for an attack on the Turkish peninsula of Gallipoli.

Colonel John Monash led his men in the attack on 26 April 1914 and his time on that bloody beach was characterised by his typically careful, strategic planning and cool determination. At Gallipoli he was promoted to brigadier general and he stayed on the peninsula until successfully pulling out all his men in a silent evacuation on 18 December 1915. After some months in Egypt guarding the Suez Canal his brigade was transferred to the battlefields of France.

In June 1916 Monash was again promoted and transferred to England to take command of the training of the 3rd Australian Division in preparation for a sustained attack on the Germans along the Hindenburg line. Now major-general, Monash returned to France and he and his men took part in the prolonged wave

A better way to do battle

Monash was never impressed by the methods used by the old-fashioned British commanders, who sent men to their deaths, wave after wave, as they had done for centuries. He knew there was a better way to win a battle and to bring as many men home as possible. He wrote:

> ... the true role of infantry was not to expend itself upon heroic physical effort, not to wither away under merciless machine-gun fire, not to impale itself on hostile bayonets, but on the contrary, to advance under the maximum possible protection of the maximum possible array of mechanical resources, in the form of guns, machine-guns, tanks, mortars and aeroplanes; to advance with as little impediment as possible; to be relieved as far as possible of the obligation to fight their way forward.[2]

Monash believed that all services should work together; that the sum of all parts would certainly be greater than each individual effort. To this end he sought the service of the new British tanks, painted each one a different colour and assigned a party of infantrymen to go into battle behind the safety of these rumbling iron monsters. The attacks were supported by aerial bombing and rolling artillery fire, the men largely unseen in the smoke of battle until, for the enemy, it was too late.

Monash, the bridge builder

RIGHT:
Fyansford Township
Photograph by John Norton, c. 1866

This photograph of Fyansford, near Geelong, shows the old timber bridge clumsily straddling the Barwon River.

(State Library of Victoria Collection)

CENTRE:
Fyansford Bridge under construction, 1896

John Monash and his wife Vic can be seen at the extreme left of this photograph of a group of construction workers and part of the concrete bridge.

(Monash University Archives, IN.202)

BELOW:
Fyansford Bridge, 1906

This photograph shows the new 'Monier' concrete bridge built by Monash and Anderson. The elegance of this modern structure appears to have been the hallmark of Monash's designs.

(State Library of Victoria Collection)

BELOW:
Breaking the Hindenburg Line
Oil on canvas by Will Longstaff, 1918
(Australian War Memorial Negative Number, ART03023)

of attacks that eventually wore the Germans down and broke through the Hindenburg Line towards the end of 1918.

With the kind of detailed planning that may have gone into the construction of a bridge, Monash prepared a plan for the destruction of the German defences at Messines Ridge. Soldiers of the 1st Australian Tunnelling Company dug under the battlefield until they reached a position beneath the German post. Several charges of more than 50,000 lbs of explosives each were laid.

On 11 June 1917 a series of nineteen massive explosions blew apart the German position and enabled the Australian and New Zealand troops to move in and capture Messines within two hours of starting the engagement. Monash planned the attack with unusual attention to detail. He made a relief map of the area and ensured that each of his officers memorised every detail of the landscape. He also insisted that every officer memorised every detail of the battle plan. He left nothing to chance.

Monash later outlined his concept for waging a successful campaign:

> A perfect battle-plan is like nothing so much as the score for an orchestral composition, where the various arms and units are the instruments, and the tasks they perform are their respective musical phrases. Every individual unit must make its entry precisely at the proper moment and play its phrase in the general harmony.[3]

Breaking the line

Monash had commanded his men on some of the most staggering victories, which swept along the Hindenburg Line in mid-1918—from his victory at Morlancourt on 10 June, to Hamel on 4 July, and the breakthrough on the Somme at the battle of Amiens on 8 August.

Monash described the battle of Hamel as: 'all over in ninety-three minutes ... the perfection of teamwork'.

After his success at Hamel, in July 1918, which marked the turning point of the campaign, Monash's battle plans and general orders for that operation were republished by British General Headquarters as a model in order writing for the entire British army.

Just before the decisive battle of Amiens in August 1918, Monash had rejected offers of British troops in support of his flanks. When he was offered Canadian troops, though, he was delighted. Monash sent this message out to all troops before the battle began:

> For the first time in the history of this Corps, all five Australian divisions will tomorrow engage in the largest and most important battle ever undertaken ... they will be supported by an exceptionally powerful artillery and by tanks and aeroplanes ... the full resources of our sister Dominion, the Canadian Corps, will also operate on our right ... Every man will carry on to the utmost of his powers until his goal is won; for the sake of Australia, the Empire and our cause ... a victory that will live forever in the history of our home land.[4]

In the course of the battle Monash used parachutes developed by the Australian Flying Corps to drop ammunition to the advancing Australian troops. He sent in the new British 'Mark-V' tanks and was impressed by the valour of the tank crews, who headed right into the heart of the battle.

The Australians and Canadians were at the front of the fighting; setting out for the German trenches at 4.30 a.m., protected by a creeping artillery barrage and dense fog, they captured the German trenches by 7.30 a.m.

The troops at the vanguard of the attack took a breather in the emptied trenches, while the 4th and 5th Divisions passed along up to the line. Then those who had been in the front struck out for their final objective. The swiftness of this battle was staggering, by the end of the day the Allies had covered nine miles, capturing 30,000 prisoners and 400 field guns.

German general Erich Ludendorff described the events of 8 August1918 as 'the Black day of the German army'. At corps headquarters on 12 August, just four days after the campaign had begun, His Majesty King George V knighted Monash in the field.

Sir John Monash was asked yet again to send his Australians in to attack the Germans, in an elevated position overlooking the open battlefield at Mont St Quentin. He was never one to send his men to a wasteful death, and planned

Master of legerdemain

Monash was a master of subterfuge. Prior to an attack on the German position he bombarded their trenches for days on end with artillery, mustard gas and smoke shells. The gas would cause the Germans to put on their face masks and the smoke would hide the advancing troops.

Monash bombarded them with the smoke and the gas always together, until he was ready to attack, then he tricked the Germans with smoke bombs only. Fearing a gas attack, they put on their cumbersome facemasks, which restricted their vision and their ability to communicate with one another. The Australians attacked under cover of the swirling smokescreen, taking the enemy completely by surprise.

Monash preferred to attack as early in the day as possible, using poor light to protect his troops from unfriendly fire. He created dummy installations, and allowed no troop movements during daylight, never indicating to the enemy that an attack was imminent.

He asked for planes to bomb Hamel, and requested older, noisier ones to distract from the sound of the tanks as they ground slowly but surely into position.

ABOVE:

French President Georges Clemenceau walking with Major-General E. E. Sinclair-Maclagan (4th divisional Co-mmander) and Lieutenant-General John Monash visit the Australian troops at the front, 7 July 1918.

(Australian War Memorial Negative Number, E02527)

this campaign very carefully. Monash, the accomplished pianist, brilliant chess player and amateur practitioner of the arts of legerdemain was about to create his own bloody, symphonic sleight of hand.

At daybreak on 31 August the hilltop of Mont St Quentin was bombarded by artillery until the 5th Brigade was ready to swoop up the hillside and capture the Germans by surprise. Rather than face the Australians in close hand-to-hand trench fighting, the Germans surrendered in their hundreds. A unit of the Prussian Guards retaliated and was momentarily successful in pushing the Australians down from the crest, but Monash fought back

BELOW:

King George V, Sir Newton Moore and Major-General John Monash review troops of the 3rd Division, Bulford, England, 27 September 1916.

After Gallipoli Monash spent several months in Suez and France, he was then transferred to England in 1916 to prepare the 3rd Division for the sustained attack along the Hindenburg Line, where the Germans surrendered in their thousands towards the end of 1918.

(Australian War Memorial Negative Number, P00997019)

again, willing his almost exhausted men back up the hill until it was secured the following day. When the 14th Brigade walked into the old walled city of Peronne, and Monash matter-of-factly informed the British commander of the Australians' success, saying: 'By the way, we are on top of Mont St Quentin',[5] no one could believe it.

Monash was next asked to take his men on the offensive against the Germans to further weaken the Hindenburg Line. The Allies did not realise it, but the Germans were almost finished: they were demoralised, and although they fought long and hard against the British troops, they had no desire to engage the Australians in battle. When the British broke through the line on 18 September the Germans surrendered: 12,000 were taken prisoner by the British and 4000 by the Australians. As the victorious Allied armies looked back along the lines of wire, concrete and steel that had cost so many lives, one German officer confessed that they had

ABOVE:
Capture of Mont St Quentin
Oil on canvas by Fred Leist, 1918
(Australian War Memorial Negative Number—ART02929)

LEFT:
General John Monash, with fellow officers at corps headquarters in France, 1918

The Australian soldier was a unique character: he ignored protocol and infuriated the British, who demanded strict adherence to recognition of rank—they rarely got it from the Australians. One British general complained to an Australian colonel: 'Not only do your men fail to salute me, they laugh at my orderlies'.

Monash knew these men, 'his wild brown men from the open spaces ... lean, hard-muscled, hard-swearing, thieves of horses and haters of discipline ... the finest and the worst soldiers that ever entered France'[6], and when he willed them forward they always fought until they won the day.

(Australian War Memorial Negative Number, EO3186)

LEFT:
Peace March, London, 19 July 1919
Monash led his victorious troops through the cheering crowds lining the streets of London
(Monash University Archives Collection)

surrendered so that they would 'not now [have to] face the Australians'.

On 6 October 1918, the commander of the French army, Marshal Foch, showed British commander Douglas Haig newspaper headlines proclaiming the Allied victory. 'Here, you have the immediate result of the British piercing the Hindenburg line! The enemy have asked for an armistice', he said.

Monash believed that the capitulation of the German army was a direct result of the persistent assault on the line by the Australians. He never wanted an all-out mass attack, but promoted the idea of a sustained series of attacks all along the line until the enemy was gradually weakened to the point of collapse. He had been proved right.

After the armistice was signed on 11 November 1918, the war was over. Monash spent the next year in charge of the demobilisation and repatriation of all Australian soldiers. He led his troops on three great marches through the streets of London in 1919, the first Anzac Day March, the Dominions March and the Peace March. He had audiences with the king and even dined informally with him. Monash returned to Australia on Boxing Day 1919. He then set about honouring the men with whom he had been honoured to serve: to this end he was instrumental in establishing the annual Anzac Day march.

Immensely proud of his men, Monash became the founder of a trust to build the Shrine of Remembrance in St Kilda Road, Melbourne, in their honour. He expressed this opinion of the Australian fighting man:

> [The Digger]—The democratic institutions under which he was reared, the advanced system of education by which he was trained—teaching him to think for himself and to apply what he had been taught to practical ends—the instinct of sport and adventure which is his natural heritage, his pride in his young country, and the opportunity which came to him of creating a great national tradition, were all factors which made him what he was.[7]

LEFT:
Flag carried by Monash during the Victory Parade in London

This red woollen flag bearing the Cross of St George has the letters AUS.I.F. stencilled in the upper canton. There is a certain coincidence in the repetition of the name St George in Monash's life.

As Knight of the Order of St Michael and St George, an address at St George's Road, Toorak was most befitting to the great general. He also carried this curiously redesigned banner of St George in the Victory Parade through London in 1919.

That the acronym for the words Australian Infantry Forces should take precedence over the cross of the Patron Saint of England was cheeky to say the least, but the 'Aussies' were notorious for their lack of deference to the 'Poms'. It seems even Monash could not resist such temptation.

(Australian War Memorial Negative Number 378215)

A leader at peace

At the end of the war Monash wrote:

> From the far off days of 1914, when the first call came, until the last shot was fired, every day was filled with loathing, horror and distress. I deplored all the time the loss of precious life, and the waste of human effort. Nothing could have been more repugnant to me than the realisation of the dreadful inefficiency of, and the misspent energy of war. Yet, it had to be, and the thought always uppermost was the earnest prayer that Australia might be forever spared such a horror on her own soil. There is, in my belief, only one way to realise such a prayer. The nation that wishes to defend its land and its honour must spare no effort, refuse no sacrifice to make itself so formidable that no enemy will dare to assail it.[8]

After the war Sir John Monash returned to civilian life, resuming his role as a civil engineer. But by now he had become one of the most admired figures in Australian public life. In 1920 he was invited by the Victorian government to take up the position of the first general manager of the newly created State Electricity Scheme. He undertook this challenge with great delight; from the turning of the first sod, to the electrification of the entire state, Monash was able to direct the affairs

Military awards

In a brilliant career that saw John Monash command Australian, British, Canadian and American troops, he was awarded honours by all the allied nations who fought in World War I.

General John Monash was awarded:

- Knight Grand Cross (Military Division) of the Most Distinguished Order of St Michael and St George
- Knight Commander (Military Division) of the Most Honourable Order of the Bath
- 1914–15 Star
- British General Service Medal
- Allied Victory Medal
- Colonial Auxiliary Forces Officer's Decoration
- Grand Officier de la Legion d'Honneur, French Republic
- Grand Officier de l'Ordre de la Couronne, Belgium
- French Croix de Guerre, with two palms
- Belgian Croix de Guerre
- American Distinguished Service Medal

OPPOSITE:
Commissioners turning the first sod for Yallourn Power Station, 5 February 1921
This group of distinguished gentlemen, their feet firmly planted in Gippsland mud, includes Sir John Monash *(second from right)* and the Hon. George Swinburne *(fourth from right).*
(State Electricity Commission of Victoria Collection)

with military precision. Industrialised Melbourne grew apace after the war ended, and Monash was aware that a reliable power source needed to be found before the state found itself in turmoil. While Yallourn Power Station was still under construction, and new rail lines were being cut through Gippsland, Monash arranged for an extension of the Newport railways power house to supply power for industrial and domestic use until Yallourn was completed. The first power from Gippsland crackled along the wires into Melbourne in 1924.

Monash was also responsible for developing the huge coal deposits for use other than power generation. As an engineer he sought new ways of using this resource; a new fuel was created from the black gold of Gippsland — briquettes — and an experimental factory was built at Yallourn. Victorians immediately took up this new fuel and Yallourn commenced manufacture on a commercial scale.

Monash worked tirelessly in the memory of his fallen comrades and instigated the Anzac Day ceremonies that grew to become a celebration of national pride and remembrance. He took a commanding role in the construction of the Shrine of Remembrance in St Kilda Road, Melbourne, and marched in the Anzac Day Parade every year until his death in 1931.

Sir John Monash died on 8 October 1931, after a short illness. He was honoured with a state funeral; his catafalque lay in state in Queen's Hall at Parliament House. From Spring Street to Brighton Cemetery, the road was lined with thousands of proud Australians who he had served, and served with. Four battalions of infantry and six squadrons of light-horsemen escorted him on his final journey.

On Monash's passing, one of the senior officers of the State Electricity Commission of Victoria wrote sentiments that could have spoken for any who had known Monash in any of the varied roles he had played:

> The whole of the employees of the commission looked upon him not only with pride as their leader but with affection as a very kind personality and his untiring and self-sacrificing devotion to duty will be a lasting inspiration to them and to their fellow citizens whom he served so well ... Great in small things, pre-eminent in great things, Sir John Monash left behind him a record alike distinguished as a leader in peace and war.[9]

RIGHT:
General Sir John Monash, Anzac Day, 1931
This was Monash's last ride at the head of the parade; he died on 8 October that year .

Over the years Monash had been a member of a staggering number of organisations, from Melbourne Rotary to the Anzac Day Commemoration Council of Victoria. He had both studied for and been an honorary recipient of an envious number of academic qualifications.

It seems that the only club he wasn't a member of was The Melbourne Club, and entry to that hallowed domain of exclusivity, unchanged since the early days of colonisation, was forever barred to him no matter how distinguished and selfless his service to king and country had been.
(National Archives Collection)

Dame Mary Gilmore

1865–1962

Dame Mary Gilmore is featured on the obverse of the $10 polymer note, first issued in 1993.

OPPOSITE:

Dame Mary Gilmore

Oil on plywood panel by Adelaide Perry, 1928

Mary was the eldest child of Donald and Mary Ann (nee Beattie) Cameron. Her mother was born in New South Wales, of Northern Irish parentage, her father was descended from Protestant highland Scots.

Mary recalled in 1903 that her mother's people were Wesleyans 'of the rigid Presbyterian kind' and that it 'was simply an accident' that her grandfather could have been called anything 'as mild as Wesleyan'.[1]

When Mary Cameron was born in 1865, her grandfather, Hugh Beattie, planted an English white poplar tree in his garden at Cotta Walla, as was his custom. The poplar grew from a cutting he had taken from Mary Reibey's garden, in her house in Newtown, Sydney.

(National Library of Australia Collection)

Socialist worker for a free Australia

BORN ON 16 AUGUST 1865 AT COTTA WALLA NEAR Goulburn, New South Wales, Mary Cameron began her schooling at a little rural school at Brucedale, near Wagga Wagga. She eventually went to a larger school in Wagga, which entailed a three-mile walk each way, every day, for her and her brother. She was a voracious reader and even at her first school the other girls would tease Mary because 'she spoke like a book'; they accused her of using 'such long words', but she replied that she 'had no intention of using out-of-way language'.

Mary attended several schools after Wagga; at Cootamundra, and later at Bungowannah near Albury. Eventually she was sent to school with an uncle who was the teacher at Yerong Creek; he had her ready for examination as a pupil teacher by the time she was sixteen — she passed with the highest grades of all in her year. Given a choice of going down to Sydney or taking a post in any of half a dozen country towns, Mary decided to stay in Wagga to be near her family, she was; after all, still just a gawky country teenager who knew little of the world other than what she had read in books.

Mary read everything from *The Koran* to Kendall, the poems of Gordon to the pages of the *Family Herald*; she spent so much of her time with her head stuck in a book, reading novels until midnight then studying until dawn, that she became quite anaemic.

RIGHT:

Dr H.V. Evatt, Albert Namatjira and Dame Mary Gilmore, c. 1950

Mary Gilmore was so highly regarded in Labor circles that all the great luminaries of the party paid homage at her table.

(Albert Namatjira Photographic Collection. By permission, National Library of Australia)

Mary's mother had to go to Wagga to feed her up and set her daughter to rights; Mary would have possibly read herself into the grave otherwise. Her landlady had even said that she was almost too scared to call her down for breakfast lest she would find her already dead.

Mary always thought of herself as a ringleader wherever she was, whether pupil or teacher. She decided not to continue as a pupil teacher and resigned to take charge of a small country school, where she fast-tracked her studies and avoided having to go to training school, which she was afraid of.

She went as assistant to Silverton in Broken Hill, and when she finally graduated took an appointment in Sydney at Stanmore in 1888.

A new, free Australia

Mary was not unusual among similarly well-educated young women of her day. She felt a burning desire for social change; she saw the inequities of established colonial society and she was determined not to accept a traditional women's role without question. Hers was a brave new world, and education, books and learning had opened the doors to it for her, and thousands of others just like her.

Mary was desperate to enter the world of letters and began to submit her work to various publishers. Careful to protect her teaching career, she wrote under various pen-names, calling herself at times Em Jaycey, Sister Jaycey and Rudione Calvert. She was invited to the home of radical publisher Louisa Lawson, where she met Louisa's son, Henry. She had quite an influence on Henry, who had also just begun to write and see his words in print. Her education and experience as a teacher was invaluable to the largely untutored Henry and he became attached to her, relying on her advice and support as a friend.

Mary began to write for radical socialist William Lane's weekly paper *Boomerang,* which commenced publication in 1887 and lasted until 1890. She then wrote for the *Worker,* which began in October 1892. Mary was increasingly drawn into William Lane's ideal of a socialist utopia, which he was convinced could never succeed in class-ridden Australia, and joined Lane and 220 other socialist radicals in the quest to 'create a perfectly equal society'. The Free Australia Movement sailed from Adelaide aboard the *Royal Tar* in 1893; bound for Lane's 'Utopia' in the republic of Paraguay, where the government had granted them 400,000 acres of land to try out their great social experiment. But the 'utopian' dream soon turned sour; Lane's dictatorial leadership and constant bickering

'Socialism in our time'

Social reformer William Lane was born in the English city of Bristol in 1861. He travelled to America when he was sixteen and worked on newspapers both there and in Canada. Lane emigrated to Australia in 1885 and worked as a journalist in Queensland.

Lane became active in the growing movement of organised labour which saw the birth of the Australian Labor Federation in 1889. Lane spread his message of radical reform through his coeditorship of the weekly journal *Boomerang,* and later with his the *Worker,* of which the motto was 'Socialism in our time'. Lane raised £30,000 to assist the London dockers' strike of 1889-90 and was there at 'the barricades' during the great maritime and pastoral strikes of 1890-91.

Disillusioned with the pace of change in Australia, he led 220 free socialists to Paraguay in 1893 to establish the commune 'Free Australia'. Within months, settlers were disenchanted with Lane's dictatorial style and left to set up a new commune at Cosmé. Mary and her new husband, William Gilmore, were part of this separatist commune.

The whole enterprise collapsed and William Lane returned to Australia in August 1899. He went back to journalism and toiled away for the rest of his days, determined to pay back the debts his utopia had incurred.

among the settlers caused most to give up after the first year, and before the end of the decade the commune was abandoned.

In Paraguay Mary married 31-year-old shearer William Gilmore, from Casterton in Victoria. They had one son, William Dysart Cameron Gilmore, who was born on 25 May 1897. After the commune collapsed, William sought work — shearing in Argentina, ranching in Patagonia — and after Mary and their son joined William in Patagonia she took a position as a governess.

Disillusioned after William Lane left and had returned to Australia to face his creditors, the Gilmores also gave up and headed for home in 1902. They travelled back to Australia via London and sailed home in the company of Henry Lawson's family, who were returning home ahead of Henry after one year of disappointment and poverty in England. On arrival in Australia, the Gilmores went to live with William's family at Casterton.

Mary had never lost the urge to write and her experiences had taught her much. Even though the socialist experiment had failed, she had not lost her enthusiasm for radical politics. In 1908 the editor of the *Australian Worker*, Hector Lamond, gave her the opportunity to contribute to the growing debate on the rights of women. Mary was given a page to herself and for the next twenty-three years she remained editor of the women's page, canvassing a wide range of social issues from economic reform to child endowment, old-age pensions to the relief of the poor, votes for women to Aboriginal rights.

Poetic licence

In 1912 the Gilmore family moved to Sydney. William continued on to Cloncurry, where he was to begin the first of the family farms in far North Queensland. Mary was happy to be back among her friends and in the company of the socialist literati. She was an inveterate letter writer and corresponded with almost every name in the artistic pantheon. She began to have her work published once again, only this time it bore her own name. The verse of Mary Gilmore was printed in the *Bulletin* and in *New Idea*; her first book of poetry, *Marri'd and Other Verses,* was published in 1910, to great public acclaim. This was followed by *The Tilted Cart* (1925), *The Wild Swan* (1930), *Under the Wilgas* (1932), *Battlefields* (1939) and *Fourteen Men* (1954). Her works of prose, *The Hound and the Road* (1922), *Old Days, Old Ways* (1934) and *More Recollections* (1935), re-created memories of the grand old days of Australia's youth into a legendary and epic saga.

For the love of 'enry

Mary Cameron met Henry Lawson at his mother's home in Sydney. Louisa Lawson was one of the more influential political radicals; she published the paper the *Republic,* and *Dawn,* a journal for women.

Henry Lawson was more than impressed by Mary, the writer from the bush, complimenting her when she wrote 'The crows kep' flyin' up, boys', saying that she had 'beaten him on [his] own ground, I haven't seen anything better'.

Some time around 1890, Henry asked Mary to marry him, but his mother sent him away to earn some money before they wed. Afraid that he may lose Mary, he tried to convince her to elope with him, but she was not ready to marry and said no. He tried to convince her to go with him, crying out to her 'You don't care for me as I care for you, or you would'. He sailed away to the Western Australian goldfields the next day, without her.

Henry wrote constantly to Mary, but she only ever received his first letter. Louisa Lawson kept all of the others from her, which she only discovered after she was called upon to assist in the arrangements for his state funeral, after his death in September 1922. She may well have wondered then what their lives may have been like if she had only said yes that night in 1890.

RIGHT:

Dame Mary Gilmore at her writing desk in her flat at King's Cross, c. 1952

Mary Gilmore remained at the centre of a world of artists, writers, political journalists and sympathisers. She corresponded constantly with Lionel Lindsay, Vance Palmer, Miles Franklin, Billy Hughes, George Robertson, Kenneth Slessor et al. The stairs to her flat at 99 Darlinghurst Road, King's Cross, drummed constantly to a steady stream of visitors paying homage at her door.

(State Library of Victoria. Reproduced by permission of the Herald & Weekly Times)

Mary Gilmore became one of the most popular writers of her time, outliving all the other 'balladists of the bush'. In 1937 she was awarded the honour of being the first woman to be appointed Dame Commander of Order of the British Empire (DBE), for her contribution to literature.

At a time when she might have been expected to slow down, Gilmore was not inclined to retire. She was a founding member of the Fellowship of Australian Writers and Sydney's Lyceum Club, and was active in the New South Wales Institute of Journalists and the Aboriginal Australian Fellowship. She continued to fire off letters to prime ministers, artists, writers, publishers, journalists, politicians, church leaders; anyone who could possibly help with any one of her many causes would receive a missive from the 'doughty Dame of Kings Cross'.

She had long lived alone; William had decided he preferred the country life and stayed on his farms. But Mary was never lonely; an endless stream of visitors climbed the stairs to her Kings Cross flat for a chat. When well-meaning friends suggested that her visitors were becoming too much for her — her housekeeper even suggested that she would shut the door against them — Dame Mary retorted: 'Well, I shall have to sit outside the door, as I would want to see them'.

Dame Mary Gilmore died from a sudden onset of broncho-pneumonia on 2 December 1962, aged ninety-five. She was honoured with a state funeral.

RIGHT:

Dame Mary Gilmore

Oil on hardboard by Sir William Dobell, 1957

This portrait was commissioned by the Australasian Book Society, to be exhibited on Gilmore's 92nd birthday.

A member of the Australian Workers Union for more than seventy years, Gilmore was also honoured by the Australian Trade Unions when they crowned her May Queen in 1961.

(© William Dobell, 1957/Licensed by VISCOPY, Sydney 2003. Art Gallery of New South Wales Collection)

No Foe will Gather our Harvest

Dame Mary Gilmore's work had an enormous impact on her Australian readers. 'No Foe will Gather our Harvest', written in 1940, echoed the prevailing sentiment throughout Australia during the dark days of World War II when the country was threatened by Japanese invasion.

General Douglas MacArthur, commander of the Allied Forces in the Pacific, was filled with praise for Dame Mary Gilmore and her patriotic call to resistance. Her other wartime poem, 'Singapore', also reached right into the heart of the Australian people.

Sons of the mountains of Scotland,
Welshmen of coomb and defile,
Breed of the moors of England,
Children of Erin's green isle,
We stand four square to the tempest,
Whatever the battering hail—
No foe shall gather our harvest,
Or sit on our stockyard rail.

Our women shall walk in honour,
Our children shall know no chain,
This land, that is ours forever,
The invader shall strike at in vain.
Anzac! ... Tobruk! ... and Kokoda! ...
Could ever the old blood fail?
No foe shall gather our harvest,
Or sit on our stockyard rail.

So–hail–fellow–met we muster,
And hail–fellow–met fall in,
Wherever the guns may thunder,
Or the rocketing air-mail spin!
Born of the soil and the whirlwind,
Though death itself be the gale —
No foe shall gather our harvest,
Or sit on our stockyard rail.

We are the sons of Australia,
Of the men who fashioned the land;
We are the sons of the women
Who walked with them hand in hand;
And we swear by the dead who bore us,
By the heroes who blazed the trail,
No foe shall gather our harvest,
Or sit on our stockyard rail.

BELOW:
The Bushwackers celebrate Dame Mary Gilmore's 90th birthday, 1956

(By permission, National Library of Australia)

Henry Lawson

1867–1922

Henry Lawson is featured on the obverse of the $10 paper note, first issued in 1966.

OPPOSITE:
Portrait of Henry Lawson
Oil on canvas by Sir John Longstaff
(By permission, National Library of Australia)

BELOW:
Louisa Lawson, Henry's mother
Louisa was always interested in politics; she encouraged Henry in his writing and steered him towards republicanism.
(State Library of New South Wales Collection)

The bard of the bush

HENRY LAWSON COULD AT TIMES BE A RATHER curmudgeonly fellow; and the cause of his bitterness was more often than not found at the bottom of a bottle. Whereas Lawson's professional sparring partner, A.B. 'Banjo' Paterson, was born into comfortable station life, Henry grew up on the New South Wales goldfields around Gulgong, a rough-and-ready place of bark huts, mud floors, and cracking shingles — and rip-roaring, hard-bitten miners from all over the world. His barefoot school days were a stark contrast to the Sydney Grammar experience enjoyed by Paterson. Like so many others who were born working class, the hard climb up the ladder to success often brought resentment; Lawson sought refuge in the socialist ideals of his mother and her comrades, and he sought solace for his own disappointment in drink.

Lawson's father, Niels Larsen, had been the quartermaster of a Norwegian ship before he had run 'off to the diggings'. In Gulgong Larsen visited a store for supplies and fell for Louisa, the storekeeper's daughter. Niels was not to make a successful go of anything in life, failing at gold mining, then at farming, and having no success as a builder either. The marriage was a mistake, and Niels spent most of his time away from Louisa and their growing number of offspring.

After the couple's second son was born the family moved into Gulgong and, at Louisa's insistence, the family name changed to Lawson, and Niels to Peter. A third son, also named Peter, was born in

A family affair

Henry Lawson was born in 1867, the son of a dirt-poor Norwegian migrant and Australian-born Louisa. When the couple's mismatched union failed in 1883, Louisa moved to Sydney, where she was joined soon after by her sixteen-year-old son Henry.

Louisa Lawson was intensely interested in matters politic. In particular she was motivated by the growing movement for women's suffrage, which sought an equal place for all women in colonial society, and she became a voice for the growing push for an Australian republic prior to Federation.

She established herself as publisher of the radical weekly paper the *Republic,* and *Dawn*, the monthly journal written especially for women. Louisa was the first to publish Henry, and was the first to release a collection of his work when she published his *Short Stories in Verse and Prose* in 1894.

Louisa Lawson placed herself in the maelstrom of the argument over women's rights that was swirling right across the globe. *Dawn* was prepared and printed entirely by women, with articles on divorce reform, suffrage, fashion, women's affairs, prose and poetry. Not surprisingly, she angered the all-male New South Wales Typographical Association, who called for a boycott of her magazine.

ABOVE:
Louisa Lawson and her son Charles William in front of their bark hut, Gulgong

Quarter-plate glass photonegative, photographed by the American & Australian Photographic Company, c. 1875

(State Library of New South Wales Collection)

Gulgong, and their father took to the bush. This time he stayed away for over three years, although he would often pass by the small post office and store, which Louisa now ran — usually on the other side of the road.

Louisa Lawson was Australian-born and she had great plans for her first-born son Henry. She was anxious for all of her children to receive a standard education and petitioned the government to provide a school in the goldmining town. Her estranged husband was given the job of building the school, and a

THIS PAGE & OPPOSITE:
Gulgong and Hill End
Photographs by Charles Bayliss, c. 1872

German-born goldminer Bernard Otto Holtermann made his fortune when a mass of gold-encrusted quartz was discovered in his 'Star of Hope' mine in 1872. He celebrated his success by appointing photographer Charles Bayliss of the American & Australian Photographic Company to record the buildings and streetscapes of the rough-and-ready goldmining towns.

These photographs from the early 1870s were used on the $10 note that bore the portrait of Henry Lawson.

LEFT:
M. T. B. Scurragh's 'Shampooing and Hairdressing Saloon', Gulgong

(Holtermann Collection, Mitchell Library, State Library of New South Wales)

poem written by Henry many years later gives an impression of his father's expertise, or lack of it:

> It was built of bark and poles, and the
> roof was full of holes,
> Where each leak in rainy weather made
> a pool:
> And the walls were mainly cracks,
> lined with calico and sack,
> There was little need for windows in that
> school.

Henry gained his love of books and literature at his mother's knee. At age thirteen, his school years were over, but he had already read the works of the greatest storytellers of the time — Charles Dickens, Edgar Allen Poe and the hugely popular authors of the first Australian serialised novels, Rolf Boldrewood and Marcus Clarke.

When one of the twins born to Louisa and Peter died, Louisa wrote a poem that was published in the Mudgee newspaper. Henry was so excited to see his mother's words in print that he rushed to his own room and wrote one of his own, which he called 'William the Conqueror'.

While his mother may have been impressed by this, the first literary effort of her eldest boy, his father said that 'it was a waste of time' and threw it in the fire.

It was around this time that Henry fell ill and lost part of his hearing. He subsequently retreated into himself, becoming aloof, living in his imagination and apart from the world. This disability was to grow gradually worse over the years, and towards the end of his days he was completely deaf.

His parents' marriage broke down completely when Henry was sixteen, and Louisa moved down to Granville near Sydney. While he stayed working on the railways with his father for a while, Henry eventually joined his mother there, and it was through her influence and encouragement that he began writing in earnest, while taking factory jobs and attending night school. He desperately wanted to go to university, and night school was the only way he could make up the years of education he had lost working on the railways and in the bush.

He had written a poem called 'The Wreck of the Derry Castle', about the wreck of a ship, and made his first attempt at getting it published. He walked down to the *Bulletin* office in Sydney but was too afraid to ask to see the editor. Hanging around on the stairs, he thrust the poem into the hands of a cleaning lady, begging her to take it to Mr Archibald, the proprietor. After Henry had left, the woman took it upstairs to J. F. Archibald, who, having read

BELOW, LEFT:
Mr Donald's Circulating Library
(Holtermann Collection. State Library of New South Wales)

BELOW, RIGHT:
Thompson & McGregor's 'Times Bakery', Herbert Street, Gulgong
(Holtermann Collection. State Library of New South Wales)

RIGHT:
J. F. Archibald and Henry Lawson, Sydney, 1918
Archibald was the publisher of the *Bulletin* who first published Lawson's poems in 1887.
(Ferguson Collection, National Library of Australia)

Lawson's unedited work, passed it over to editor Fred Broomfield, who said he could fix it up and prepare it for publication.

Lawson had his poems, 'Song of the Republic' and 'The Wreck of the Derry Castle' published in the *Bulletin* in 1887. Other nationalistic verse, 'Sons of the South', 'The Hymn of the Socialists', 'Flag of the Southern Cross' and 'Distant Drum' were also published in 1887; bringing his republican views to a society eager for a truly independent Australia.

Professor J. Le Gay Brereton of Sydney University read 'Derry Castle' in the *Bulletin* on 24 December 1887, and was impressed by the work of this new writer. He wrote to Lawson and invited him to the university; this was to be the first meeting in what became a lifelong friendship. Le Gay Brereton was surprised when a mere slip of a lad entered his office. He was shocked that one so young had been able to write a work with such powers of observation: 'he felt the poet had the gift of making others see what the poet had seen'.[1] Brereton said that Henry's description of people drowning had given him nightmares.

The meeting at the university must have seemed like a dream come true, but Lawson was never to gain entry into that hallowed place of learning; he had tried three times to matriculate and failed. It seemed that the academic life was not for this boy from the bush; he was from the school of hard knocks, and his lessons were to be learnt in the roofless classroom of the broad and star-lit skies and the university of the open road.

Henry went up to Newcastle to work as a clerk, but the desk-bound life was not for him; he hated it. He left his job and returned to Sydney, where he began the almost hopeless task of finding himself another job. In the early

Selected verses from 'Faces in the Street', 1888

They lie, the men who tell us, for reasons of their own,
That want is here a stranger, and that misery's unknown;
For where the nearest suburb and the city proper meet
My window-sill is level with the faces in the street —
        Drifting past, drifting past,
        To the beat of weary feet —
While I sorrow for those owners of the faces in the street.

And so it must be while the world goes rolling round its course,
The warning pen shall write in vain, the warning voice grow hoarse,
For not until a city feels Red Revolution's feet
Shall its sad people miss awhile the terrors of the street —
        The dreadful everlasting strife
        For scarcely clothes and meat
In that pent track of living death — the city's cruel street.

mornings he loitered around the *Sydney Morning Herald* building waiting for the 'Situations Vacant' listings to be posted.

It was there that he saw the unemployed and down at heel — victims of the collapse of the economy that had followed the boom years of the rush to gold. These same people were to become the inspiration for his paean to the dispossessed worker, 'Faces in the Street', written years later.

Louisa sent Henry down to Melbourne for treatment for his advancing deafness, but nothing could be done for him. He stayed there for a time, but was again so unsuccessful at the job he had taken — retouching photographs in a photographer's studio — that he packed that in and headed back to New South Wales again.

He went back to work on the railways with his father, where the reticent young lad soon fell in with a group of workers who became his first real mates. These men of the bush showed Lawson both the hard realities and delights of life under the stars. They also taught him how to drink. His father died while Henry was working with him on the railways. His time toiling alongside these rough working men had a great impact on his later writings; his first published work of prose was called 'His Father's Mates'.

The radicals

With some money left to her after her husband died, Louisa bought a printing press, which she installed in a room in her cottage at Granville. Always interested in the world of ideas, and caught up in the nascent spirit of radical republicanism that was abroad among the free thinkers in pre-Federation Australia, Louisa Lawson established her own journals; first, the political weekly the *Republican* in 1887, and, *Dawn*, a monthly journal for women published from 1890–1905.

In the boarding house that Louisa ran in Sydney Henry met the prominent figures of the Australian socialist movement. Such figures left an indelible mark on the spirit of the young man and he was to envision his Australia for ever after through his desire for a free republic.

By this time Lawson was coming into contact with other writers; notable among them was Mary Cameron, a young woman who

LEFT:
Bust of Henry Lawson
Tasmanian blackwood carving by Otto Bettmann, c. 1900
(National Library of Australia Collection)

shared his egalitarian, socialist and republican views. Later known as Mary Gilmore, this talented young schoolteacher from the southern New South Wales town of Goulburn helped him develop his writing technique.

Henry soon fell for the educated Mary Cameron — she seemed to have all that he thought he was missing — and he eventually asked for her hand. Louisa Lawson stood between Henry and Mary; she sent him away to the Western Australian goldfields, ostensibly to earn enough money to be able to marry. While Henry was away Louisa drove a wedge between the young writers, not passing on the letters Henry sent to Mary. When he returned, Mary had already gone with William Lane, and the Free Australia Movement, to the South American Republic of Paraguay.

Like so many other republican Australians Lawson was derisive of the English royals while at the same time taking a swipe at those who sought their favour and approval. They were critical of Sir Henry Parkes, who would not openly confirm his republicanism, preferring to grovel before the Crown as trinkets, knighthoods and titles were distributed with abandon across the colonies at the time of Queen Victoria's Jubilee.

Lawson openly mocked Queen Victoria, the 'widow of Windsor', and wrote a comic poem making fun of the Prince of Wales, wondering 'how he'd fit the throne where sits his royal mummy'.[2] In his 'A Birthday Ode', penned to celebrate the Jubilee year, he described Victoria as 'that cold and selfish woman whom the English call "The Queen"… that dull and brainless woman … The dull, yet gilded dummy …'[3]

On the Bulletin *track*

The *Bulletin* gave Lawson and another writer, Jim Grahame, £5 each and a train ticket to travel to Bourke in the far west of New South Wales, and packed them off to report on the seemingly endless drought of 1892-3. The two young writers picked up jobs as they went — as house painters and as shearing-shed rouseabouts — and from this trip, which eventually took them as far as Queensland, Henry returned with a large amount of material. He soon crafted his experiences into expressive prose and verse; while some of these early stories were published in the *Worker*, most appeared in his later published collections.

Henry had seen the reality of bush life at first hand; the impact of the harsh environment on the lives of the outback dwellers, and the language of the bush, became grist to his mill. With his themes of 'a fair go for all' and

Song of the Republic

Lawson's republican feelings were evident in much of his work. His sympathy with the ordinary person was the hallmark of his stories, his antipathy to 'royalty' a sneer.

In the 1890s he wrote that 'England's red flag' would bring 'hatred and worse with it', that England had 'but a good-natured contempt for [Australians]'. He added that the only flag that should be flying over Australia should be the flag that called the Ballarat diggers of 1854 to protest: 'that stubborn old rag/the rebel flag, the bonny bright flag of the Southern Cross'.

Sons of the South, awake! arise!
Sons of the South, and do.
Banish from under your bonny skies
Those old-world errors and wrongs and lies
Making a hell of Paradise
That belongs to your sons and you.

Sons of the South, make choice between
Sons of the South, choose true,
The Land of Morn and the Land of E'en,
The old dead Tree and the Young tree Green,
The land that belongs to the Lord and the
Queen, And the land that belongs to you.

— *Song of the Republic, 1887*

the strong bond of mateship, his work touched a nerve in all Australians.

It was the common touch, his typically Australian, wry good humour and heartfelt sympathy for the plight of his fellow man, that assured him a welcome place in the heart of his ordinary readers. Lawson's Australia was ever the domain of the dirt-poor farmer, the common man and the irreverent larrikin.

In 1895 Lawson fell in love with Bertha Bredt, the eighteen-year-old stepdaughter of the proprietor of a radical bookshop in Castlereagh Street in Sydney. He succeeded in winning her hand, and against all advice and with only £10 borrowed from another writer in his pocket, Lawson married Bertha on 15 April 1896. George Robertson, of Angus and Robertson, publisher of Henry's first book *In the Days When the World Was Wide*, advised Bertha that 'He's a genius, and you know what geniuses are — they can never make a woman happy'.[4]

Robertson gave Lawson £50 as an advance on royalties for this first book; Lawson had never seen so much money at one time and decided then and there to take his bride away to Western Australia to join the last rush for gold in the 1890s. But Henry never went in search of gold; instead they lived in a tent in Perth, where he wrote some articles for the *Western Mail* and sent poems back to the *Bulletin*. As he seemed to be spending too much of his time propping up the bar with the local newspapermen, Bertha thought that it was time they headed back to Sydney. It was at this time that Lawson's second book, *Where the Billy Boils*, was published.

Back in Sydney it was not long before Lawson was back to his old ways, mixing with his old comrades the radical socialists, living the bohemian life and drinking his royalties away.

Bertha convinced J. F. Archibald to help the couple get away from this distracting company, and he secured for them a berth on a ship bound for New Zealand, and was able to assist Bertha in obtaining a teaching position in country school. Henry, now freed from the distractions of Sydney, produced some of his finest work, including 'Joe Wilson and His Mates' and 'Verses Popular and Humorous'; he stayed off the grog for two years.

In a curious denial of his republican leanings, Lawson sought the assistance of the

RIGHT:
The young Henry Lawson

At twenty years old the almost untutored young writer from the goldfields was a regular contributor to the bushman's bible, 'The Bully'.

(National Library of Australia Collection)

BELOW:
Henry Lawson
Cartoon by David Low, c.1920
(National Library of Australia Collection)

Governor of New South Wales, Lord Beauchamp, when he wanted to travel to England in 1901; he was convinced he would have a greater success with his writing there. He did sail away and lived in the land of the 'dull and gilded dummy'.

Although he had long protested against the monarchy, Lawson was transfixed by those great days of Empire at the turn of the century. He said that he had 'gone to England prejudiced against the English, and with great Republican ideas',[5] but the longer he stayed, the greater was his admiration for them.

The Lawsons were desperately poor in England and it was only with an advance on royalties from the upcoming publication in England of a retitled edition of *Children of the Bush* that Bertha and the children were able to return home. Henry followed them on the next boat bound for Australia.

Under the pressure of the death of a child, constant poverty and Henry's alcoholism, the marriage could not survive. When the family's furniture was taken in lieu of unpaid rent, it was the last straw.

After the break-up Henry remained close to his three children, and when his daughter Bertha graduated from Sydney University with a Bachelor of Arts he was filled with pride. Such an honour had always been denied him and he sent to the newspaper a crumpled photograph of her that he carried with him, hoping to see it in print; he wanted to show Sydney society that at last there was one educated Lawson of whom Louisa would be proud.

Lawson drifted in and out of various positions that his supporters made available to him, but he was no longer tied to the needs of his family. Although still without much in his pockets, he was at last a true freelance writer bound to no desk. As a result of his addiction to alcohol, he drifted in and out of hospital. After an excessive bout of boozing he was admitted to hospital in 1921. His friends decided that he needed their help to survive;

The Star of Australia

We boast no more of our bloodless flag that
  rose from nation's slime;
Better a shred of a deep-dyed rag from the
  storms of a golden time.
From grander clouds in our peaceful skies
  than ever were before
I tell you the Star of the South shall rise—
  in the lurid clouds of war.
— *The Star of Australia (excerpt), 1895*

BELOW:
Henry Lawson's funeral procession, Sydney, September 1922
(State Library of Victoria Collection)

they planned a recovery excursion to Lord Howe Island to help him dry out, but within hours of his release from hospital, he was back on the booze again.

Reflecting on his weakness and the family he had loved but left behind, Lawson wrote:

They shall feel it, they shall know it,
Who, when from the sky of azure that
dread thunderbolt was hurled,
Made me drunkard who was sober,
Made me devil who was poet,
Made the girl-wife and boy-husband man
and woman of the world.

Lawson died on 2 September 1922. He was honoured with a state funeral. Thousands lined the footpaths of Sydney to watch the final journey of the much-loved 'bard of the bush', Henry Lawson; the hearse drove his casket past those 'faces in the street' that he had once immortalised. He was buried at Waverley; his tombstone rests on a slight rise overlooking the South Pacific Ocean.

Henry Lawson was born poor and died poor, but the 'bard of the bush' left a rich treasury of the written word. His vision laid the very foundations of the Australian character that endured right through until the end of the twentieth century.

Lawson's Australia still exists today; the bush is little changed — gum trees still shed their bark, and cockatoos and kookaburras screech and squawk in their lofty branches, horses are still saddled in their dusty yards and stockmen still sit in their sweat, stockwhips held at the ready in a sunburnt grip. Henry Lawson conjured up the image of his age and all Australia was crafted by his pen.

More than any other writer of his time, Henry Lawson managed to touch the hearts of the ordinary man and woman in the street with his irreverence towards 'the nobs' and 'the royals', and his lifelong desire for an Australian republic governed by Australians for the benefit of all.

David Unaipon

1872 – 1967

Storyteller of the Dreamtime

David Unaipon is featured on the face of the $50 polymer note, first issued in 1995.

OF ALL PEOPLE REPRESENTED ON AUSTRALIA'S DECIMAL banknotes David (Ngunaitponi) Unaipon is the only Indigenous Australian. Unaipon was born at Raukkan Mission (Point McLeay), on the Lower Murray River in South Australia, on 28 September 1872. His father, James Ngunaitponi, was a Ngarrindjeri man, and was the first Indigenous convert to the evangelistic ministry of the Congregational Church. His mother, Nymbulda, and his father both spoke the Yarraldi native tongue.

David Unaipon was born at the confluence of two worlds, at a time when well-meaning missionaries sought to bring the Australian natives to Christ and often paid little heed to time-honoured ceremony, native tongue or religious customs. To some white men, the native was at best a 'noble savage' who needed salvation through Christ, to others he was part of a lost culture that could best benefit by assimilation into white society. There were even some who thought that breeding out the dying race was the only means of saving white society from the embarrassment its own treatment of Indigenous Australians caused.

The South Australian Congregational Church established the mission to the Lower Murray Aboriginal tribes at Point McLeay on Lake Alexandrina in 1858, when the influential missionary George Taplin began his work with the local Aboriginal people. The Aborigines Friends' Association, based in South Australia, developed a long

OPPOSITE:

David (Ngunaitponi) Unaipon

Aboriginal author, inventor and spokesman David Unaipon was a Ngarrindjeri man. He married a Tangani woman, Katherine Carter Sumner (Nymbulda), in 1902. The couple had one son.

First schooled on Raukkan Mission at Point McLeay, and later in Adelaide at the home of C. B. Young, a prominent supporter of the Aborigines Friends' Association, David Unaipon was a man caught between two cultures and smart enough to make the best of both.

He became the first Indigenous Australian author ever to have his works published by the 'European' press, although for the best part of half a century he received no recognition for this work.

(Photograph courtesy of the State Library of South Australia, SLSA: B7326. By permission, Mrs Alma Katinyeri, Tailem Bend)

RIGHT:

Point McLeay (Raukkan) Mission Station

In 1858 the mission station was established at Lake Alexandrina on the lower Murray River where it runs into the Coorong.

David Unaipon's father was the first Indigenous Australian convert to the Congregational Church and he became the first native missionary. Just like his father and mother, who were both educated at the mission, it soon became apparent that in young David there was a bright mind, with an aptitude for learning that set him apart from others.

(Photograph courtesy of the State Library of South Australia, SLSA: B9777. By permission, Raukkan Community Council)

association with the mission; after David Unaipon had spent several years at the mission school he was taken to Adelaide, aged thirteen, to work for C. B. Young and his family, who were also prominent members of the Association.

As a boy, Unaipon demonstrated a thirst for knowledge that set him apart from others. It was in Young's home that he was given an eclectic, classical education; he took an avid interest in philosophy, science and music in particular. He made the most of the many opportunities offered to him; an avaricious reader, he soon became obsessed with scientific journals, memorising descriptions of inventions and all kinds of engineering discoveries. He spent hours in the Museum of South Australia, where he was able to study the relics of his own culture and, as an intelligent young man straddling two worlds, was able to see both the contrasts and the similarities between the cultures he studied.

Unaipon was greatly influenced by the time he spent in Adelaide, yet he always viewed the world through Indigenous eyes. His Aboriginal heritage always influenced the work he created in all aspects, whether scientific, literary or cultural.

Although he had no real understanding of anything other than rudimentary arithmetic, Unaipon soon began to create his own inventions and devised all kinds of solutions to engineering problems. He patented his designs for a better shearer's mechanical handpiece in 1909, and also produced designs for a centrifugal motor, a multi-radial wheel and a mechanical propulsion device. He even predicted the development of the helicopter, as early as 1914, using the principle of the boomerang as the basic concept for his design. Unfortunately for Unaipon, and for Australia, he was never able to secure the

ABOVE:

Reverend George Taplin, c.1870

(Photograph courtesy of the State Library of South Australia, SLSA: PRG 1258/2/1955.)

RIGHT:

Aborigines mourn the passing of Reverend George Taplin who died in1879, c. 1880

Aborigines of the Point McLeay mission mourn the passing of Congregational minister George Taplin, who founded the Mission Station in 1858.

(Photograph courtesy of the State Library of South Australia, SLSA: B8414. By permission, Raukkan Community Council)

much-needed financial backing that would have enabled him to pursue these ideas.

Although he became recognised for some of his innovative designs — even dubbed 'Australia's Leonardo' in his time — it was as a representative of Indigenous people that Unaipon first came to public notice. He was often called upon to represent the Aboriginal people in various royal commissions and inquiries into issues of Aboriginal welfare.

Unaipon assisted the Bleakley inquiry into Aboriginal welfare in 1928–29, and in 1934 recommended that the Commonwealth assume control over Aboriginal affairs, taking responsibility away from the states, and an independent board be established to replace the office of chief protector of Aborigines.

Unaipon was employed by the Aborigines Friends' Association and travelled widely throughout south-eastern Australia lecturing and preaching on the need for 'sympathetic co-operation' between European and Indigenous Australians. He promoted equal rights for both.

ABOVE:
Point McLeay, c. 1879

(Photograph courtesy of the State Library of South Australia, SLSA: B 5463. By permission, Raukkan Community Council)

LEFT:
Aboriginal residents of the mission station pose in front of one of the thatched-roof accommodation buildings, c. 1885

(Photograph courtesy of the State Library of South Australia, SLSA: PRG 1258/2/1989. By permission, Raukkan Community Council)

RIGHT:
Point McLeay Mission greeting card, c.1900

(Photograph courtesy of the State Library of South Australia, SLSA: PRG 1258/2/2002. By permission, Raukkan Community Council)

As he toured throughout the south-eastern states Unaipon also lectured on Aboriginal legends and customs, and attempted to develop a greater spirit of understanding between the cultures. He began to collect the stories of Aboriginal culture, and soon began to commit them to paper, with the intention of seeking their publication in a single volume. His first published work was an article titled 'Aboriginals: Their Traditions and Customs', published in the Sydney *Daily Telegraph* on 2 August 1924. 'The Story of the Mungingee' was published in *Home* magazine in February the following year, and a slim, fifteen-page booklet titled 'Native Legends' was published in 1929.

Unaipon began working on a large collection of stories which he was under contract to produce for publisher Angus and Robertson Ltd, but for one reason or another, it was not published in Australia as had been intended. Instead, *Myths and Legends of the Australian Aboriginals* was first published in London in 1930, but, curiously, David Unaipon was not noted as the author of the work.

Edinburgh-trained medical officer, coroner and amateur anthropologist William Ramsay Smith, a man who had been dismissed from the British Medical Association for his alleged mishandling of Indigenous human remains, was credited as the author of this volume produced by English publisher George G. Harrap. Ramsay Smith had met the English publisher in Adelaide when Harrap was collecting stories for a series of works on tribal myths and legends from around the world. Quite the opportunist, Ramsay Smith began a correspondence with George Robertson in

Voice of the Great Spirit

In Unaipon's manuscript for the book *Myths and Legends of the Australian Aboriginals*, the story titled 'The Voice of the Great Spirit' begins:

> It is interesting to learn how all races of men have wrestled with the problem of good and evil. The Australian Aborigines have a greater and deeper sense of morality and religion than is generally known: this is one of the stories that is handed down from generation to generation by my people.

It was said that Unaipon wrote in a style reminiscent of John Milton, whose verse he had memorised.

Aware of the importance of his people offering their traditional stories for appreciation and understanding in the wider world, Unaipon wrote: 'As a full-blooded member of my race I think I may claim to be the first — but I hope, not the last — to produce an enduring record of our customs, beliefs and imaginings.'

Sydney, hoping to get his hands on some of the stories already published, and was advised of the intended publication of Unaipon's writings, under the author's own name.

Ramsay Smith schemed to darken Unaipon's reputation, suggesting him to be a 'typically' wayward fellow who could not be relied upon to meet the demands of the Sydney publisher, until, in the end, Angus and Robertson offered the copyright to Ramsay Smith.

Several volumes were printed over the years, starting with the Harrap edition in 1930. American hardbacks, mass-market paperback facsimile editions, reprints, and even a beautifully illustrated Japanese edition of six of the stories, were all published without ever giving credit to the original author. It was not until much later that this aberration was set to rights.

Ramsay Smith died in 1937 and the copyright in his version lapsed in 1962. David Unaipon died in 1967, his copyright also lapsing twenty-five years later, in 1992. The intellectual and moral rights to this important collection of Aboriginal legends have reverted to the David Unaipon Estate, of which his extended family is custodian. Almost seventy-five years since the work's first publication, the rights are at last back in the hands of his own people, the Ngarrindjeri, where it began.

The handwritten 80,000-word manuscript 'Myths and Legends of the Australian Aboriginals' is held today in the collection of the Mitchell Library in New South Wales. For his efforts, Unaipon was paid two guineas for every thousand words, a standard fee at the time of his writing.

Although David Unaipon never earned any recognition for this work published during his lifetime, he was awarded a Coronation Medal in 1953. In 1985, eighteen years after his death on 7 February 1967, he was awarded the Fellowship of Australian Writers' Patricia Weickhardt Award for Aboriginal writers.

David Unaipon is buried in the cemetery at Point McLeay, overlooking the Murray River where it runs into the Coorong.

LEFT:

Portrait of David Unaipon

This photograph was intended for reproduction on the frontispiece to Unaipon's book, *Myths and Legends of the Australian Aboriginals*; it was never published by Angus and Robertson, who had commissioned the work and had paid the author two guineas for every thousand of his 80,000 handwritten words.

(Mitchell Library, State Library of New South Wales Collection)

Reverend John Flynn

1880–1951

Reverend John Flynn is featured on the obverse of the $20 polymer note, first issued in 1994.

'We shall cast our mantle of safety over the inland'

— *The Flying Doctor Service*

JOHN FLYNN WAS BORN IN 1880 IN THE TINY CENTRAL Victorian goldfields town of Moliagul. The area is known for its red-gravelled earth, stripped by mining of its precious soils, and its gnarled, black-trunked, iron-bark trees.

Moliagul does have one other claim to fame: it was there that on 5 February 1869 John Deason and Richard Oates, two miners from the Island of Tresco, pulled from the earth the largest gold nugget ever found in the world. They named it the 'Welcome Stranger'. Although this discovery took place a decade before John Flynn was born, the event left its mark on the district and all who lived there.

Today, there are two monuments in Moliagul: one to the discovery of the richest nugget ever found, the other to honour the birthplace of the man whose selfless humanity enriched the entire nation.

After he finished his secondary schooling in 1898, John Flynn spent four years as a teacher with the Victorian Education Department, until he felt called to a different kind of service. In 1902 he decided to begin training to become a Presbyterian minister and, at first, financed his studies working at Church Home Missionary centres around Victoria. In 1907 he began a four-year course in theology at Ormond College, at the University of Melbourne, graduating in 1910.

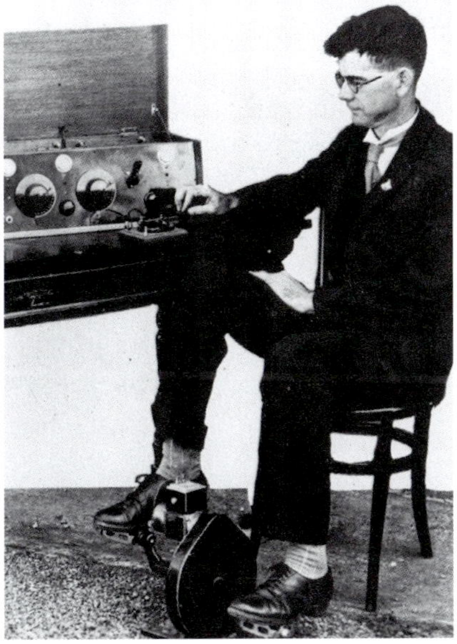

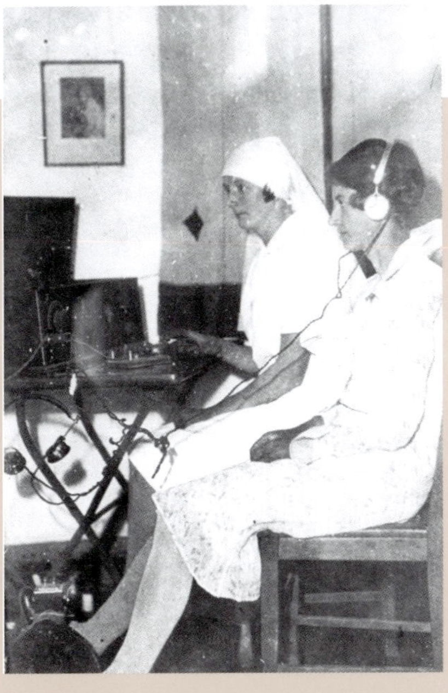

Above Left:

Alfred Traeger at the pedal wireless

The pedal radio was a godsend to the isolated homesteaders, making instantaneous communication across the vast outback possible for the first time.

Left:

Australian Inland Mission nurses using pedal wireless

Opposite:

John Flynn, aged 37

In 1911 Reverend John Flynn was appointed to Beltana Mission in South Australia's far north. The following year he was made the first superintendent of the newly formed Australian Inland Mission, referred to as the 'bush department' of the Presbyterian Church.

It was his work on the mission that inspired him to find a better way to provide medical assistance to the settlers in the outback in times of emergency and distress.

(All photographs, John Blakeman Collection, Northern Territory Library)

Flynn had already begun to seek ways of offering assistance to the people of the outback and in 1910 published *The Bushman's Companion*, a collection of articles with advice and instruction on matters medical, spiritual, domestic and educational. Around the same time, C. W. E. Bean published his *On the Wool Track*, an account of the hard times in the bush and the development of an individual Australian character forged in the outback. Mary Grant Bruce also published her *Little Bush Maid* in that same year. This spate of publishing reflected young Australia's desire to tell its own stories in its own voice, and in a language that spoke to the heart of its own experience. This simple, honest approach characterised Flynn's vision for an appropriate service for all living in the outback.

In 1911 John Flynn began his work with the Presbyterian Church in South Australia, when he was ordained as a minister and appointed to the Smith of Dunesk Mission at Beltana in the state's north-west. It was in this tiny remote community that Flynn saw the rigours of outback life for himself. This was no longer the romantic, poetic vision of Lawson or Paterson that he had so enjoyed reading to his pupils from his schoolmaster's desk; this was not Clancy's 'sunlit plains' — it was more like 'the land that time forgot'. The isolation made the living hard, and survival in times of emergency even harder.

ABOVE:
Arrival of supplies, Moolawatana, South Australia, c. 1933

When John Flynn was first appointed to the Smith of Dunesk Mission in South Australia's north-west, no motor vehicle had ever crossed the country.

Residents of the outback relied on camel or mule trains to bring them supplies and to connect them with others in their region. The advent of the pedal radio, combined with the aerial medical service, changed that forever.

(National Library of Australia Collection)

The pedal wireless

Apart from the vision of John Flynn, the most important contribution to the improvement of life in the outback came from electronics enthusiast Alfred Traeger. Traeger was born in Dimboola, in Victoria's vast wheat and sheep-grazing district, in the north-west of the state. He grew up accustomed to the long distances travelled and the isolation endured by settlers in the far-flung corners of the states.

Radio transmission was changing communication across Australia and Traeger constructed his own receiver when he was only twelve years old. He had created a people-powered radio transmitter before he joined with Flynn's mission, but it was not the most efficient machine for its eventual application. Traeger's early machine required the efforts of two people to operate it: one to turn the generating handle and the other to operate the Morse-code key.

When this was applied to Flynn's 'doctors of the airways', it was likely that in the case of an emergency only one person would be able to work the machine while the other lay injured or incapacitated. Traeger had a brainwave and adapted bicycle technology to power his electrical device. The pedal radio only required the foot-power of one person, who could tap out a message at the same time. It was not long before a keyboard was added

LEFT:
Alf Traeger at the pedal wireless
(DD Smith Collection, Northern Territory Library)

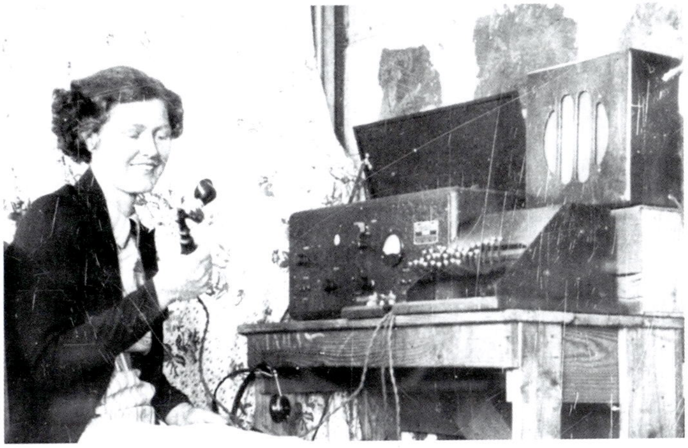

BELOW, LEFT:
Pedal wireless operator at work, 1936
Miss Jessie Chalmers of MacDonald Downs Station operates a wireless supplied by the flying doctor. The table was made by John Flynn from the case in which Alfred Traeger had sent the set from Adelaide.
(John Blakeman Collection, Northern Territory Library)

Flynn soon learned that life in the outback meant that even the simplest of injuries or ailments could bring death, that it could take weeks by camel to bring a sick stockman or a pregnant woman to the mission hospital; for many, that journey could well prove to be their last. He searched for a way to secure a better, safer future for his 'flock'.

The Presbyterian Church commissioned Flynn to report on the needs, both physical and spiritual, of those living on remote stations. After presenting his findings to the church in 1912, he was appointed as superintendent of a new ministry to the outback: the Australian Inland Mission (AIM). This mission was to minister to remote areas at a time when supplies and communications between homesteads and communities still relied on camel trains, mules and horse-drawn coaches. Flynn recruited what were to become known as 'patrol padres' or 'boundary riders', ministers who travelled on horseback or camel, and he began to see the establishment of a network of nursing homes across the outback.

Up until the 1920s no one had ever driven a car across the outback, but after World War I a few intrepid adventurers made the first four-wheeled excursions into the hot and dusty interior, making their way across the centre from north to south. Flynn was presented with an old motor vehicle, which he had fitted out like an ambulance, and he carried patients from their homesteads into hospital care.

to the transmitter, to convert keystrokes to the appropriate Morse command, relieving the untrained operator of any need to understand Morse. This made the pedal wireless accessible to almost anybody. It was the application of the wireless, combined with the aerial medical service, that revolutionised communication in the outback.

The first 50-watt transmitter was set up in the Presbyterian Church at Cloncurry in north-western Queensland, and pedal wireless sets were distributed to stations within transmission range. By the mid-1930s voice communication was available and the sets were adapted so that they could also be powered by car batteries.

The wireless sets were soon being used for all sorts of other applications. One of the most important was the establishment of the 'School of the Air', which began transmission on 8 June 1951; its first broadcast was from the Flying Doctor Service base at Alice Springs. Although now known officially as the 'Distance Education Service', the school still broadcasts under the sobriquet 'School of the Air'.

It was only after the end of World War I that aircraft were seen as a possible means of transport, or at least for supply and quick communication between settled areas and the outback. But the adoption of aircraft as the primary means of taking medical services to patients in remote areas was still a long way behind the introduction of the automobile.

Flyn had been impressed by reports from the European war which told of the way that aircraft had been used to transport wounded from the battleground to field hospitals. He had been corresponding with young Victorian medical student Lieutenant Clifford Peel, who was interested in Flynn's work in the outback. Peel had joined the Australian Air Force and was on his way to France when he wrote to Flynn in November 1917. Peel suggested that aircraft could be Flynn's answer to bringing medicine to the people in remote areas and for transporting those in dire need into nursing homes. Peel shared with Flynn his vision of an 'airborne doctor', telling Flynn that he could see: '... a missionary doctor administer-

ABOVE:

The flying doctor refuels at an outback station, c. 1951

(Mayse Young Collection, Northern Territory Library)

LEFT:

(From left): Flynn, 'Skipper' Partridge and 'Old Man' Chalmers erect a radio mast at MacDonald Downs Station in 1936

Chalmers had trekked overland from Queensland, with his family and a flock of sheep, to take up MacDonald Downs in 1924.

Building a network across the red centre was hard work, and Flynn never shied away from putting his shoulder to the wheel, especially if it meant helping out his 'human flock'.

(John Blakeman Collection, Northern Territory Library)

ing to the needs of the men and women scattered between Wyndham and Cloncurry, Darwin and Maree'.

Peel advised Flynn on the costs of such a service, the flying capacities of the various machines available and the support facilities needed to keep it all running. Flynn was so excited by this idea that he published the concept in the church's magazine, the *Inlander,* in 1917, only months before Peel was shot out of the French skies while flying over German lines just before the end of World War I.

It had been the sad case of Western Australian stockman Jimmy Darcy that convinced Flynn he must find a way to help those in need of urgent medical attention. Jimmy Darcy was hurt in a fall in August 1917. He was taken by friends to Halls Creek, thirty miles away from where he had been found lying badly injured; this part of the journey took twelve hours.

Only the postmaster knew any first aid and he concluded that Jimmy Darcy needed urgent medical attention. He tried to make contact with the only two doctors in the Kimberley Region at Wyndham and Derby, but to no avail. He then telegraphed his old first aid instructor, 12,000 miles away in Perth. Following the instructions tapped out to him by Morse code, the postmaster subjected poor Jimmy Darcy to two painful and difficult operations conducted with a penknife.

Dr Holland from Perth then set out for Halls Creek, making the ten-day journey first by cattle boat,T-model Ford, then by horse-drawn sulky, making the last few miles on foot. When he finally arrived Holland discovered that although the operations had been successful, Darcy had died the day before of malaria and an abscessed appendix.

This sad story reached the newspapers in the capital cities and even shouldered news of the war from the front page. It showed city dwellers and country folk alike the war at home that needed to be fought—the war against isolation, injury and disease.

Flynn took up Peel's vision and melded it into his own; it was another decade before he was able to send his first plane into the skies over Central Australia. He spent that decade touring the country raising funds for his grand vision of a 'flying doctor service' that would 'cast a mantle of safety over the inland'.

Among Flynn's supporters in these early days were Hugh McKay, the manufacturer of the Sunshine Harvester; W. Hudson Fysh of Qantas; and Dr George Simpson, a Melbourne doctor who had been inspired by Flynn's vision when he heard him on his fund-raising circuit years before.

The moderator

In 1939 the Very Reverend John Flynn was appointed to the position of Moderator-General of the Presbyterian Church in Australia for an initial term of three years.

While this was a great honour for the outback missionary, members of his scattered flock were afraid that they had lost their friend to the city. But Flynn was dedicated to his ministry to the people of the outback and remained superintendent of the Australian Inland Mission up until just before he died in 1951.

(John Blakeman Collection, Northern Territory Library)

Hudson Fysh was a returned World War I flying ace who had begun an air service flying out of Cloncurry, carrying passengers, mail and supplies across Queensland and the Northern Territory: the acronym Qantas (Queensland and Northern Territory Aerial Services) was to become the saviour of hundreds of isolated settlers in the years that followed.

On 15 May 1928 an aerial medical service was established, with a one-year trial operating out of Cloncurry in Queensland. The first flight was in response to a call two days later when it flew out of Cloncurry to Julia Creek. Dr Keith St Vincent Welch and pilot Arthur Affleck were dispatched to save the life of a man who had a cut throat. Fifty flights were made in that first year; 18,000 miles were flown, 225 patients were treated and at least four lives were saved.

At fifty-one years old John Flynn married Jean Baird, secretary of the Australian Inland Mission, in 1931. This no-nonsense girl, used to the ways of the outback, was a tremendous support to Flynn during the hard years of the Great Depression as he struggled to keep the service in the air. At the time the couple wed the mission had a network of ten small hospitals scattered across Central Australia; pilots and doctors were attracted to the service by the power of Flynn's vision and it continued to grow despite the economic constraints of the time.

By 1934 the aerial medical service had expanded across the entire continent, and established its first Western Australian medical centre at Port Hedland.

The church handed the service over to the administration of a new organisation called the Australian Aerial Medical Service, which expanded operations to include bases in the Centre at Alice Springs and Broken Hill; in the west at Kalgoorlie, Meekathara, Port Hedland and Wyndham; and Charters Towers and Townsville in Queensland's far north.

In honour of his great service to the people of Australia's outback, sixty-year-old John Flynn was made an Officer of the Order of the British Empire (OBE) in 1939.

The service was renamed the Flying Doctor Service in 1949, with the prefix Royal granted by the young Queen Elizabeth in 1955. Throughout this time the service relied on public donations, trusts and monies raised through public appeals for its survival. State and federal governments only supported the service with irregularly granted subsidies.

At the age of seventy, Flynn decided that it was time for him to step down. He informed the church that he would not renominate for

RIGHT:

Prime Minister Robert Menzies attends the consecration of the John Flynn Memorial Church in Alice Springs, 1955

Such was the national sorrow at the Reverend John Flynn's passing that the prime minister attended the consecration of this modern church built to honour Flynn. Menzies remarked that the Royal Flying Doctor Service had made 'the greatest single contribution to the effective settlement of the far distant back country that we have witnessed in our time'.

(Walton Collection, Northern Territory Library)

the position of superintendent of the mission, a position he had held for almost forty years.

It was not long after this that he passed away in Sydney, on 5 May 1951. Flynn was given a rare and unusual funeral service. As his ashes were laid to rest four miles from Alice Springs, the service was broadcast across the nation: 630 pedal radios, scattered across the vastness of the Central Australian outback, lay silent in tribute to the passing of the Very Reverend John Flynn.

ABOVE:
Dr George Simpson (left), who had supported Flynn from the start, Mrs Simpson and the Reverend John Flynn
(National Archives of Australia Collection)

Flynn's outback memorial

John Flynn had requested that he be laid to rest in the very heart of his beloved outback. On 23 May 1951 his ashes were interred beneath a huge boulder, in the shadow of Mt Gillan, four miles from Alice Springs. Out on the red-earthed plain beneath the towering gums, his resting place reflects his birthplace half a country away.

At a lonely crossroad in the Central Victorian goldfields stands a second monument: a propeller mounted on a simple obelisk. While it is an appropriate symbol to mark the life of this extraordinary man, it does look strangely incongruous on this quiet goldfields intersection.

(NT Government Photographer, Northern Territory Library)

Sir Douglas Mawson

1882–1958

Sir Douglas Mawson is featured on the face of the $100 paper note, first issued in 1996.

'Australia's present position in the Antarctic is due entirely to the foresight, imagination, energy and stimulation of Sir Douglas Mawson.' — *Phillip Law*

Opposite:
'The Dux'
Photograph by Frank Hurley

Mawson was feted as a hero after his epic voyage in 1911–12. Stranded alone in the snow, his body in a state of physical exhaustion, he crawled his way back to base, dragging his mineral-laden sledge behind him. The once-strapping, strongly built man, whose film-star good looks were the stuff that heroes were made of, was reduced to an unrecognisable skeleton. When the first rescuer who rushed to his aid brushed the ice from Mawson's face he cried out: 'My God! Which one are you?'

Mawson was known affectionately as 'The Dux' by his men on the first all-Australian polar expedition of 1911–14.

(Australian Antarctic Division Archive, photo Frank Hurley, 1931. Cat. No. 722C1)

When Robert and Margaret Mawson left their home in England in 1884 to migrate to the colonies, they had no idea that the younger of the two small boys they carried with them would add to the British Empire, as it then was, and to the future Commonwealth of Australia, a land mass a hundred times larger than all of Great Britain and almost as large as continental Australia itself, nor that he would be honoured as a knight of the realm for his efforts.

Douglas, the second son of Robert and Margaret Mawson, was born in Yorkshire on 5 May 1882. Upon their arrival in Sydney the family settled into Rooty Hill, where Douglas began his schooling. He later went to the renowned Fort Street Model School in Sydney and he proved to be an excellent pupil. He gained a place studying mining engineering at the University of Sydney and graduated in 1902.

Douglas Mawson's first taste of scientific exploration came the following year, when he joined an expedition to the New Hebrides that

Right:
King George Land, 50 miles from the south magnetic pole
(National Archives of Australia Collection)

BELOW:

T. W. Edgeworth David

Crayon drawing by George Marston, 1908

Edgeworth David, who had been Mawson's teacher at the University of Sydney, was fifty years old when he joined Shackleton's expedition. Alongside men half his age, afflicted with snow blindness on the way back from the pole, he passed leadership of the return journey over to Mawson, who navigated them all safely back to base.

(National Library of Australia Collection)

was going to make the first geological survey of the islands.

T. W. Edgeworth David, Mawson's professor of geology at the University of Sydney, was the motivating influence in Mawson's early career. Edgeworth David was a passionate teacher who believed in the value of excursions into the field; it was under his tuition that Mawson first developed an interest in the effects of the slow movement of glaciers on the formation of the Australian landscape.

Mawson took a position as lecturer at the University of Adelaide in 1905, and it was from there that he continued his research into glaciation. On his many trips to the Flinders Ranges he observed the physical evidence of the power of the incredibly slow-moving rivers of ice that had scraped the land millions of years before, dragging and depositing huge boulders across the now-desert landscape.

Mawson wanted to know more, but the only place where he could study similar phenomena was in Antarctica. The opportunity to do so was soon made available to him.

Shackleton

English explorer Ernest Shackleton was in Australia attempting to raise funds for a British-led expedition to Antarctica. During his visit to Adelaide, Mawson and Edgeworth

LEFT:

Shackleton's Antarctic explorer, the steam-powered sailing vessel the Nimrod

British explorer Ernest Shackleton led the 1907–9 voyage to the South Pole. His desire to be the first to the pole was thwarted when appalling weather called the quest to a halt only 180 miles short of his prize.

(National Library of Australia Collection)

David met with him and were invited to join his party. Shackleton was really only interested in getting to the South Pole before anybody else, he had little interest in scientific study, but included the two university men in his party to give his expedition a veneer of scientific merit which he hoped would help him secure the funds he needed.

Shackleton's vessel, the *Nimrod,* left New Zealand on New Year's Day 1908. The expeditionary party first pitched camp on Ross Island in Antarctica and was able to make just one short expedition before the five long months of the polar night fell.

On 10 March 1908, Edgeworth David and Mawson stood on the rim of Mount Erebus, Antarctica's only active volcano. As Mawson looked down into the boiling lava, a constant plume of steam shot hundreds of yards into the freezing air, ice crystals forming almost immediately and being deposited on the crater's rim — he was transfixed. Antarctica had Mawson in its thrall; he was to return several times over the next few years, but on his next expedition it was to all but claim his life.

Shackleton's expedition had gone to Antarctica early in the year to enable the party to acclimatise, and be prepared to take advantage of the good weather as soon as it broke after the five winter months of darkness. Shackleton wanted to head out for the pole as early as possible, making his return to base before the short Antarctic summer ended.

With the arrival of good weather Shackleton headed for the pole; Edgeworth David, Mawson and another member of the exploration party, Alistair Mackay, took off on an expedition of their own to the south magnetic pole on 26 September. The three men set out on their journey of more than 2000 kilometres dragging their sledges behind them. They had decided against taking dogs, as this would have meant carrying a lot of extra supplies to feed them as well. As it turned out, they had to put themselves on half-rations within a month, as they had eaten their way through their provisions far more quickly than they had expected to. Dragging all they had for their survival across the vast icy wilderness was gruelling.

All three men had lucky escapes from disaster. First Edgeworth David fell through the ice when a hole opened beneath his feet. He thrust his arms out, just stopping himself from disappearing into a cravass. The surface of the

LEFT:

Inside the living quarters of the main hut

Photograph by Frank Hurley, 1911-14

While the quarters was reasonably large, it had to accommodate quite a large body of men.

When the weather prevented any activity outside, boredom was the main enemy of those trapped inside. The men were kept busy: they celebrated birthdays and anniversaries in fine style; they performed at musical soirees, whether they could play an instrument or not; and they tended to their own gear.

Mawson ensured that each man under his command was responsible for his own harness and tackle, lest no man should ever feel the guilt of another's death through inattention to the safety of his harness. This proved to be very good advice; Mawson himself was saved at least three times by the strength of his harness.

(State Library of New South Wales Collection)

ice was seared with long fissures, which could not be seen because snow was constantly falling, forming a seemingly secure crust over the deep and deadly cracks. Next, Mackay fell through an ice bridge while hunting penguin. The fissure was filled with water but he was pulled free before he froze to death. Mawson also crashed through the ice, but was saved by the harness of his sled as he dangled beneath it. Edgeworth David and Mackay were able to haul him to safety.

By 15 January 1909 the team had got close enough to the south magnetic pole that they left their sledges and hurried on by foot. Mawson was responsible for taking their bearings and when the needle on his compass pointed directly to the ground they stopped; they had at last reached their goal.

At the south magnetic pole on the following day, the trio, weak from hunger and the rigours of their three-month trek across 1000 kilometres of treacherous ice and snow, stood together for a ceremonial portrait. They raised the Union Jack and, with a string attached to the camera shutter, Edgeworth David took a photograph of them all: Alaister Forbes Mackay, Douglas Mawson and himself, the first men ever to reach magnetic south. On this day they claimed the area for the British Empire in the name of King Edward VII.

They returned to their sledges and began the 1000-kilometre return expedition back to meet the *Nimrod* at the coast. Edgeworth David was fifty years old when he began this expedition and the physical demands of the gruelling journey had taken their toll. By the time they had reached the pole he was exhausted and on the return trek he was blinded by the glare of the snow and ice. He handed over the leadership of their small party to Mawson, who led them back safely to the *Nimrod* by 5 February 1909.

Shackleton had not had the same success. When the *Nimrod* picked up his party one month later, he could only report that they had got within 180 kilometres of the pole. They had trekked more than 2700 kilometres, a journey lasting 128 days; fast running out of food, and absolutely exhausted, they had been forced to turn back short of their goal. Time was against them, and they knew that to press on into the coming winter weather would have only one certain result: a lonely, freezing death in a vast white wasteland.

When the *Nimrod* eventually sailed back into the warm port of home all on board were given a hero's welcome. Edgeworth David heaped praise on his former pupil, saying:

> Mawson was really the soul of the march to the Magnetic Pole. In him we have an

RIGHT:

First at the South Magnetic Pole, from left: A. Forbes Mackay, T.W. Edgeworth David and Douglas Mawson, 15 January 1909

This photograph was taken by Edgeworth David on the day that the flag of Empire flew for the first time at the south magnetic pole. He attached a string to the camera shutter, stood back with his comrades and recorded their proud moment for posterity.

Once they had reached their goal they turned back for the coast, their rations almost gone.

Unfortunately the leader of their expeditionary team to the south, the English explorer Ernest Shackleton, had no similar photograph to record his success; he had failed to reach his objective and headed back to base before the weather closed in on his party.

(Australian Antarctic Division Archive, photo by T W Edgeworth David. Cat. No. 731D4)

BELOW:
The Air-tractor
Photograph by Frank Hurley, c.1911-14
The all-Australasian expedition was the first to take a plane to Antarctica, although it never left the ground.
(State Library of New South Wales Collection)

Australian Nansen, a man of infinite resource, splendid spirit, marvellous physique, an indifference to frost and cold that was astonishing, all the attributes of the great explorer.

The second expedition

Only twelve months later, yet another British explorer, Robert Falcon Scott, prepared his expedition to the South Pole. Like Shackleton, Scott hoped to take history's accolade as the first man to the pole. Mawson travelled to England to meet Scott, only to find that Scott was not at all interested in Mawson's scientific aims. Although Scott promised Mawson that he could be among the party that would plant the flag when they reached their goal, he was not convinced. Mawson returned to Australia disappointed.

Shackleton was also trying to mount a second expedition and Mawson went again to England, in February 1911, to put his plans before him. Shackleton failed to raise the necessary funds; it looked as though Mawson was never to get to Antarctica again.

Scott was in Australia raising funds for his expedition by the time Mawson returned home. By now, Mawson had decided that he would try to form his own all-Australasian expedition to explore Antarctica. He showed great respect for the English explorer by waiting until Scott had completed his tour before he began fundraising for his own expedition.

By the end of the year Mawson had raised almost the full £50,000 that he needed to take his thirty-two-man team to the Antarctic. They had secured the vessel *Aurora* and sailed from Hobart on 2 December 1911 bound, first, for Macquarie Island, halfway between Australia and Antarctica.

At Macquarie base camp they set up the first ever radio transmitter for the relay of messages from Antarctica to Australia. Mawson was always keen to adopt new technologies and the wireless was just one example of his interest. The expedition was also the first to take an aircraft to the Antarctic, but it was damaged before they even left Australia. This did not stop Mawson; he simply had the wings removed and the aircraft came in very handy in the snow as a motorised sledge.

When the *Aurora* arrived on the Antarctic coast, Mawson was frustrated to find that

Right:
Photographer Frank Hurley washing cinematographic film after development in the Antarctic on board the Aurora
Photograph by Frank Hurley, 1911-14
(State Library of New South Wales Collection)

Scott had made his base at Cape Adare, at exactly the same spot Mawson had planned.

When Mawson was in England and considering joining Scott's expedition, Scott had told him that Cape Adare would not have been a suitable place for a base camp. Disappointed with Scott's narrow vision, Mawson had decided to mount his own expedition after this meeting, and he was not happy at all to find the Englishman at this preferred campsite. Mawson had to find another suitable land mass where he could set up camp.

As they sailed across Commonwealth Bay they saw two huge glaciers pushing out into the sea; it was on these ice floes only months later that Mawson's team was to first meet with tragedy.

They settled at a place Mawson named Cape Denison; after all of their supplies had been unloaded the *Aurora* sailed away, not to return to Antarctica until the end of the following summer in January 1913.

They set about erecting the pre-fabricated huts they had brought with them and establishing their camp in what was (unknown to them at the time) the windiest place on earth. Mawson had set up where the winds blew straight from the pole; winds of up to 300 kilometres per hour that would blow a man off his feet battered the camp constantly. The explorers could hardly even walk outside the huts; when they did venture out to check their scientific instruments or to feed the dogs, they had to crawl on hands and knees or walk straight into the wind, when possible, laying into it at an angle of forty-five degrees.

The party waited out the long, dark months of the polar night until November, when

Frank Hurley

Twenty-six-year-old Sydney-sider Frank Hurley wrote to Douglas Mawson offering his services as a photographer for the second Antarctic expedition.

In his letter dated 29 September 1911 he offered his services free of charge. His mother also wrote to Mawson, begging that Frank not be taken to the pole; she said he was too weak to stand up to the rigours of such an adventure. In contrast, Hurley wrote: 'I am 26 years of age — unmarried, and have had a good share of roughing it'. Hurley had experience with photo-micrography, and held a Certificate in Electrics from Sydney Technical College.

In another letter, this time from The Gaumont Co. (Cinematographers), Mawson was advised that Hurley was the best man for the job. Gaumont advised Mawson that while Hurley had little experience at that time with motion picture cameras: 'by the time that we have got through with him, he will know perfectly well what is to be done and how to get the best results with the Cinematograph camera'.

Their letter also stated that as far as Gaumont knew, there was no physical impediment to Hurley joining the expedition.

exploration began in earnest. Five separate parties set out to explore the continent: one ventured south to the magnetic pole; three set out to explore the west; and Mawson took the most dangerous mission of all, heading as far east as possible. Two others went with him: Swiss ski champion Dr Xavier Mertz, who was a lawyer with mountaineering experience, and Lieutenant Belgrave Ninnis of the British Royal Fusiliers, who had experience with huskies.

On 10 November 1912 Mawson, Mertz and Ninnis headed out for the east with three sledges pulled by teams of six Greenland huskies apiece. Mawson's last venture had ensured that this time he wasn't going to be caught dragging his sledge for weeks on end — at least, that's what he thought as they set out.

A week later they saw a black form in the distance and when they eventually got up close they discovered that it was the tip of a mountain sticking out of the snow. They named the point Aurora Peak and noted its position, as it would serve as a landmark for the return journey.

It took them almost a month to cross the first glacier they had seen from the bay. They had to climb up, down and around huge ice boulders, which littered the glacier surface, all the time taking care to avoid the seemingly bottomless crevasses that cut across their path. Having found their way safely across the first glacier, they were kept snow-bound in their tents for three days by a blizzard. They talked of turning back but decided to press on for at least a few more days and try to get as far east as possible before they had to make their run back to base to meet the *Aurora*.

They were picking their way across the second of the two glaciers they had spotted from the *Aurora*, when tragedy struck. Mertz was in the lead, with Mawson following and Ninnis coming along behind. They had decided that Mertz should go ahead on skis and Mawson would lead the way for Ninnis, who had the sledge with the best dogs and most of the provisions. The glacier was unpredictable and the weight of Ninnis's sledge caused them to take the precaution of blazing a trail before he came along.

It was 14 December 1912, an unusually sunny day, and the temperature had risen to 21 degrees Fahrenheit. They were travelling at a great pace when suddenly Mertz stopped in his tracks. He had looked behind and seen only a single sledge: Ninnis had simply disappeared. Mertz and Mawson rushed back and saw that Ninnis had stepped into a crevasse and taken the sledge and dogs with him.

LEFT:
Building the main hut

The main hut was a three-roomed rectangle measuring 24 x 42 feet, the pyramid-shaped roof straddled the building; its long, enclosed eaves formed a verandah that went all the way around, doubling as the supply store.

Inside the largest room was the combined kitchen, dining and recreation room, which was lined with bunks. A smaller room housed the workshop, wireless and engine room, and an adjoining porch which led to the outside housed the latrine and cellar door.

(State Library of New South Wales Collection)

They peered down into the gaping hole, its shimmering blue walls turned to pitch black as it stretched away deep into the ice. On a ledge fifty yards below they saw one dog, struggling and whimpering, its back broken by the fall. Further down another dog lay dead. But there was no sign or sound of Ninnis; the young man they had nicknamed 'Cherub' was lost. Mawson and Mertz stayed at the crevasse calling out his name for almost three hours before they gave up. While they grieved for the loss of their young companion, they had also lost their best dogs and two weeks supply of food.

Just as Mawson finished reading the burial service committing young Ninnis to his icy grave, Mertz cried out to the sky: 'I know it is the hand of God; but why?' Just as he looked into the blue canopy of the Antarctic heavens a petrel was seen hovering overhead; it was the first living thing they had seen since they left the coast. As the bird wheeled and turned away Mertz proclaimed that it was the spirit of Ninnis; he accepted the tragic death of his companion. Mertz and Mawson decided to head back to the coast. They had ten days worth of food left in their kit, with 315 miles still to go before they would reach base.

By Christmas Day they had made little progress; the remaining dogs were not as fit as those lost with Ninnis, and the men were not as fit as they had been when they set out. Their rations were fast disappearing and they were left with very little choice but to eat the dogs. On Christmas Day 1912 Mawson and Mertz sat in their tent to a dinner of boiled dog bone stew and broken biscuits, and toasted each other with dog soup.

By the beginning of January Mertz, usually a fit and healthy fellow, became gravely ill. He asked Mawson to stay in camp for a few days, but Mawson knew that they would have to continue their march back to the coast or they would run out of both food and dogs altogether. On 6 January 1913 he put Mertz on his sledge and dragged him along; they had only two days' worth of food left and still 100 miles to go. They could not waste the good weather; even then, it was only possible to cover about eight miles per day.

Both men were suffering the effects of vitamin A poisoning caused by eating the dogs' livers. They did not know to avoid the poisonous livers of the dogs, and in an attempt to

RIGHT:

Lieutenant Belgrave Ninnis of the Royal Fuseliers

Baby-faced Belgrave Ninnis was nick-named 'Cherub', for obvious reasons. He was the youngest member of Mawson's party and was the first to die.

(National Archives of Australia Collection)

save themselves from starvation had in fact condemned themselves to a painful demise.

Mertz became delirious, and descended into insanity; before he died on 7 January he was so disturbed that he even bit off a finger from his own hand. Mawson read the second burial service of the expedition and was then alone. By now he too was suffering just as Mertz had before he died; his body was wracked by the effects of the poisoning, from hunger and from sheer exhaustion. Yet he struck out determinedly for the coast.

By now his skin was beginning to hang from his flesh in shreds; the soles of his feet had completely detached themselves and he tied them back on with the spare wick of his lamp, putting on all his socks at once in an attempt to keep his soles attached to his feet. His hair fell out completely and he developed such a terrible pain in his right side that he was unable to stand erect. Mawson was convinced that he too would meet his end in the empty wilderness.

To lessen his load he cut the remaining sledge in half and set off yet again. Disaster struck when he crashed through the crust of snow and fell into a crevasse. Although he felt sure that he was about to crash to his death, he was pulled up suddenly by the harness attached to the sledge, which had become jammed in a snowdrift. He hauled himself up slowly hand over hand, until he reached the lip of the crevasse. His body weakened and wracked with pain, he tried to pull himself over the edge when the crumbling snow gave way again. He fell back into the crevasse, to be caught by his harness once more.

As Mawson dangled fourteen feet below the surface he thought of simply slipping from the harness and putting an end to his agony. But it was not the character of Douglas Mawson to give in. Again, with his hands torn and bleeding, he hauled himself to the surface, and this time he was able to scramble out onto the snow before collapsing into unconsciousness.

After he awoke, Mawson took stock of himself and proceeded to make ready for the rest of his journey. Such was the indomitable spirit of Douglas Mawson that he made a sail for the sledge, and made his harness into a ladder in case he fell again, which he did several times; each time his sledge jammed into the snow and he was able to climb to safety.

LEFT:
Mertz and 'Baselisk'
Photograph by Charles Laseron, 1913

Greenland huskies were taken to Antarctica because the strong, reliable and friendly dogs were perfectly at home in the frozen environment; they were able to sleep outside even when they were covered with snow.

When Mawson was in England, the proposed expedition had created so much public interest that Nellie Melba encouraged Russian ballerina Anna Pavlova to visit the ruggedly handsome Australian explorer.

The great dancer patted one of the huskies and the dog was duly named Pavlova in her honour. It is doubtful that she was ever aware that once they had become trapped in the snow, their food gone, the starving explorers had Pavlova for dinner.

(National Library of Australia Collection)

RIGHT:
At Aladdin's Cave in drifting snow
Photograph by Douglas Mawson, 1911

Aladdin's Cave was a forward supply depot nine kilometres from main base. It was cut straight into the face of the ice as it swept up from Cape Denison to the Antarctic plateau. Shelves could be cut directly into the ice walls rather like an igloo.

It was at Aladdin's Cave on 1 February 1912 that Mawson found a pineapple sitting on an ice-shelf, as well as other supplies, left for him by the rescue party that he had missed by only five hours.

A blizzard forced him to remain in the cave for six days before he was able to make his last, desperate bid for the safety of main base.

(State Library of New South Wales Collection)

OPPOSITE:
The 'Aurora' in heavy pack ice north off Termination ice tongue—Queen Mary Land
Photograph by Frank Hurley, 1911-14

(National Library of Australia Collection)

Two weeks late for his rendezvous with the *Aurora* and with only two pounds of food left, Mawson spotted a dark object ahead. When he pulled himself close enough he saw that it was a column of ice blocks on top of which sat a black-wrapped package of food left by a search party. Inside the package were parcels of food wrapped in brightly coloured cloth and a message with the time and date. Mawson had only missed the party by five hours. The note gave Mawson directions to Aladdin's Cave, a supply dump still thirty-seven kilometres away. The note also told Mawson that all of the other expeditions had returned safely and that the *Aurora* was waiting for him.

Mawson reached Aladdin's Cave on 1 February 1912, but there was nobody there to greet him. At least there was food, and a stove, and he was protected from the fierce winds that blew without let for the first week of that month. He wrote the same entry in his diary every day that week: 'Blizzard, rising at times to hurricane'.

He was stuck in the cave for six days before a break in the weather made it possible for him to make a bid for the coast. When he finally reached the point where the ice cap sloped away to the sea, he spotted a tiny speck in the distance. The *Aurora* had set sail for a rendezvous with others on the Shackleton Shelf, and he was left alone on the ice. Convinced that he would be left for another year in Antarctica, if he survived at all, Mawson made his way slowly down to the base camp.

To his astonishment, he saw some men working around the camp; the rescue party

'Paquita' bags

After his first Antarctic voyage Mawson had gone back to Australia to continue his geological work. While working in the Barrier Ranges north of Broken Hill in New South Wales he met Paquita Delprat, the daughter of the general manager of the Broken Hill Proprietary Company.

In 1911 Mawson and Delprat were engaged to be married. Neither could foresee the events that would happen in the time between the happy engagement and their wedding two years later. Mawson almost lost his life and he doubted that Delprat should ever want to marry him, considering the condition he was in afterwards. He sent her a radio message offering to release her from the engagement; while he let her know that he was getting better, he told her that he had lost his hair. She replied: 'Deeply thankful you are safe. Warmest welcome awaits your hairless return. Contract same as ever only more so.'

The expedition took food supplies to Antarctica wrapped in coloured bags made by Miss Delprat. Known by the men as 'Paquita bags', the bright materials cheered them when they were stuck inside sheltering from the endless, white, blizzardly weather. It was the bright red food bags that she had made that had raised Mawson's spirits when he staggered alone and almost defeated into Aladdin's Cave on 1 February.

ABOVE:
A 'bad light' (snowy weather), tent-clothes, etc, out to dry, 1 December 1912

Drawing by Chas. T. Harrison, artist to the Second Party, Australasian Antarctic Expedition, 1911-14

(State Library of New South Wales Collection)

had not given him up and were prepared to spend another year on the ice in the hope that he was not lost. He raised his weary arms and waved to them. When he had caught their eye and knew he had been seen he collapsed on to his sledge and waited for them to bring him in. The first man to reach Mawson, brushing the ice away from his face and seeing the condition he was in, cried out: 'My God! Which one are you?' Mawson was almost an unrecognisable skeleton.

The *Aurora* was contacted by radio and turned back to pick them up, but the weather was so rough that no boat was able to make land. Mawson and the rescue party were left at the camp for another year. It was just as well, for Mawson might not have survived the rough voyage back to Australia. At the best of times the voyage in the *Aurora* was a tough experience; a man in his condition would have done it very hard.

Recovering at the camp, he gradually regained his strength; the effects of Vitamin A poisoning took a long while to wear off, but gradually his hair began to grow back, his skin repaired itself and his appetite returned.

A chilly dip

Just after the men had finished constructing the main hut, they began to assemble the stove but could not find all the parts. The stove was possibly the most important piece of equipment to their survival, and it would not work without its vital parts.

One of the men remembered seeing a box fall into the water as they unloaded the *Aurora* weeks before. Mawson made a quick decision, stripped off his clothes and dived into the freezing ocean again and again until he brought up a heavy crate. The men were stunned at his bravado, and shocked when they broke the crate open to discover that it was packed with tins of jam.

After they had composed themselves from their laughter at Mawson's icy dip for a pot of jam, they searched the hut properly and found the missing stove parts well hidden among their supplies.

He honoured his lost companions by naming the glaciers where they had lost their lives in their memory — Mertz and Ninnis Glaciers both appear on maps of Antarctica today.

A hero's return

While the reason for his survey of the icy continent was the scientific study of the glaciers and to take mineral samples in the hope that the great land mass could at some time in the future be used as a source of wealth production for the Empire, Mawson brought little back other than his memories and experience forged through hardship and sorrow.

He did have his notebooks and mineral samples, which he had dragged across the ice and snow packed into his cut-down sledge. Even though he had been at the depths of despair for his survival, he never abandoned the very reason why he had gone there in the first place.

Although twelve months earlier Mawson had written in his diary that 'a terrible chapter of my life is finished', he did not abandon Antarctica. In 1929–30 and 1930–31 he led return expeditions of combined British, Australian and New Zealand research teams.

These BANZARE (British, Australian, New Zealand Research Expedition) parties made two voyages on board Scott's ill-fated ship the *Discovery*, visiting the Crozet and Kerguelen Islands and Heard Island. They mapped a large portion of the Antarctic coast and proclaimed a large section of the landmass for Great Britain, this time for King George V. The BANZARE expeditions were the first to use an aircraft to conduct aerial surveys of the Antarctic continent.

BELOW:
Mawson poses among members of the BANZARE expedition on board the Discovery
Photograph by Frank Hurley, 1931
(Australian Antarctic Division Archive, photo Frank Hurley, 1931. Cat. No. 739C4)

It was also the first time that radio had been used to broadcast the voice of an explorer in the course of his exploration. A short-wave broadcasting wireless set had been installed aboard the *Discovery*, where Mawson and others could speak to a listening audience back home eager for tales of discovery and danger from the Antarctic.

Mawson always maintained that his expeditions were for scientific purposes only. While he never promoted the land as fit for mineral exploitation and did not foresee a time when there would be any permanent settlement there, he did offer the following opinion on the potential of the Antarctic waters:

> ... there is one product in Antarctica, which ought to be developed in the early future. The waters round the coast of the unknown continent teem with life. The equatorial waters are not more fully stocked with fish of all kinds than the far southern seas. It requires no stretch of the imagination to foresee the time when the coasts of the snow-bound country will be one of the chief sources of food supply for the world'.[1]

In 1933 the Australian government was ceded control over the areas claimed by Mawson for Britain, and in 1936 this area of more than 6.5 million square kilometres, more than three-quarters the size of Australia itself, was renamed the Australian Antarctic Territory.

Mawson never returned to Antarctica after 1931, but he continued to promote interest in the Territory right up until his death at his home in Adelaide on 14 December 1958.

BELOW:

Cheering the flag overlooking Proclamation Harbour, 13 January 1930

The *Discovery* can be seen in the distance as Mawson (third from right) and his colleagues raise the flag on Enderby Land and proclaimed it for King George V.

(State Library of Victoria Collection)

Top:

The successful explorers at the South Pole, 14 December 1911

Photograph by Roald Amundsen, 1911

(National Library of Australia Collection)

Above:

Scott's party at Amundsen's tent

Photograph by Lieutenant 'Birdie' Henry Robertson Bowers, 18 January 1912

The men in this photograph all perished on the journey back to the coast. They are from left: Captain Robert Falcon Scott, Lieutenant Titus Lawrence Edward Grace Oates, Dr Edward Adrian Wilson and petty officer Edgar Evans. What a shame for these proud and patriotic Englishmen to have passed into history posed beneath the flag of another country.

(National Library of Australia Collection)

Norwegian Roald Amundsen is first to the South Pole

Captain Robert Scott's expedition failed to be the first to reach the South Pole. When they got there they were dismayed to discover a Norwegian flag already fluttering in the wind. Roald Amundsen had reached the South Pole on 14 December 1911, the same day that Belgrave Ninnis had plunged to his death. Scott's party never made the journey out.

The frozen bodies of Captain Robert Scott and two of his companions, Dr Wilson and Lieutenant Bowers, were found by a rescue party in their snow-covered tent on 10 February 1912.

A diary found in the tent left details of how the rest of the party had died, including the heroic end of Captain Oates, who, crippled by frostbite, had been begging the others to leave him behind. Unable to take it any more, Oates stepped out of the tent into a blizzard, leaving with the words: 'I am just going outside, I may be some time'. He was never seen again.

Sir Charles Kingsford Smith

1897–1935

Sir Charles Kingsford Smith is featured on the face of the $20 paper note, first issued in 1966.

Larrikin lord of the skies

WHEN THE NEWLY FORMED BONDI SURF-LIFESAVING Club performed its first ever rescue on 3 December 1906, a spluttering, but adventurous, nine-year-old lad was pulled from the water. The boy who survived this near drowning went on to capture the imagination of all Australians, and earn the admiration of aviators the entire world over. Born before humans had even taken their first faltering leaps into the air, Charlie Kingsford Smith — Smithy — was to make his name as the man who took Australia up into the clouds, breaking record after record, linking Australia to the rest of the world with a speed typical of the modern age.

Smithy was born in Hamilton, Queensland, on 9 February 1897, the fourth son of bank manager William Kingsford Smith and his wife Catherine. The family travelled to Vancouver on banking business in 1903; returning to Australia two years later, they settled in Sydney. It was in the 'boiling' surf at the beachside suburb of Bondi that young Charlie was to take one risk too many, and was caught in a dangerous rip. He was rescued; one of his mates drowned.

He was not an overly distinguished scholar, so Charlie Kingsford Smith left school at sixteen and began an electrician's apprenticeship. He soon saved enough money to purchase a second-hand motorcycle, and the flashy young teenager roared around the streets of Sydney, showing off his style.

In 1914, when Charlie was still only seventeen, war with Germany was declared. Hundreds of dashing young men lined up at the recruiting centres and clamoured for the king's uniform, but Charlie was rejected for being too small. However, he persisted; he wanted to get among the action, so on the morning

OPPOSITE:
Charles Kingsford Smith — 'Smithy'
Oil on canvas by Frank Dunne, 1935

Cheeky Charlie Kingsford Smith was at heart a loveable larrikin.

When he first took to the skies, aged only nineteen, flying was a recent phenomenon. The dashing young aviators were like gallant knights of the bright blue heavens: they soared like birds, flirting with death at every turn.

Smithy loved the attention: he sparkled under the spotlight of public approval, but was depressed when things didn't go his way, and there were many times over his long and brilliant flying career that he tasted the bitter pill of disappointment.

(National Library of Australia Collection)

RIGHT:
Sir Charles Kingsford Smith, MC, AFC
Photograph by Dr Julian Smith

On 13 July 1917, the second day after he first took to the skies over the Western Front in World War I, Smithy put a halt to a ground assault by German troops by strafing them with machine-gun fire. He also shot an enemy plane out of the skies on the same day, when eight British planes engaged with a twenty-strong German convoy.

In four weeks of aerial battle Smithy had taken four victories against the enemy aircraft.

(Australian War Memorial Negative Number A03349)

of his eighteenth birthday he was waiting outside the recruiting office when it opened.

Two months later he was on board a troopship bound for Egypt. He was sent to Gallipoli, where he served as an infantryman; after the withdrawal of all Allied troops from the peninsula in December 1915 he was sent to France, where he was able to use his motorcycling skills, honed in the streets of Sydney, when he was transferred to the Motorcycle Despatch Corps.

It was not long before he was invited to apply for a commission in the Royal Flying Corps. Aircraft were just beginning to be used in military service, mainly for reconnaissance and balloon attacks, but the flying corps was rapidly evolving into a fighting unit. Machine guns were being fitted to the flimsy craft for the first time, and hand-held bombs were dropped as the planes flew low over enemy lines. Both sides of the conflict were turning the skies over France into an aerial battlefield, and young daredevils like Charlie Kingsford Smith were in their element. Although training for the young pilots was very basic, within two months he was in the air. The pilots almost had to learn to fly their machines as they sat in the cockpit, one finger on the trigger, the other on the joystick, while all about the enemy buzzed like a swarm of hornets.

Charlie was awarded a Military Cross when he shot down a German plane and brought a ground assault to a halt as he swooped over the enemy, ripping them apart with his machine-gun fire. He was wounded in this attack; he was shot in the legs and lost three of his toes as a result. He had to stand supported by crutches to receive his medal from King George V. He spent the rest of his war as captain-instructor, developing his knowledge of flying technique as he taught others.

After the war

The war was over on 11 November 1918. Everyone was heading for home, but not Captain Charles Kingsford Smith, MC RFC; he remained in England. Although there were no ready employment opportunities for ex-RFC pilots, the air force was disposing of its old wartime planes.

With and two other ex-pilots, Cyril Maddocks and Val Ruddle, Charlie Kingsford-Smith bought two De Havilland Sixes and established an aerial taxi service in England. They didn't last long in business: the old planes were worn out and maintenance was beyond them—and they had too many crashes. The public was not confident using this type of rough-and-ready aerial transportation, preferring to keep their feet firmly on the ground.

RIGHT:
Pilot's jacket worn by Charles Kingsford Smith

Smithy's first real flying lessons came when he was aloft, at last alone, over the Western Front.

While his old chums were stuck in the stinking mud of the front-line trenches, Smithy was up in the clouds with the birds, bombs and bullets, and some of those came pretty close. This jacket still bears a mark left by a machine-gun bullet near the neck.

(National Library of Australia Collection)

When the American flyers Alcock and Brown made the first aerial Atlantic crossing in June 1919, in the stunning time of sixteen-and-a-half hours, the world was amazed. The age of flight had begun in earnest. The Australian government offered £10,000 to the aviators who could be the first to fly from England to Australia in less than thirty days.

Smithy was desperate to make this his prize. He and his partners, Maddocks and Ruddle, decided to sell one of their old planes and purchase a twin-engined Blackburn Kangaroo for their attempt at the record-breaking flight. They were bitterly disappointed when Australian Prime Minister Billy Hughes refused them permission to enter the race. He told the young pilots that they had neither the experience, the financial backing nor the navigational skills to consider the attempt. Smithy had to keep his feet on the ground while the prize went to two other Australians: brothers Ross and Keith Smith from Adelaide.

An envious and disappointed Charles Kingsford Smith left Australia and joined an aerial circus in America, flying from town to town, barnstorming, performing 'aerobatics' and taking joy rides. He nearly came to grief when he had to hang upside down from the undercarriage of the plane he was flying; not accounting for the slipstream, he almost didn't make it back into the cockpit, just getting back in time to pull the plane up and away from disaster.

He flew for Hollywood in the silent movies, and even flew low over Californian rice farms to frighten ducks out of the water. But for the decorated aviator who had flown and won over the battlefields of France, this was disappointing stuff indeed.

On 1 January 1921 Smithy sailed for home, determined to build a business based on aviation. He began flying for Digger Aviation, a company set up by an old Royal Flying Corps mate, but this venture didn't last long either. On one flight the passengers were horrified when they saw bits of wing falling off in mid-air. The gallant 'lords of the sky' simply loved flying; keeping the planes in safe, airworthy condition to ensure public confidence was another matter altogether.

By the end of 1921 Smithy was flying for Royal Flying Corps veteran Major Norman Brierly, who was setting up the Western Australian Airways mail service. He flew from Perth to small towns right across the north of the state, setting every record for flights into these remote outback communities. He continued to chase his dream of having his own company, but the reckless daredevil nature of his youth plagued his good intentions.

LEFT:

The victorious aviator, Keith Smith and his Vickers Vimy on the airfield at Mascot

With Keith Smith is Mawson's Antarctic photographer Frank Hurley, showing the cameras used in the record-breaking flight from England to Australia in 1919.

Ex-Royal Flying Corps pilot Ross, and his brother Keith Smith, who had been refused a commission to the corps as he was considered unfit, were the first to fly the England to Australia route in less than thirty days. Charles Kingsford Smith was refused entry to the race on the grounds that he didn't have the resources to start, let alone finish. In the end they all wrote their names into aviation's record book.

From left: Mechanic Sergeant J. Bennett; photographer Captain Frank Hurley; Pilot Keith Smith and mechanic Sergeant W. Shiers.

(Australian War Memorial Collection)

RIGHT:

Smithy beside the World War I Bristol Tourer purchased from Western Australian Airlines' Major Brierly in 1927

Smithy and another Royal Flying Corps veteran, Keith Anderson, purchased a Bristol Tourer and set up their own company, the Interstate Flying Service, in 1927. Their best customers were country bookmakers who wanted to get to remote country race-tracks, and from one to another, as quickly as possible.

(State Library of New South Wales Collection)

Disappointed when new businesses were started, and closed just as quickly, Smithy would simply set his sights on yet another flying record, each time setting the bar a little higher. No challenge was too great or too dangerous for him, no matter what was happening on the ground.

Hinkler does it on his own

Australian airman Lieutenant Bert Hinkler made the first solo flight from England to Australia, touching down in Darwin at 6 p.m. on 22 February 1922.The former Royal Navy and Royal Air Force pilot completed the journey, in his sixty-horsepower Avro Avian, in less than fifteen-and-a-half days. Flying without any official support was an expensive business, and Hinkler was relieved when Australian Prime Minister Stanley Bruce offered him a cheque for £2000 to mark his achievement.

In 1925 Smithy and Keith Anderson, another old mate from the Royal Flying Corps, bought the Gascoyne Transport Co. in Carnavon, Western Australia, which they sold two years later, making a profit of £2300. On 28 January 1927 the pair flew east to Sydney in their own three-seater Bristol Tourer, purchased with the profits of the sale, where they set up their own company, the Interstate Flying Service.

In 1926 Smithy had met aviator and businessman Charles Ulm in Sydney, and his fortunes were changed. Ulm shared Smithy's dream of establishing a successful air transport service flying routes all over Australia. To promote their new business venture, Smithy and Ulm attempted a record-breaking long-distance flight circumnavigating the entire continent. They flew from Sydney to Brisbane, Longreach, Camooweal, Darwin, Broome, Carnarvon, Perth, Adelaide, Melbourne and back to Sydney, in ten days and five hours, almost halving the previous record; 50,000 people turned out in Sydney to cheer them as they landed. The New South Wales government granted them £3500, with which they bought themselves a newer plane.

Smithy and Ulm set their sights on making a grand gesture: they decided to attempt the

RIGHT:

Studio portrait of Smithy (left) and Ulm taken just after the Trans-Pacific flight, 1928

Smithy and Ulm ran short of funds after they bought a Fokker monoplane from Arctic explorer Sir George Wilkes. American industrialist G. Allan Hancock purchased the plane from the 'down-and-out' Australians then promptly handed it straight back, telling them to 'fly it to Australia'.

When they landed in Brisbane at 10.14 a.m. on 9 June 1928, they were handed a cable in which they read that Hancock had returned ownership of the plane to them and that their accumulated debts of £10,000 had been taken care of.

(National Library of Australia Collection)

first flight across the Pacific. They sailed for America to raise funds for this great adventure. Just after they set foot on American soil seven pilots were killed in an air race to Hawaii; the public quickly lost its taste for aerial adventure. The Australians found it very difficult to interest anyone at all in their quest, until they met wealthy American shipbuilder Captain Allan Hancock. Hancock bought their Fokker monoplane—which they had purchased from Australian Arctic explorer Sir George Wilkes—and promptly handed it back, instructing them 'to fly it to Australia'. They named it the *Southern Cross*, a name that in time was to become possibly even more familiar than their own.

Smithy and Ulm replaced the single motor on the Fokker with three Wright Whirlwind engines; they quadrupled the fuel capacity and fitted modern radio and navigational equipment. They recruited two Americans, navigator Harry Lyon and radio operator Jim Warner, for the flight. When they took off on 31 May 1928, the huge *Southern Cross* lumbered into the skies off the Californian coast with 8000 nautical miles ahead of them.

Inside the aircraft the noise created by the three huge motors was so loud that no one could talk or hear at all; all communication had to be written on paper. The vibrations almost rattled their teeth from their gums. Smithy and Ulm sat up front in a semi-open cockpit exposed to the wind; it was freezing cold and rained for the twenty-seven hours it took to reach Hawaii. When the intrepid aviators stepped from the aircraft to greet the huge crowd that had gathered to welcome them they could not hear a word spoken: all four of them had been temporarily deafened by the noise of the Wright Whirlwind engines.

They took off again and headed, first to Fiji, then on to reach Brisbane, just eighty-three hours and eleven minutes after leaving San Francisco. On 10 June they flew to Sydney,

BELOW:
The heroes of the Pacific skies

From left: navigator Captain Harry Lyon; copilot Charles Ulm; pilot Charles Kingsford Smith; radio operator John Warner.

They flew from California to Australia in 83 hours, landing in Brisbane on 9 June 1928.

(National Archives of Australia Collection)

BELOW:

The Southern Cross *over Fairburn, Canberra 1928*

The *Southern Cross* was a huge plane for its day. The Dutch-made Fokker monoplane was fitted with three Wright Whirlwind engines, its fuel capacity quadrupled, and modern navigational gear fitted for the attempt on the first trans-Pacific aerial crossing.

(Australian War Memorial Negative Number 098187)

where a crowd of 300,000 welcomed the *Southern Cross* home. The roads leading from Sydney to Mascot Aerodrome were blocked for miles around. Smithy was made Honorary Squadron Leader in the Royal Australian Air Force and was awarded the Air Force Cross; £20,000 was raised to help cover expenses.

At last Smithy had earned the place that Prime Minister Hughes had denied him almost a decade before; his name was added to the honour roll of the Australian Smiths who had conquered the southern skies.

The victorious aviators couldn't stop there. In another attempt to prove the viability of long-distance passenger and mail services, Smithy and Ulm flew nonstop from Melbourne to Perth. On 8 August 1928 the pair crossed the continent from east to west, battling howling winds and squalling rain to reach Perth in twenty-three hours.

They next attempted to cross the notoriously dangerous skies over the Tasman Sea to New Zealand. They took off from Richmond in New South Wales in fine weather. The pleasant flight soon turned to terror as they hit a violent storm not long after they had left Australia behind. The plane rose and fell hundreds of feet at a time, rain lashed and hail battered the fuselage, the navigation instruments failed and the altimeter froze. Yet Smithy flew on into the eye of the storm. When the plane was heard circling over Wellington early the following morning people rushed from their beds, still in their pyjamas, to cheer them on. They touched down in Christchurch that morning, fourteen hours and twenty-five minutes after leaving Richmond. The return flight took twenty-three hours, as they flew into head winds all the way. They set down on the Richmond runway with only ten minutes worth of fuel left.

Touchdown at Coffee Royal

To bring attention to their enterprise and prove themselves to be among the best aviators in the world, Smithy and Ulm decided to attempt the long-distance flying record from England to Australia.

On 31 March 1929 they prepared their island hop to England, flying first from Sydney to Wyndham in Western Australia. As they crossed the desert they flew into a violent electrical storm. Rain lashed at the cockpit and red dust swirled high into the air; the

long-range radio aerial fell off, making navigation almost impossible. Unable to see through the clouds of dust, and with fuel running low, they decided to search for somewhere to land. The *Southern Cross* was put down on the mud flats of a riverbed filled with crocodiles. Neither Smithy nor Ulm knew where they were, nor did anybody else.

A massive aerial search was launched as planes took to the skies to comb the desert route for Australia's most charismatic aviators. On the ground, Smithy and Ulm set about repairing the little damage done to the plane on their muddy landing. Stranded as they were, they were forced to live on the meagre supplies on board: some beans, baby food, coffee and brandy. Smithy nicknamed the place 'Coffee Royal' and this name became synonymous with one of the most difficult periods of his career.

Old friends from the Royal Flying Corps, Keith Anderson and Bobby Hitchcock, joined in the aerial search but, unfortunately, engine failure also forced them into a desert landing. By the time their *Kookaburra* was located weeks later, both men had starved to death; no one had been out searching for them.

Rumours spread around Australia that Smithy had gone missing as a publicity stunt to draw attention to this latest adventure. If so, the publicity was of the wrong kind for Smithy and Ulm. Even though an official inquiry into the 'Coffee Royal' affair exonerated both of them of any deception which could have contributed to the death of their old flying companions, it took years before Smithy regained his good reputation.

The pair continued on their quest and flew the Australia to London route in the *Southern Cross* in the record time of twelve days and eighteen hours. Smithy wanted to fly from England to America and complete the first round-the-world flight, but 'the old bus', as he called the *Southern Cross*, was not up to it. The old Fokker was ready for a remake and the manufacturer in the Netherlands offered to give its most famous aircraft a complete overhaul, free of charge.

They left the 'old bus' at Fokker in Holland. Ulm returned home, while Smithy went to America to plan his next adventure. On the ocean voyage back to Australia from America he met Melbourne girl Mary Powell, and they fell in love. They were married on 10 December 1930.

The birth of ANA

Smithy and Ulm founded Australian National Airways (ANA) in 1930, and began to ferry mail between capital cities. They tried to

LEFT:

The De Havilland DH 61 Canberra *that discovered the lost aviators stranded at 'Coffee Royal' on 12 April 1929*

Photograph by Albert James Perier

A massive air search was mounted to look for Smithy and Ulm, who had gone missing en route from Sydney to Wyndham to begin their attempt at the long-distance flying record in 1929.

(State Library of New South Wales Collection)

BELOW:

Arrival of the Southern Cross *in Sydney on the first trans-Pacific flight, 10 June 1928*

When the plane taxied across the tarmac, Atlantic Oil Company executive Captain Clive Chateau ran out to warn the lines of policemen guarding the plane to beware of the still-spinning, unseen propellers, so unused was the general public to the sight of a plane on the ground.

This commemorative photograph bears the signatures of the flight crew aboard that historic flight: (from left) J. Warner, C. T. P. Ulm, C. E. Kingsford Smith and H. W. Lyon.

(State Library of New South Wales Collection)

establish a mail service between Australia and England but could not get the government to support their scheme. It may have been Smithy's larrikin spirit that kept the government at bay; while all were excited by his exploits as he centred world attention on his record-breaking achievements, at the same time there were other less flamboyant aviators building up solid businesses and gaining official support for their fledgling industry.

A new plane, the *Southern Cloud,* flew ANA's first official flight from Sydney to Brisbane on New Year's Day 1930; ANA carried 8000 passengers in the first few months and while the passenger business seemed to be going well, Smithy went back to England, his eyes set again on the record books. The *Southern Cross* looked as good as new when, on 23 June 1930, Smithy and radio operator Bill Stannage took off from the beach of Galway Bay in Ireland on their attempt at the first east–west crossing of the Atlantic, a journey of 3040 kilometres.

The weather deteriorated as they flew into low mist over the northern seas, and it soon became impossible to navigate; the compasses went berserk, and although they were assisted by radio reports from ships who could hear them overhead, they really had little idea of their exact position. Smithy was flying blind.

After thirty-one hours, with the plane's fuel tanks almost empty, the lights of Newfoundland flickered below. Smithy had never been more relieved to make a touchdown than this one on Canadian soil.

But it seemed no record was enough for him. Within weeks he was back in Holland to take delivery of a new plane he named *Southern Cross Junior*, taking to the skies almost immediately in an attempt to break Hinkler's record. Smithy flew *Southern Cross Junior* to Australia in a new record time for a solo flight, taking five and a half days off Hinkler's time.

Records were crashing, but so were some of Smithy's passenger craft. On 21 March 1931 the flagship of ANA, the *Southern Cloud,* went missing with two crew and six passengers on board. Smithy took to the skies and searched the air route for days. There had been reports of a sighting near Mount Kosciuszko, but no trace of the missing plane was found. This disaster almost ruined ANA's reputation; it seems that the public perception was that ANA may have been taking too many risks while Smithy was chasing too many prizes. After the loss of *Southern Cloud,* his commercial venture suffered; ANA lost its customers first, its capital second. The business lost £10,000 and barely managed to survive the economic depression of the 1930s.

Smithy still had his heart set on the big mail run to England; he was convinced that he needed a solid long-term government contract to solve all his financial worries. When a British Imperial Airways mail flight crashed in Timor in August 1930, Smithy rushed to the island to complete the run. In his attempt to prove his capabilities in the provision of an Australian-based mail service, he flew Christmas mail to and from Britain, but he still couldn't land that vital contract.

He tried again to use a record-breaking flight as proof of his abilities. He made another attempt on the solo record, flying *Southern Cross Junior* from England to Australia. He had no luck at all in making good time on this flight: he was arrested and jailed in Turkey for three days, then tropical storms forced him into a jungle landing in Malaya. He had lost so much time a new record was not possible. He gave up and returned to Australia by boat.

Smithy and Ulm had tried their best to impress the Australian government but were disappointed again when the much-sought-after mail contract was awarded to Hudson Fysh of Qantas and to British Imperial Airways.

But although he couldn't get the backing he needed to create a sustainable business for

Right:

The ANA School of Flying, Mascot

Photograph by Sam Hood, c. 1930

A Gypsy Moth Aircraft is christened on the tarmac outside Smithy's ANA hangar at Mascot airfield in Sydney in the mid-1930s.

Even after his knighthood in 1932, when he had received an award of £3000 from the Australian government, the Depression years left Smithy constantly strapped for cash. In an effort to improve his often disappointing cash flow, Smithy accepted an appointment to the Vacuum Oil Company as an aviation consultant and created his own flying school in Sydney.

(State Library of New South Wales Collection)

himself, he was still Charles Kingsford Smith, the loveable 'Smithy' who had established and broken more records than any other aviator of his day. No one could take these achievements from him, and no one was honoured more than him. In June 1932, Smithy received a knighthood from King George V for his services to aviation.

The Australian government awarded him £3000, but he still needed more capital to fully establish his aerial service. He joined the Vacuum Oil Company as an aviation consultant and established a flying school in Sydney.

But the record book still beckoned. He made yet another attempt on the solo England to Australia record, flying his new Percival Gull, *Miss Southern Cross,* and reached Wyndham, setting a new record.

In March 1934 the announcement of an air race to celebrate the centenary of the City of Melbourne caused Smithy to make a decision that put him at odds with his once-loyal Australian fans. Desperate to win this race, Smithy bought himself a new plane, which he called *Anzac.* The Australian government refused to allow him to bestow this hallowed name on the American-built Lockheed Altair. Miffed by this rebuttal, Smithy renamed the pretty single-winged, super-charged speedster *Lady Southern Cross.* Although it was the fastest machine that he had ever flown, he was never to compete in the centenary race.

Owing to cracks which appeared in the plane's fuselage on the flight to England before the race, Smithy pulled out at the last minute; the newspapers reported that owing to the fuss over the name he had pulled out in spite, and claimed that he was too cowardly to compete. He even received 'white feather' letters in the mail. The public fascination with Smithy was almost at an end.

At thirty-two years of age, Smithy was in trouble; almost bankrupt and almost out of favour, he decided to make one last attempt to restore his reputation. With P. G. 'Bill' Taylor as his copilot, he made the first ever reverse trans-Pacific crossing, flying from Australia to America in October 1934.

While in California he heard the news that Ulm and two other airmen were missing on a flight to Hawaii. Smithy organised search flights in a vain attempt to locate his old friend's *Stella Australia,* lost somewhere over the vast eastern Pacific. Dejected by the loss of Ulm, and his failure to secure finances, Smithy sailed back to Sydney.

The *Southern Cross* took to the skies one last time when Smithy planned to celebrate the king's silver jubilee by flying a special mail run across the Tasman. On 15 May 1935 the

LEFT:

The flashy legend Smithy and the Lockheed Altair he named Lady Southern Cross

When Smithy purchased the very quick, super-charged Lockheed Altair for his tilt at the centenary air race from London to Melbourne, he first named it *Anzac.* The Australian government would not allow him to use this name for an American-built plane.

(National Archives of Australia Collection)

'old bus' was halfway across the Tasman sea when a piece of exhaust broke away, tearing off a piece of a propeller, which in turn damaged one of the engines. The plane began to lose height as the oil pressure in the other engines dropped to alarming levels. It seemed as if they were about to ditch into the sea. Copilot P. G. Taylor stepped out onto the wing carrying a thermos flask; he drained oil from the damaged engine, transferring it back to the others, which were now overheating. Taylor repeated this manoeuvre five more times. The mail was ditched into the ocean as the 'old bus' almost skimmed the waves as they limped back to Sydney.

Taylor was awarded the George Cross for his bravery over the Tasman, and the Australian government purchased the *Southern Cross* from Smithy and retired the historic craft to Eagle Farm Airport in Brisbane.

The *Lady Southern Cross* was still in California, unsold. Smithy shipped her to England, ready for one last record attempt before he retired from competition. It seems that Smithy was never satisfied; he just couldn't keep his feet on the ground or take his eyes from the prize. But now, close to bankruptcy again, he was ready to give the game away — after one last race against himself. He knew that his time at the top was fast fading away, and the demands of his failed business ventures had simply become too great. He confided to a friend just before take-off on 25 October 1935: 'the pressures are becoming too great'.

Despite this obvious decline, he took once more to the skies. With Tommy Pethybridge by his side, where once Charlie Ulm had sat, he pushed the *Lady Southern Cross* to try to beat the standing record of seventy-one hours for the England–Australia route. They reached Allahabad on 7 November, but were never heard of again. Somewhere between Rangoon and Singapore, Smithy and his plane simply disappeared. No trace was found of the *Lady Southern Cross* or her pilots, even though hundreds of searchers scoured the area in British bombers and flying boats right up until the end of November.

The loveable larrikin of the skies was lost forever. However, the spirit of the great aviator survived; his dream of passenger flights and cargo services crisscrossing the globe became a reality. It may have taken better businessmen than Charles Kingsford Smith to make it happen, but it took an Aussie larrikin to show them how it could be done in the first place.

RIGHT:
Sir Charles Kingsford Smith

Just before the *Lady Southern Cross* disappeared over the Bay of Bengal, one of the other pilots in the same air race, Jeremy Melrose, looked up and out of his cockpit and saw the plane overhead. That was at 1.30 a.m., just out from Calcutta over the Avdam Sea. The plane was sighted again at about 2.50 a.m. out of Rangoon, but was never seen again.

When Melrose landed his Percival Gull in Singapore the next day, he was alarmed to discover that the *Lady Southern Cross* had not beaten him in. He had probably been the last to see Kingsford Smith alive.

Eighteen months later, the port wheel of the *Lady Southern Cross* washed up on an island in the Bay of Bengal.

(National Archives of Australia Collection)

Howard Florey

1898–1968

Howard Florey is featured on the face of the $50 paper note, first issued in 1974.

BELOW:
'Floss'
When Howard Florey was a child, his older sisters liked to dress him up as 'Little Lord Fauntleroy', insisting that he kept his hair long so that they could curl it, completing their charming creation.
(Barr Smith Library Collection, University of Adelaide. Gift of Dr Gardiner)

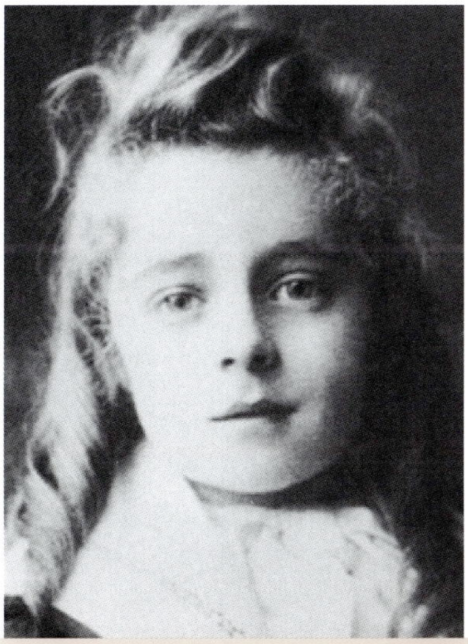

The bushranger of research

THERE ARE THOSE BORN INTO WEALTH WHO DO LITTLE more with their lives than squander their inheritance. There are others born into poverty who, through hard work or good fortune, climb to the top of the pile. There are few like Howard Florey, who started life in wealth and privilege, watched it all disappear before his very eyes, but continued anyway, never missing a beat — working tirelessly to fulfil his destiny.

Before Howard Florey had even started to go to school, his four older sisters, Anne, Charlotte, Hilda and Valetta, who all doted on their little brother, would dress him up, insisting that he let his hair grow long so they could curl it and turn him into their own version of 'Little Lord Fauntleroy'. Florey began his schooling at a small Adelaide school in Unley Park, where his name was corrupted to 'Florrie', then 'Florence' and lastly to 'Floss'. In 1908 he began at exclusive Kyre College. His hair was cut before he joined the bigger boys at Kyre, but the nickname 'Floss' went with him; in fact, it stayed with him all his life — even his wife referred to him as 'Floss'.

At school Florey was an exceptional student; he excelled in everything. He was in all the sporting teams, a champion at every game or track event he attempted. In 1911 he was sent to St Peter's College, one of South Australia's best schools at that time. Young Floss was getting the best that money could buy, and his father's footwear business, the *Standard Shoe & Leather Company* — the biggest

A family business won and lost

Howard Florey was born in Adelaide on 24 September 1898. He was the fifth child and only son of bootmaker Joseph Florey, who had migrated to the colony in 1882 from Standlake in Oxfordshire.

The family had only been in the colony for four years when Joseph's first wife, Charlotte, died from consumption, a condition she had when they first migrated. Three years after her death, Joseph married the daughter of the widowed housekeeper whom he had employed to care for Charlotte in her time of illness. Howard's mother, Joseph's second wife, was Australian-born twenty-six-year-old Bertha Wadham, an energetic and enterprising young woman. Together the couple built a flourishing bootmaking and general footwear business, first with the *Enterprise Boot Factory* and later in 1897 when they owned the *Standard Shoe & Leather Company*. Florey's footware empire was not only known across the colony of South Australia but right across the continent, with factories in Perth and Melbourne. He was soon the biggest footwear manufacturer in southern Australia, with hundreds of employees and an income that made him a very wealthy man.

But their good fortune did not last forever. While Howard was in his second year at the University of Adelaide in 1918 the business collapsed, and the family fortune was lost.

OPPOSITE:
Portrait of Howard Florey, 1960
(National Library of Australia Collection)

manufacturer in southern Australia — was certainly providing plenty of that.

At the end of his first year at St Peter's, Florey came first in physics and chemistry. One day he came home from school and asked his mother what she would give him if he won the Farrer Scholarship; she replied that she would give him fifty pounds. 'Hand it over,' said Floss, 'I've won it!' For the next few years Floss paid his way at school by repeatedly winning scholarships.

St Peter's was modelled on the style of an English boarding school; and there were some eccentric 'English types' who were inspiring teachers. 'Sneaker' Thompson was Floss's chemistry teacher, so named because he crept about the corridors in rubber-soled shoes, and from 'Sneaker' Florey developed a love of scientific research. It was around this time that he told his sister Hilda, who had begun her studies in medicine at the University of Adelaide, that he didn't want to go into their father's business — he 'wanted to be another Pasteur'.

This was just as well, as the footwear company went bust when Floss was in his second year at university. His father had expanded the business just a little too fast and had entered a partnership with his accountant, O. M. Harry. Harry had been systematically driving down production and quality in the Melbourne factory in the hope that he could write down the

Above:

The Florey family ready for a spin in Joseph's* Darracq *motorcar, c. 1907

Joseph is at the wheel of the *Darracq*, Anne is beside him in the front seat. Hilda, Howard and Valetta are in the back. Howard's mother Bertha and sister Charlotte are seated on the verandah of their country house Nankerri in Belair.

Right:

Letterhead of the Standard Shoe & Leather Company of Adelaide and Melbourne

(Photograph & letterhead courtesy Barr Smith Library Collection, University of Adelaide. Gift of Dr Gardiner.)

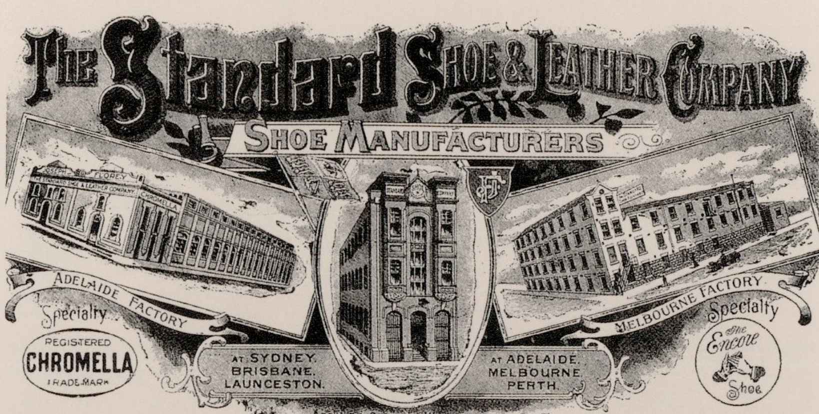

RIGHT:
Ethel Hayter Reed, c. 1920
Ethel was attractive, intelligent, ambitious, and well-to-do. Her ambitions were thwarted by ill health even before she travelled to England to marry Howard Florey.
(Barr Smith Library Collection, University of Adelaide. Gift of Dr Gardiner)

value of the business and buy it out cheaply from under Florey. Unbeknowns to Florey, the swindler had also established a number of retail outlets in Perth, which were mainly operated by members of Harry's own family. Joseph Florey died suddenly of a heart attack in September 1918 while he was in Melbourne in a last attempt to save his company from destruction.

Everything had to be sold up to pay probate on what was left of the Joseph Florey empire. The family was forced to leave the mansion, Coreega, in Adelaide's exclusive, leafy suburb of Mitcham, and moved into a small bungalow in Glen Osmond, not far from where Howard Florey had been born.

These dramatic events did not deter the Florey offspring from their goals. Howard continued to excel at his classes and won enough scholarships to allow him to complete his medical degree. Towards the end of his studies he formed a friendship with another medical student, Ethel Hayter Reed. She was intelligent, ambitious and very attractive, and she and Howard were soul mates from the start.

All Rhodes lead to Oxford

Floss didn't want to become a practising MD; just as he had told his sister Hilda years before, he was committed to the life of the scientist and the research laboratory. To this end he needed to take on further study; he applied for a Rhodes scholarship and was successful. He really didn't have enough money to get himself to England so he took a job as ship's doctor aboard the SS *Otira* and sailed from Australia on 11 December 1921.

In England at last, the opportunities were laid out before him. But the boy from the 'colonies' felt like a duck out of water around the sophisticated English scholars when he first arrived among the seven-hundred-year-old 'dreaming spires' of Oxford. He was quite alone in England, and he wrote hundreds of letters to Ethel, who rapidly became his only lifeline to Australia.

Ethel Hayter Reed

Like Howard Florey, Ethel Hayter Reed came from a well-to-do family in Adelaide. Her father was the manager of the Bank of Australia. Her mother was from the established du Ve family, and was immensely proud of her French ancestry.

Ethel's father disapproved when she began to study medicine at the University of Adelaide. The only female in her class, she was an excellent student and graduated in 1924. She began her professional career as house surgeon at Royal Adelaide Hospital in 1926.

At an early age she developed otosclerosis, and slowly started to go deaf. She was also prone to pleurisy and feared that she would succumb to tuberculosis. Although she appeared to be fit, healthy and rather feisty, her predisposition to ill health caused her to become a bit of a loner. Howard seemed drawn to Ethel for her determination to succeed in a world of her own as much, if not more than, for any romantic reason.

Howard and Ethel married in London in 1927 but the lack of romance in their relationship soon turned the marriage sour. While they stayed together they effectively lived apart, yet Ethel continued to work alongside Howard, assisting in his research.

Right:

Howard Florey on board the Polar Bjorn, *1924*

Florey (right) sporting the 'splendid beard' he grew on his expedition to the icy wilderness of the Arctic Circle in 1924.

(Barr Smith Library Collection, University of Adelaide. Gift of Dr Gardiner.)

Studying under eminent physiologist Sir Charles Sherrington, Florey was encouraged to consider pathology as a career and Sherrington recommended him for a position at the 'rival' university, Cambridge. Nearing the end of his time at Cambridge, Florey was awarded a Rockefeller Scholarship to study in America in 1925. He wrote to Ethel and proposed to her, by post, suggesting that:

> If I get the Fellowship, I might go to America with Mr Rockefeller's bounty, and as they pay more to a married man I can see no adequate proposal why you shouldn't come too'.[1]

Was there ever any more romantic proposal than this? The rather businesslike proposal should not have surprised Ethel, who had earlier received a letter from Florey suggesting that theirs was a cerebral relationship rather than one based on sexual attraction:

> Sex, as can be demonstrated by recording drums and electricity, is our greatest stimulating force. The struggle of youth in our civilisation is to suppress it and make other interests loom large, some minds—and I hope ours are among them—can perceive beauty in biology or chemistry—but anything romantically or 'humanly' beautiful will probably stir us more.[2]

It is hardly surprising that Ethel did not rush to join her 'paramour' on his trip to America. In fact, it took quite some coaxing to get her to agree to wed at all. It would seem that was she first delayed in her decision by concerns over her state of health, and Howard was doing little to paint a rosy picture of life in England; she complained that the 'rain leaked out' of one of his gloomy letters, and that 'the gloom had made her weep before her examinations'.[3]

In spite of her misgivings and against the best advice of her mentor Sir Trent de Crespigny, the house physician at Adelaide hospital, who was also concerned for her health—some enlarged glands removed from Ethel's neck had proved to be tuberculous—Ethel was quite determined to go to England. Floss and Ethel were married in London in a

A vacation in the Arctic

Florey didn't waste any of the spare time he had in England: he travelled widely throughout the countryside, visited Europe and even joined an expedition to the Arctic on board the Norwegian whaler *Polar Bjorn* in 1924.

Oxford provided eight members of the expedition; Florey was medical officer. Cambridge provided another three team members, and there were also four dog teams, one of which was handled by Captain Hanssen, who had been with Amundsen at the South Pole. The expedition was the first to take an aeroplane into the Arctic Circle, which Florey later described as a complete nuisance; the plane crashed on its first flight and it took a rescue party two days to locate the crew. The expedition to study the natural history, geology and glaciology of Spitsbergen was not much of a success, but Florey enjoyed himself immensely. There was very little call for his medical services, other than attending to a boil on Hanssen's face and diagnosing a case of pleurisy, so he spent most of his time taking in the exquisite beauty of the polar wilderness—and even 'growing a splendid beard'.[4]

The memory of this adventure stayed with him all his life. He even named his daughter Paquita, after the wife of that 'other' South Australian polar explorer, Sir Douglas Mawson.

LEFT:
Bacteriologist Alexander Fleming
Photograph by Howard Coster
Scottish-born Fleming did the first work on the lysozyme he named *Penicillium notatum.*
(National Portrait Gallery, London)

quiet ceremony on 19 October 1927, where de Crespigny gave the bride away.

Although they had corresponded for years, when the couple finally began to live together they discovered that they knew little about each other at all. The only real bond they had was their professional interest, and this was no basis for a contented union. Although they had two children — Paquita born in 1929 and Charles in 1934 — the home was never a happy one, and the marriage survived in name only.

Florey was increasingly disappointed with the match that he had pursued for so long by mail. He had built up an image of Ethel as the ideal partner that he had fallen in love with. Although the marriage had broken down, they agreed to stay together and Ethel continued to work with Howard in the laboratory. She was immensely proud of her husband, yet jealous of his success at the same time. While she knew that her health would not permit her to pursue a career on her own, as she would have wished, her marriage to the successful research scientist gave her financial security and professional cachet. Without any official appointment to the Oxford hospital, where Howard now worked, she was still regarded as his assistant, and it was only after the children were evacuated during World War II that she was able to throw herself fully into their research.

In 1927 Florey was awarded the Huddersfield Lectureship in Special Pathology at Cambridge University. He was delighted to be back at Cambridge, as it offered him every advantage over his previous position at London Hospital, better facilities for his research and a stimulating academic environment in which he could immerse himself totally; and the weather was better for Ethel's health as well.

Looking for little bugs

After his trip to the Arctic Circle in 1921, Howard Florey suffered from periodic bouts of indigestion. He didn't know whether it was his appendix, a gastric ulcer or simply

Alexander Fleming 1881–1955

Scottish-born Alexander Fleming worked his entire life in the Innoculation department at St Mary's Hospital, London. A talented bacteriologist, he was studying a harmless bacteria in a petrie dish when he accidentally sneezed over it. He later noticed that the bacteria had stopped growing where he had sneezed. He then took a test tube which held a cloudy mixture of bacteria and dropped some of own snot into it. Fleming recalled that 'It went as clear as gin'.

Fleming discovered that the enzyme he later named 'lysozyme' (*lyse* means dissolve in Latin) existed naturally in tears, bodily mucus, saliva and egg whites.

It was some time later, in 1928, that Fleming noticed a spore of mould growing on a dirty laboratory plate; the spore was destroying the bacteria growing near it. Fleming made a juice from the mould and applied it to an open sore; it killed the microbes that caused the infection.

He named the juice *Penicillium notatum,* submitted a report of his experiments to the scientific journals, then turned his mind to other things, concluding that the production of penicillin was too problematic to make it of any practical use to mankind.

'dyspepsia'. His own discomfort led him to examine the medical journals. He came upon reports of the work of Scottish-born scientist Alexander Fleming, who had investigated the effect of enzymes in the fight against bacteria. Fleming had discovered an enzyme called 'Lysozyme', found in mucus, that had a profound effect on the growth of bacteria.

Florey immediately carried out experimentation on lysozymes to see how they behaved in the human body. His motives were not purely selfish in trying to find a cure for his own indigestion; the coming tensions across Europe and the impending outbreak of war had meant that the search for any means to stave off infection was a high priority for medical researchers. Florey was only too aware of the devastating loss of life and limb in World War I that could have been prevented if only an effective method of arresting infection could have been found. He had seen the disabled soldiers who had come back from the front at the end of the war just as he was finishing his secondary schooling when many of his mates had rushed to join the fray.

In 1938, just before the outbreak of World War II, Florey asked Sir Hugh Cairns, a doctor also from Adelaide who was with the Australian Medical Corps in World War I, what he would like to have in his kit for the coming war that he didn't have in the last and Cairns replied: 'Some means of controlling infection, so many lives were lost — so many limbs too. A small wound could keep men laid up for months if it got infected. If we could prevent that, we could get men back into the fight and change the outcome of the war very quickly'. Florey decided to make that 'his personal war effort'; he told Cairns of his interest in Fleming's discoveries and that it was 'looking promising'.

But Florey did not stand still for very long. In 1932 he accepted the position of chair of pathology at Sheffield University, where in his first year alone he produced more than thirty papers about his work there. Three years later he was back at Oxford, this time as head of the William Dunn School of Pathology. In only ten years the 34-year-old 'bushranger' from Adelaide had gone from undergraduate to Head of School in one of the two most prestigious universities in the world.

Floss's personal war effort

The skies were darkening over Europe and Florey was determined to honour his commitment to Sir Hugh Cairns. His search for a means of arresting infection was intensified. Florey began to assemble a team of similarly minded scientists, believing that several

Laboratory assistant Jim Kent

Things did not always run smoothly for the demanding and often ill-tempered 'Don' Howard Florey. He had difficulty getting hold of and retaining good assistants. One fellow who assisted him at Cambridge later refused to work with him on the grounds that he had been pushed too hard. Florey decided to build his own team.

In 1927 fourteen-year-old Jim Kent walked into Florey's life. Not long after he had returned to Cambridge Florey noticed a lad sweeping leaves outside his laboratory window. He called him in and asked if he liked working with animals. Kent replied 'Yes sir, I do love animals — I'd like to be a vet one day'. Florey asked 'Would you like to work for me? You'll get plenty of animal work if you do'.[5] From that brief encounter began the longest professional relationship of their careers.

Although Florey had to fight many times to keep Kent, they worked together for forty years. Kent developed management skills that had a vital impact on Florey's research output, and, possibly more importantly, he understood Florey's method of working, was willing to work long hours beside his 'firebrand' of a master, and tolerated his bad temper.

LEFT:
Biochemist Ernst Boris Chain
Photograph by Wolfgang Suschitsky
Born of a German mother and a Russian father, Chain fled to England just ahead of Hitler's rise to power.
(Copyright Wolfgang Suschitsky. National Portrait Gallery, London)

scientists working towards the same goal, pooling their ideas and bouncing off one another, would achieve much more than the same minds working in isolation. This method of working was unique in university circles, where many thought that teaching was the primary role of the institution, and it needed a lot of financial support to ensure its success. Florey was determined to raise the funds necessary to keep his laboratory humming: he simply went out and badgered government, philanthropists and the private sector for money. For this he earned the sobriquet 'the bushranger of research'.

He began to build his team, starting with his laboratory assistant, Jim Kent; next he added brilliant German biochemist Ernst Chain. Bacteriologists A. D. Gardner and Jean Orr-Ewing, who were already at the William Dunn school, joined in. Edward Abraham and Norman Heatley, two more biochemists, joined Chain in his work, and when pathologist Margaret Jennings became Florey's assistant in 1936, the team was complete.

Florey set Chain to work on lysozymes, but he found little that would help them make a drug that could fight bacteria and that was both safe and effective under different applications. The pair scoured every scientific article on antibacterial substances they could find and narrowed the field down to three possibilities, one of which was *P. notatum*.

When Germany invaded Poland on 24 August 1939 Florey redoubled his efforts in his personal war against infection. Money was always his biggest problem; with the country throwing all of its resources into the war there was little left for medical research. He wrote to the British Medical Research Council, which had previously supported his work, and received a cheque for £25, barely enough to pay the salary of one man for a month. He wrote to the Rockefeller Foundation in New York and, as the Americans were not involved in the war at that stage, received a grant from them for more money than he had asked.

Ernst Boris Chain

German Jew Ernst Chain fled to England on 30 January 1933 ahead of the advance of Nazism, when 'Europe was plunged into a darkness in comparison to which the Middle Ages now appear as a blaze of light'.[6]

Chain was a brilliant biochemist who had been studying snake venoms, attempting to find the vital ingredient in venom that poisoned human tissue. He had been recommended to Florey by Sir Frederick Gowland Hopkins, who had read his PhD thesis at Cambridge. Hopkins described Chain as also having 'remarkable genius as a musician [that] has made him acceptable in some social circles … a point I think is not without some importance'.[7]

The son of a German mother and a Russian father, Chain was an accomplished musician. He had thought to become a concert pianist but the excitement of the laboratory had drawn him from the stage.

With his bristling, hirsute upper lip, resembling the moustache sported by Albert Einstein, Chain was also the epitome of the 'mad' scientist: excitable, temperamental and passionate about his work, he would pace the floor arguing with himself until he had sorted the problem out in his mind, then return to his test tubes. Chain and Florey were ideally suited: both men were eccentric, both were outsiders, and both were brilliant.

A sample of penicillium was located in a laboratory store and Chain began his experiments, attempting to grow enough of the mould to obtain samples of its juice. They began by adding sugar, salt, meat extract and even a 'soup' of Marmite to the liquid the mould grew in. They needed a huge amount of mould to provide the 'juice' from which the penicillium was extracted before they could even begin to analyse what it was that made it so effective against bacteria. It took months to get enough to make even one gram of the freeze-dried powder.

Cambridge-educated Dr Norman Heatley was the team's fix-it man and he created a production line in the lab made from of all kinds of bits and pieces: an old bathtub, milk churns and any old receptacle that could be used to grow mould in. When they had enough of the then impure dried brown powder (pure penicillin is snowy white) they began the first trial, on a batch of laboratory mice.

On 25 May 1940 Jim Kent prepared eight white mice for injection, first with a lethal dose of Streptococci bacteria. Then four were given penicillin, two given a single dose, the other pair a smaller dose followed by repeated doses every two hours. While Kent made tea over his Bunsen burner, Florey watched the mice all afternoon, recording every detail. Later in the afternoon, Florey recorded that the four injected with the bacteria were looking decidedly unwell; the others were unchanged. At three minutes to midnight the first mouse died, and by 3.28 a.m. the following morning all four that had not received any penicillin were dead. The four that had received the antibacterial injection were as lively as ever.

On Sunday morning Florey, Chain and Heatley were witness to what they all described as a miracle. Penicillin did arrest infection, and could save lives, if only they could manufacture enough of it for human trial. But first they needed to learn as much as they could about its properties and determine the appropriate dosage for all kinds of conditions. Literally hundreds of mice were bred for these trials, injected and tested; the results mounted up in pages of pages of scientific records. So dedicated were they to the search for the drug that Florey and Kent were sleeping in the laboratory, spending seven days a week at their vital task.

They had completed the trials on mice and had proof that penicillin did not only clean wounds, but that it was also capable of curing infections deep within the body. The next thing they needed to do was to prepare a sufficient quantity of the drug for human trials.

Mr Fix-it — Norman Heatley

To complement his research, Florey needed a laboratory engineer capable of attending to their every need. He knew the man he wanted: Norman Heatley, who was just completing his science degree at St John's College, Cambridge. There was no immediate prospect for Heatley at Cambridge, so he was happy to go to Oxford and join 'the team'.

Although there was an attempt to lure Heatley away to work on a Rockefeller Scholarship in Copenhagen, Florey convinced him to stay and work with him on *P. notatum*. Heatley was an expert in the lab; versatile and ingenious, he could put his mind to any task — glass-blowing, plumbing, carpentry, electrics — it was 'Mr Fix-it', Norman Heatley, who kept the lab working twenty-four hours a day.

Sad case of PC Alexander

To grow sufficient mould for human trials, Heatley designed a special 'mould' dish rather like a hospital bedpan. On Christmas Eve 1940 he took delivery of 174 ceramic pans from a pottery in Burslem and on Christmas Day seeded them with mould spores. They needed to make 500 litres of mould juice each week. A team of six girls was employed to keep the production line going, draining the pans of juice and reseeding constantly around the clock. Known as 'the penicillin girls', they became famous for this work.

By February Florey decided that he had enough of the freeze-dried powder to make his first trial. The only thing they needed was a patient; as Florey said, they needed someone with nothing to lose and everything to gain.

They came upon the case of a forty-three-year-old policeman, Albert Alexander, who lay dying in hospital. For two months he had suffered from an infection that had begun with a small sore at the corner of his mouth, which had started with a scratch from a rose thorn. He was in a shocking state: the bacteria (staphylococcus and streptococcus) had infected his entire system, and his body was covered with oozing sores. His left eye had become so badly infected and filled with pus it had to be removed. The infection had taken over his lungs and his right eye was also beginning to suppurate. There was no real hope of a recovery for Albert Alexander.

Dr Charles Fletcher had only recently been introduced to Florey, who had asked him if he could find a suitable patient for the first trial. As it turned out, Fletcher had the honour of being the first to trial penicillin. He gave Albert Alexander an intravenous injection of 200 milligrams of penicillin on 12 February 1941; this was the largest dose ever given and he followed it up with further doses of 100 milligrams every three hours. Within a day Albert's condition had changed markedly; within four days his temperature had dropped to normal and he was sitting up eating a meal. By the end of a week his remaining eye had almost returned to normal. The prognosis for Albert now seemed to be quite good. Unfortunately, the supply of available penicillin had all but been exhausted; for the last five days of his treatment the drug was being recycled, taken from his urine, back to the laboratory, extracted and reinjected into his system.

Even though Albert was on the mend for a week or so, without any further possibility of treatment the lung infection returned and he died on 15 March 1941. Although they had been unable to save Albert Alexander's life,

Family practice

The Florey siblings all followed their own path in society, except Charlotte, who was totally dominated by her mother and remained the 'house drudge'.

Hilda took up her studies of medicine at the University of Adelaide in 1912. First in her class in her final year, she was awarded the Davis Thomas Scholarship and graduated MD BSc in November. She met and married Dr John Gardner in Ballarat and went to live with him in Melbourne. After Joseph Florey passed away, Hilda's mother Bertha went to live in Melbourne, staying with her for the rest of her days. Hilda became one of the leading clinical pathologists in Australia.

Anne took up nursing when she was thirty years old, after she became friends with a nurse engaged to care for Howard when he had contracted pneumonia. Desperate to get away from Adelaide, she enrolled as a student nurse in Launceston. Working with the Queen Alexandra Nursing Service in the Middle East during the war, she was awarded the Royal Red Cross Medal. Valetta had studied at the Elder Conservatorium and had begun a promising career as a concert pianist but was frustrated by deeply webbed fingers which restricted her hand span. In the end she gave it all away and seemed happy enough to be idle at home.

Florey had proven that penicillin was safe to administer over a prolonged period without any toxic effects. The only problem they had was how to make enough of the powder, as Albert had also shown how the drug passed very quickly through the patient's system. Florey said that it was 'like trying to fill a bath with the plug out'.[8]

Further trials were conducted on other severely ill patients. The next was a fifteen-year-old boy who had developed a streptococcal infection after a hip operation; he was cured. Next, a forty-two-year-old labourer had a four-inch carbuncle on his back disappear within a week. Not all cases were as successful: sometimes the patient was too far gone before treatment could be started.

Getting to America

After Florey published the results of these first, rather limited, human trials, he needed to conduct full-scale trials in order to be able to convince the scientific world. He went to the British drug companies for their support, but as everyone was directing all their resources towards the war effort, they were not prepared to fund research. Florey once again looked to America. He contacted the Rockefeller Foundation again and it agreed to fund a trip to the United States.

Travel to America during wartime was not easy; the departure date was so secret that even Heatley, who was to accompany Florey, did not know he was going until Florey telephoned him on 30 May 1941 and told him 'to polish up the bags'. There were weeks of paperwork, clearances and permits ahead of them, but on 26 June 1941 Ethel drove Howard and Heatley to Bristol; next day they took off from Whitchurch airfield in a blacked-out plane headed for Lisbon. After four days enjoying the sunshine in Lisbon, they boarded a clipper flight to New York.

With the increased bombings in London and the major industrial cities Florey had become so concerned that England was about to be invaded by the Germans that his scientists all took the precaution of hiding dried spores of *P. notatum* inside their coat linings. As Florey and Heatley sat inside the plane they were afraid that they could be shot out of the sky. They did not want to see the papers and samples they clutched to their knees fall into the hands of the enemy. The scientists had resolved never to let the findings of their research fall into the hands of the enemy, but they didn't want to see all of their work disappear without trace; their coat linings were to be the last line of resistance in the protection of *P. notatum.*

No German connection!

The international scientific community is made up of researchers from all over the world committed to a common cause: the advancement of knowledge. Reports are published for all to see — there is no embargo on knowledge.

It was in this climate that Florey became quite afraid that the Germans were likely to get their hands on his discovery and gear up for production, which would have a devastating effect on the Allied war efforts.

As he had been unable to convince British manufacturers to take an interest in his 'wonder drug', Florey became increasingly concerned that the Germans, who had the best chemical industry in the world at that time, would get hold of the results of his research.

He instructed the National Type Collection Laboratories 'not to issue cultures of *P. notatum* to anyone with possible enemy connections'. A similar letter was sent to Fleming. Ernst Chain convinced Florey that he should patent his discovery; this idea was rejected by the university administration, which viewed the function of academic research as being 'to make discoveries and to give them freely to the world ... patent applications by Oxford workers is unethical'.[9]

As long as that world didn't include the Germans, for the duration of the war at least.

Immediately after they arrived they got straight down to work. They literally dropped their bags at their hotel and proceeded to the Rockefeller Foundation for their first meeting with Dr Alan Gregg, head of the natural sciences division; Gregg had certainly done his homework — he knew as much about Florey's work as Florey did himself, and more.

Although most of those Florey met from the scientific community were impressed by his ideas, few of the pharmaceutical manufacturers were falling over themselves to help. One described Florey as 'a carpet bag salesman trying to promote a crazy idea for some ulterior motive'. It was not until he had enlisted the support of A. N. Richards, an old friend he had worked with in 1926, and who was now the chairman of the medical research committee in the Office of Scientific Research and Development, that he was able to make any headway at all. Richards approached the four largest drug manufacturers in America and suggested to them that there was the possibility of financial support from the government if they agreed to help. By the time he had arranged a meeting with them all, America had been drawn into the war when the Japanese bombed Pearl Harbor in December 1941. All of a sudden, everyone was interested and the production of a drug such as Florey's became of national importance.

Florey had already returned to Oxford alone, disappointed that he had not convinced the Americans to back his research any further. Heatley stayed on at the Northern Regional Research Laboratory, 280 kilometres north of Chicago, at Peoria, where work had been done on moulds; he stayed behind to teach them everything that the Oxford team had learned.

It was at Peoria in America's corn-growing heartland that some of the most important discoveries were made. They discovered that by feeding the mould syrup made from corn they could produce more than ten times the penicillin they had previously been able to make. This meant that instead of needing 2000 litres of juice to feed the mould they only needed 200 litres to produce the same amount of penicillin. This was a major breakthrough.

LEFT:
The Lord Florey
Portrait by Allan Gwynne-Jones
Oil on canvas, 1963
(University of Adelaide Art Collection)

One of the laboratory assistants had the job of gathering mould from anywhere she could: dirty dishes, rubbish bins, even old shoes. At the Peoria fruit market one day she came across a mouldy cantaloupe covered in a thick fur; juice grown from this mould proved to be twice as strong as any other previously used.

But Florey still had not been able to trial his drug sufficiently to convince those who could sanction his discovery and bring penicillin to a waiting world. He was becoming increasingly irritated that the only time that doctors would turn to his discovery was after all else had failed; that Florey's 'corpse reviver' was called for as a last resort. The fact that it did work under these circumstances began to impress even the most sceptical of clinicians.

Lambert's miracle

In July 1942 Harry Lambert, a friend of Alexander Fleming, was dying of meningitis. Fleming begged Florey for his help. Florey took the first train up to London with his entire supply of penicillin; he instructed Fleming on the appropriate dosage and method of injection and left him to it. Within a few days Lambert had completely recovered; his streptococcal infection had been eliminated. This had happened at St Mary's, where Fleming had first discovered the lysozyme he had called *P. notatum.* Naturally, St Mary's was keen to extract as much publicity out of this miracle as it could, and at the same time promote the brilliance of its own research scientist. The *Times* published an article on 30 August headed *'Penicillium'*; this article 'drew attention to a remarkable new therapeutic substance',[10] and while it espoused the exciting potential of the new wonder drug it avoided mentioning its discoverer, or where it had been discovered. A letter appeared the next day, from St Mary's, letting the public know that it was their research scientist Fleming, who had made the discovery of the wonder drug.

All of the newspapers carried the story of the wonder drug. Headlines such as 'LIVES SAVED BY PENICILLIN' were splashed across the newsstands. The whole world was ready to accept the new lifesaver. When reporters clamoured at Fleming's door he tried to point out that it was the Oxford team under the leadership of Howard Florey that was really responsible. But when they tried to interview Florey, he refused to speak to them, afraid that the resulting publicity would create a demand that he could never hope to satisfy. Without any communication from Florey, attention centred on Fleming, who simply gave up trying to correct the stories that were written about him and 'his discovery'.

Ethel finds her niche at last

After the outbreak of war, the Florey children were evacuated to America and Ethel was able to fully apply herself to assisting Howard in the laboratory. He gave her the task of running clinical trials and this proved to be the thing missing from her life — the career she had left in Australia when she decided to marry.

Although she had no official appointment to the Oxford team, she was regarded as Florey's assistant just the same. It was Ethel who conducted the clinical trials: she selected the patients, organised the tests, controlled the treatment and wrote the reports. She was 'on call' twenty-fours hours a day. It was a common sight to see her cycling around Oxford with her basket filled with bottles of urine taken from patients under treatment so that the valuable penicillin could be recycled.

Ethel was never free from medical problems herself: she suffered from respiratory problems, hypertension and incipient heart failure. An operation in 1957 to relieve her deafness was unsuccessful. A heart attack in 1965 didn't stop her from travelling to America on a lecture tour, and then on to Australia to visit her family. Ethel died suddenly on 10 October 1966 after a trip to America for her son's wedding.

The Americans pressed on with their research and found penicillin to be of greater value than they had ever considered possible. The American drug manufacturers had begun in earnest and were producing huge quantities of the drug. It took a while, but the British eventually got their factories into production.

In May 1943 Howard Florey, accompanied by Sir Hugh Cairns, visited the North African battlefield, where the pair conducted trials of the drug on injured soldiers. The results were just as they had expected, and as Florey had promised Cairns all those years before. Florey made a trip to Russia later that year as part of an Anglo-American mission to assist the Russians in their war against the Germans with the latest in Western medical advances, penicillin being the most important of all.

Recognition

King George VI made Howard Florey a Knight Commander of the British Empire (KBE) in June 1944. He returned to Australia, for only his second visit, shortly after, to assist in the production of penicillin at home. While in Australia he was asked by the government to advise on the creation of a new national university in Canberra and was keen to help. He returned in 1958 to officially open the John Curtin School of Medicine.

While the controversy continued over who actually discovered penicillin, the scientific community had no doubts who deserved the honours. In October 1945 Florey, Chain and Fleming all shared in the Nobel Prize for Medicine. In 1946 philanthropist Lord Nuffield offered Florey £50,000 in recognition of his sterling work throughout the war. Never seeking personal reward for himself, Florey used the money to establish research fellowships for young scientists.

In 1965 Florey was created a 'life peer' and took the title of Baron Florey of Adelaide and Marston: Adelaide for his place of birth and Marston for the village where he lived in Oxford. Just when most thought he was about to retire, he accepted the position of provost of Queen's College at Oxford. He was the first, and only, Australian to be elected president of the 340-year-old Royal Society. This was his greatest honour.

On a trip back to Australia in June 1967 Florey suffered the first of two heart attacks. The second came seven months later, after he had returned to Oxford. Howard Florey died in his bed in the provost's lodgings on 21 February 1968. Margaret Jennings, his second wife, was at his side, just as she had been at his side in the laboratory for the last thirty-two years of his life.

Margaret Jennings — Lady Florey

Dr Margaret Jennings, wife of gastroenterologist Dr D.A. Jennings, joined Florey's team in Oxford while Florey was in Australia in 1936 to see his mother just before she died.

Upon his return to the Dunn School at Oxford Florey started her off working on mucous secretions with him. Jennings stayed working beside him for thirty-two years, marrying him in the last year of his life.

Although the few months they had as man and wife brought great happiness to them both, it is sad that Howard had to wait so long for contentment in his personal life. Margaret was with him when he died of a heart attack on 21 February 1968.

Lady Florey died twenty-six years later in 1994.

(Barr Smith Library Collection, University of Adelaide. Gift of Dr Gardiner.)

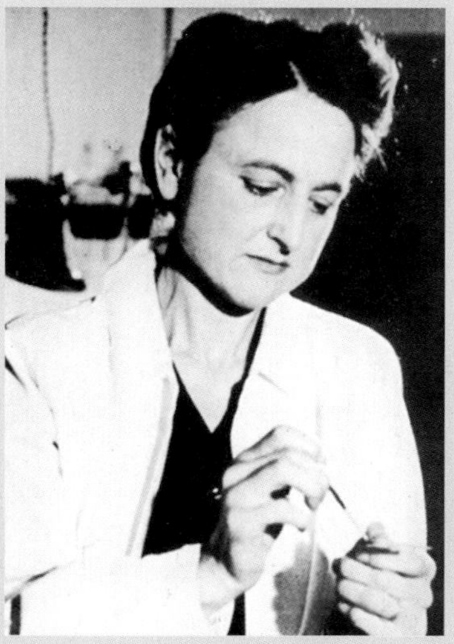

Sir Ian Clunies-Ross

1899 – 1959

Sir Ian Clunies-Ross is featured on the obverse of the $50 paper note, first issued in 1974.

OPPOSITE:
Sir Ian Clunies-Ross
Sir Ian Clunies-Ross had a distinguished career, not so much for his work as a research scientist, but for his management of others and his role as a facilitator in bringing science to the fore in Australian life.

His administration of the Commonwealth Scientific and Industrial Research Organisation (CSIRO) saw Australia change from a state dependent on other countries for a lead in science and manufacturing industry, to become a leader in international scientific research.

The organisation dominated Australian research under the leadership of Ian Clunies-Ross, creating hundreds of agricultural research stations right across the country. Through Clunies-Ross's membership of the International Wool Secretariat, Australian wool was taken to the world.

At one stage, attempting to highlight the uses of new, lightweight wools, the secretariat was even able to persuade the Queen of England and Mrs Roosevelt, wife of the American president, to appear in woollen dresses in the middle of summer. The secretariat concluded that it was happy with the result and that it had no 'suspicion that the comfort of either distinguished wearer was in any way affected other than for good'.
(National Library of Australia Collection)

The man from CSIRO

DURING WORLD WAR I IT BECAME ABUNDANTLY CLEAR to the Australian government that it could no longer rely on 'old Europe' for the supply of goods and services. Australia's isolation from troubled Europe meant that it could no longer remain a client state: it needed to take immediate steps to control its own agricultural, scientific and manufacturing destiny.

To this end, Prime Minister Billy Hughes created the Advisory Council on Science and Industry in 1916, which became the office of Council for Scientific and Industrial Research (CSIR) a decade later; CSIR was established to assist primary industry through scientific research. It was another twenty years before its charter was broadened to include secondary industry, under the acronym CSIRO.

Agriculture — pests and parasites

The first parasitologist appointed to the research team at CSIR was young graduate veterinarian Ian Clunies-Ross, who began a thirty-year relationship with the organisation in 1926.

Ian Clunies-Ross was born on 22 February 1899 in Bathurst, in central New South Wales. He was four years old when his family moved to the Sydney suburb of Ashfield, halfway between central Sydney and Parramatta, after his father had taken a position as a lecturer in the department of chemistry and metallurgy at East Sydney Technical College. It was in the open paddocks and bushland around Ashfield that Ian developed a lifelong passion for nature. Ian and his three older brothers were taught at home by their parents for the first few years of their school days and as lessons usually finished around lunchtime they had plenty of time to explore the world around them. Their mother, Hannah, let them go as they liked: she tolerated their collection of fantail pigeons, boxes of insects and buckets of frogs, but 'drew the line at poisonous snakes in the house'.

Like their father, William, who had a great interest in natural science — he kept records for the Geographical Society, collected rocks, plants and reptiles, even allowing himself to be bitten by an Australian Black Snake to prove the species was suffering from an unfair reputation — the boys studied all that was around them. Their father had no pretensions at all; he was typical of the austere and conservative Scot steeped in his Christian faith. Hannah was much more liberal, although careful of manners, cultured and conscious of accent and style. Where William favoured Disraeli, Hannah preferred Gladstone; he favoured a state education for his boys, she preferred to send them to a private school. Such contrary outlooks led to their eldest sons, Allen and Egerton, attending Sydney High while Robert and Ian were enrolled as day-boys at Newington Methodist College.

While the boys were still at Newington their father died of cancer, leaving the family in distressed circumstances. With the outbreak of war, the three older boys joined up immediately. Egerton had been a part-time soldier and went to war with a commission; the others were sent as privates to France.

Egerton and Robert never came home; weakened by an earlier bout of typhoid, Egerton contracted pneumonic influenza and died. Robert was killed in battle. Hannah travelled to England in 1919 to return to Australia by troopship alongside Allen, her only surviving veteran of World War I. Ian had reached eighteen years of age and was keen to enlist before he entered university, but Hannah had exercised her right to keep him away from the battlefield, as he was not yet twenty-one.

Although his father, who believed in the working man's college system, had objected to him doing so, Ian Clunies-Ross enrolled at the University of Sydney in 1917. Four years later, in 1921, he graduated with honours in veterinary science. He began his working career as a research fellow at the Walter and Eliza Hall Institute of Medical Research in Melbourne, returning later to Sydney to take up the position of lecturer in the faculty of veterinary science at the University of Sydney. While he was at Walter and Eliza Hall Clunies-Ross arranged to spend some of his time overseas. He worked at the Moleno Institute of Parasitology at Cambridge and the School of Tropical Medicine in London. His research was in the field of parasitology, and he set his mind to finding a solution to the control of liver fluke and the hydatid parasite, two of the biggest concerns for Australian pastoralists at that time.

He made the trip to England accompanied by his mother and on his way home, a year later, travelled through Hungary and Poland with ship's doctor Charles Huxtable, whose friendship he had made on the journey over. He also visited research facilities in Texas and Louisiana on his circuitous route home.

When he got back to Sydney in 1925, Clunies-Ross set himself up in a veterinary practice in College Street, in the heart of Sydney, but his inability to secure enough clients to enable him to pay the rent soon saw him return to academia.

The curious seagoing clan of Clunies-Ross

Ian's father William John Clunies-Ross was born and bred in London. At the time his wife Hannah Elizabeth (Tilley) gave birth to Ian, their fourth and youngest child, William was head of Bathurst Technical college in central New South Wales. Australian-born Hannah Tilley had also been a schoolteacher before the pair married.

William had travelled to the colony of New South Wales at the age of thirty-three aboard a sailing ship captained by his brother Alfred. Their father, Robert Clunies-Ross, was a sea captain himself who had been born in Shetland in 1790.

His father's brother John was the Clunies-Ross who settled on the Cocos-Keeling Islands with his family, and ship's crew, in 1826, establishing their own little 'Malay Kingdom'. A descendant, George Clunies-Ross, was granted the islands in perpetuity by Queen Victoria in 1886; the British government was then keen to exploit the vast phosphate deposits on Christmas Island and it was annexed in November 1888.

The Tilleys were a mixture of Hampshire farmers, distressed gentry and Protestant Irish evangelists from County Tipperary; they included one brother who had ended up in Berlin where he established a school teaching German to English-speaking students.

Clunies-Ross joined the Council for Scientific and Industrial Research (CSIR) when it was established in 1926 and stayed until 1937. During his time at CSIR he had been director of the McMaster Animal Health Laboratory and president of the Australian Veterinary Association. During his first term at CSIR he spent one year at Tokyo Imperial University, conducting parasitological research at the Research Institute of Infectious Diseases.

He resigned his position at CSIR to join the International Wool Secretariat, which had been created in response to the rapid acceptance of synthetic fibres in the global market during World War II. This posed a serious threat to the survival of wool production and manufacturing as a viable industry for the future.

By 1940 Clunies-Ross was back at the University of Sydney, accepting an appointment as professor of veterinary science, a position he held until 1946. These were again war years, and while at the University of Sydney he was appointed adviser to the pastoral industry, to the department of war organisation of industry, and director of scientific manpower. Just as Prime Minister Hughes had seen the need for Australia to stand on its own two feet during the 1914–18 war, later governments had recognised the positive role that science could play in the development of the manufacturing industry in particular as it geared up, once again, for the war effort.

CSIRO

At the end of World War II Clunies-Ross was back at CSIR when he was appointed executive officer in 1946. He became chairman of a new body after CSIR had outgrown its original charter and changed to become the Commonwealth Scientific and Industrial Research Organisation (CSIRO) in 1949. Clunies-Ross remained in this position until his death in 1959.

His time at the helm of CSIRO saw its domination of the academic world of scientific research in Australia. Since it had broadened to include secondary industry in 1936, the institute had diversified to include plant and animal breeding, pasture management, pest and disease control, paper manufacture, mineral exploration, wool and textiles research, solar energy, radio astronomy, atomic absorption and spectrophotometry.

Throughout his professional life Ian Clunies-Ross sought to bring Australian science to international attention. He was committed to the development of Australia as an educated society, a society that pooled its natural advantages, with the managed exploitation of its

LEFT:
Sir Ian Clunies-Ross

Not long after he returned to Australia in 1925, Ian was invited to spend the weekend at Mount Kembla on the New South Wales south coast. He travelled down by train in the company of final-year university student Janet Carter, whom he had knowledge of, but had never met.

Ian was never sure whether he would ever marry, and although he and Janet formed a strong bond over the next two years after that first holiday weekend, they resolved to stop seeing each other for three months. The trial separation must have proved too much, as they were married on 6 October 1927. They did, however, wait until after Ian had been appointed to CSIR, and after his mother had decided to make another trip to England once they had married.

(State Library of New South Wales Collection)

BELOW:
Rabbiters display their catch at Murrangowar in Victoria

(Museum of Victoria Collection)

(State Library of Victoria Collection)

First, catch your rabbit!

Rabbits were unknown in Australia until 1859, when Victorian grazier Thomas Austin, keen for some shooting sport, released the first pair.

Before a decade had passed, more than 20,000 rabbits were shot on Austin's property alone, and rabbiting became a necessary pastime for almost every Australian who tried to make a living from the land. The scourge was no longer any cause or sport, and needless to say, the name Thomas Austin never entered the lexicon of Australia's great colonial benefactors.

For the better part of the following century Australian farmers and graziers sought any means at all to eradicate this furry pest. Fences were run up over hundreds of miles to stop the rabbits' onward march; poisons were dropped in pasture land; steel-jawed traps lay yawning at burrow holes; ferrets flung their way along the underground tunnels as the little beasts raced to the openings, netted before they fell prey to rows of razor sharp teeth. But the little bunny continued to breed and breed, ever resourceful, ever one step ahead of the hunter and the next bit of technology designed to bring about its doom. Until there was 'Myxo'.

In 1918 a Brazilian scientist identified the South American rabbit virus 'myxoma' and suggested that it be tried in Australia. Following the release of myxomatosis by CSIRO in 1950, to devastating effect among the rabbit population along the Murray-Darling basin, the *Weekly Times* of 14 March 1951, reported that:

> Myxomatosis is doing to the rabbit population around Corowa what the Black Plague did to the people of Europe in the 14th century.

Although the *Weekly Times* did go on to point out the 'C.S.I.R.O. says there is no danger of the disease spreading to other animals [and that] it will infect only rabbits', a coincidental outbreak of human encephalitis along the Murray River had the rural population in a panic.

To quell the panic, CSIRO scientists injected themselves with a large dose of the virus to prove its safety. But the public was not convinced until the scientists had revealed their identities: people wanted visible proof that these three men were still alive and well. Ian Clunies-Ross, Macfarlane Burnet and Frank Fenner duly revealed themselves; Fenner recalled that the only visible sign of trauma was Clunies-Ross bleeding from a cut caused by a broken syringe tip.

BELOW:
Meeting of Executive & Chiefs CSIRO, 1949
As a result of the paranoia during the cold war this executive, including Clunies-Ross, front row, centre, were accused of being communist symapthisers.
(National Library of Australia Collection)

resources and the best of scientific knowledge and expertise. Through his example he sought to build the confidence of the community in science as a harbinger of economic growth and social wellbeing.

In his continued quest to establish the prescience of Australian science on the international forum Clunies-Ross served as a delegate to the League of Nations Assembly in 1938 and as president of the Australian Institute of International Affairs from 1941 to 1945.

During a forty-year career at the forefront of Australian science Ian Clunies-Ross published sixty research papers. He was awarded a doctorate of veterinary science in 1928, the Gold Medal of the Royal Society of England, the James Cook Medal, and was a foundation fellow of the Australian Academy of Science in 1954. He was also made Knight Commander (KCMG) in 1954.

Reds under the bed

In July 1949 a CSIRO scientist in London distributed leaflets which attacked the Australian government's handling of the miners' union during a coal strike. This action embarrassed the executive of the CSIRO, who, in not dismissing the scientist on the spot, were accused of being communist sympathisers. This had come hot on the heels of concerns by several members of federal parliament the previous year when a junior officer, working in forestry research, was found to be an active member of the Communist Party. In a mad world searching everywhere for 'reds under the bed' the US government became concerned about sharing information on atomic research with Australian scientists. Unlike the public service, CSIRO had no political test to an appointment and bound its employees to secrecy only if they were working on defence research.

This stressful situation aggravated an angina condition that Sir Ian Clunies-Ross had been carrying for some years. Although he was advised to be careful, he continued to represent Australian science and education abroad. After a trip to India and Pakistan in 1958 he suffered a mild stroke, and later in the year he had his first coronary attack.

His recovery was slow and he decided to make some time for himself. He began work on an autobiography and to take some walking exercise to rebuild his strength, but a second heart attack laid him low. Sir Ian Clunies-Ross died in Melbourne on 20 June 1959. His shortened life had been one of total dedication to the advancement of scientific knowledge and to Australia as an educated nation ready to take its place among all others.

Decimalisation — 14 February 1966

Australian currency was decimalised on 14 February 1966. Leading up to the changeover from the old English nomenclature of pounds, shillings and pence to dollars and cents, there had been considerable discussion regarding the appropriate name for the new currency.

Prime Minister Menzies tied his colours to the monarchist mast when he proposed that the basic unit should be called the Royal; howls of protest rebuffed his suggestion.

The decision was made to call the basic unit the 'dollar'. This was in itself controversial at the time, as it seemed to tie Australia's future, ideologically, to the fortunes of the United States of America.

The original $1 note was replaced in May 1984 by a $1 coin; the $2 note was also replaced by a smaller coin in June 1988. The world's first polymer notes were introduced in January 1988 with the release of the $10 bicentennial note. These 'plastic' notes were promoted as virtually indestructible; the first thing many did when they got hold of one of them was try to tear them; many succeeded.

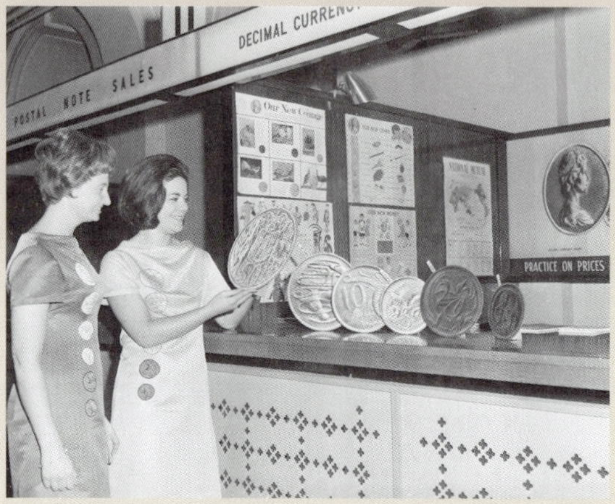

ABOVE:
'Dollar Girls' on duty at a post office, with giant replicas of the new Australian decimal coins released on 14 February 1966
(National Archives of Australia Collection)

The first paper notes

$1 — The Queen of England and the Commonwealth, Elizabeth II, was featured on the first $1 paper bill; the Australian Coat of Arms is in the background. *(1966-74 paper, designed by Gordon Andrews)*

$1 *obverse* — Features an Aboriginal design adapted from bark paintings and cave paintings from Arnhem Land.

$2 — Pastoralist John Charles Macarthur. Features a merino ram and woven woollen material. *(1966-74 paper, 1974-88 polymer, designed by Gordon Andrews)*

$2 *obverse* — Agriculturalist William James Farrer. Features ears of Federation wheat.

$5 — Botanist Sir Joseph Banks. Features botanical sketches of native Australian fauna.
(1966-74 paper, 1974-92 polymer, designed by Gordon Andrews)

$5 *obverse* — Philanthropist Caroline Chisholm. Features the Sydney Rocks area, a migrant ship and faces of the girls Chisholm sought to serve.

$10 — Emancipist architect Francis Greenway. Features detail of buildings designed by Greenway in Sydney, Parramatta and Windsor, New South Wales.
(1966-74 paper, 1974-93 polymer, designed by Gordon Andrews)

$10 *obverse* — Journalist, author, republican and poet Henry Lawson. Features details of images from the Holtermann Collection of photographs of the Hill End and Gulgong goldfields, New South Wales.

$20 — Aviator Sir Charles Kingsford Smith. Features propeller movements.
(1966-74 paper, 1974-94 polymer, designed by Gordon Andrews)

$20 *obverse* — Inventor Lawrence Hargrave. Features designs for box kites and flying machines.

.

$50 — Medical researcher Howard Florey. Features petrie dishes with *Penicillium notatum* bacteria.
(1974-95 paper, designed by Gordon Andrews)

$50 *obverse* — Veterinarian, parasitologist, scientific researcher and administrator Sir Ian Clunies-Ross. Features Parkes radio telescope.

$10 Bicentennial commemorative issue — Features Captain James Cook's bark HMS *Endeavour* and images of Australian exploration and migration in the nineteenth century. An image of Cook is set in the hologram.
(1988 polymer, designed by Harry Williamson)

Obverse — This controversial design was withdrawn following a dispute over the rights to reproduce images from traditional Aboriginal culture. It shows a min min figure, a decorative corroboree stick and traditional tribal body painting.

$100 — Antarctic explorer Sir Douglas Mawson. Features the Mertz glacier tongue.
(1996 paper, designed by Harry Williamson)

$100 *obverse* — Astronomer John Tebbutt. Features the observatory and library Tebbutt built at Peninsula House, Windsor, New South Wales.

Polymer notes 1993-present

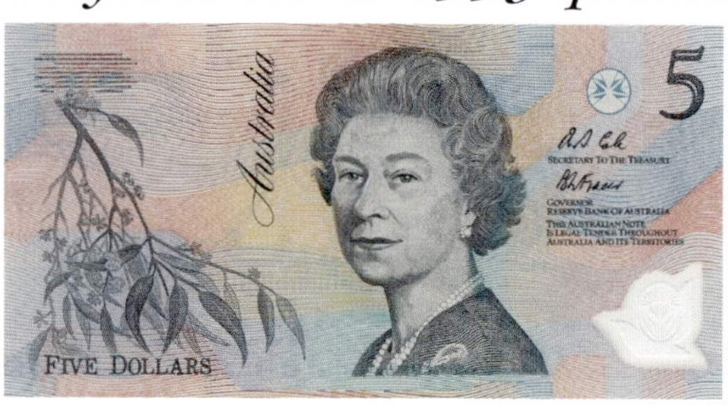

$5 — Queen of Australia, Elizabeth II. Features a sprig of wattle, Australia's national floral emblem.
(1995-2001 polymer, designed by Bruce Stewart)

$5 *obverse* — The new Australian Parliament House, Canberra, opened in 1988.

$5 Federation note — Parliamentarian Sir Henry Parkes. Features a public school building; the opening of the first parliament in the Exhibition Building, Melbourne; Federation Cupola, Centennial Park, Sydney; Federation Star; emblems of the States of the Federated Commonwealth of Australia.
(2001 polymer, designed by Garry Emery)

$5 *obverse* — Women's rights activist Catherine Helen Spence.

$10 — Journalist, author, poet and war correspondent Andrew Barton 'Banjo' Paterson, 1864-1941. Features a sprig of wattle, the man from Snowy River and 'Waltzing Matilda' music sheet.
(1993 polymer, designed by Max Robinson)

$10 *obverse* — Republican, political activist, civil rights agitator, author and poet Dame Mary Gilmore. Features portrait painted by Sir William Dobell and bullock-wagon.

$20 — Emancipist, businesswoman and merchant Mary Reibey. Features merchant trading vessel; George Street, Sydney, warehouse.
(1994 polymer, designed by Garry Emery)

$20 *obverse* — Missionary, visionary and cleric Reverend John Flynn. Features 'Flying Doctor' aerial ambulance; pedal radio; numbered medical poster used for remote diagnosis; camel transport.

$50 — Aboriginal inventor, author and anthropologist David Unaipon. Features designs for mechanical shears; engine; outback mission; Dreamtime story.
(1995 polymer, designed by Brian Sadgrove)

$50 *obverse* — Parliamentarian, social rights worker, women's rights activist and feminist Dame Edith Cowan. Features Western Australian parliament building; woman and family; woman at podium.

$100 — Opera singer Dame Nellie Melba.
(1996 polymer, designed by Bruce Stewart)

$100 *obverse* — Engineer and soldier Sir John Monash. Features Anzac 'Rising Sun' badge; Light Horsemen 1st AIF; Private Simpson and his donkey; Howitzer in action at the battle of the Somme.

Bibliography

BARNARD, MARJORIE. *Australia's First Architect — Francis Greenway*, Longmans, Sydney, 1961.

BEAGLEHOLE, J.C. *The Endeavour Journal of Joseph Banks, 1768-1771*, Angus and Robertson, Sydney, 1962.

BHATHAL, RAGBIR. *Australian Astronomer — John Tebbutt*, Simon & Schuster, Sydney, 1996.

BLAIR, DAVID. *The History of Australia*, McGready, Thompson and Niven, Glasgow, 1878.

CAMPBELL. R. & HARVIE, P. *Singer of the Bush. A.B. 'Banjo' Paterson. Complete Works 1885-1900,* Lansdowne Press, Sydney, 1983.

CHAMBERS, NEIL (ED.), *The Letters of Joseph Banks, A selection, 1768-1820,* Imperial College Press, London, 2000.

CLARK, C. M. H. *Select documents in Australian History, 1851-1900*, Angus and Robertson, Sydney, 1955.

ELLIS, M. H. *Francis Greenway, His Life and Times*, Angus and Robertson, Sydney, 1949.

HETHERINGTON, JOHN. *Melba. A biography*, F.W. Cheshire, Melbourne, 1967.

HOBAN, MARY. *Fifty-one Pieces of Wedding Cake. A biography of Caroline Chisholm*, Lowden Publishing Co., Kilmore, 1973.

KIDDLE, MARGARET. *Caroline Chisholm*, Melbourne University Press, 1950.

LLOYD, CHRISTOPHER (ED.). *The Voyages of Captain James Cook Round the World,* The Cresset Press, London, 1949.

MARTIN, A.W. *Henry Parkes. A Biography*, Melbourne University Press, 1980.

MACDOUGALL, A. K. *Australians at War. A Pictorial History.* The Five Mile Press, Melbourne, 2002.

MACDOUGALL, A. K. *The Great Treasury of Australian Folklore*, The Five Mile Press, Melbourne, 2002.

MACFARLANE, G. *Howard Florey. The Making of a Scientist*, Oxford University Press, London, 1979.

MARGERY, SUSAN. *Unbridling the Tongues of Women — A biogaphy of Catherine Helen Spence,* Hale & Iremonger, Sydney, 1985.

MAWSON, SIR DOUGLAS. *The home of the blizzard: being the story of the Australasian Antarctic expedition, 1911-1914,* Heinemann, London, 1915.

MELBA, DAME NELLIE. *Melodies and Memories,* Thomas Nelson, Australia 1980.

NORTHWOOD, VERNON. *Monash,* State Electricity Commission of Victoria, Melbourne, 1961.

OLDFIELD, AUDREY. *The Great Republic of the Southern Seas*, Hale & Iremonger, Alexandria, 1999.

OLLIF, LORNA. *Andrew B. Paterson*, Twayne Publishers Inc., New York, 1971.

PORTUS, G.V. *50 Famous Australians*, Colorgravure Publications, Melbourne, 1951.

ROSS, JOHN (ed.). *Chronicle of Australia,* Penguin, Ringwood, 2000.

RUSSELL, ARCHER. *William James Farrer, A Biography,* F.W. Cheshire, Melbourne, 1949.

SEMMLER, CLEMENT. *A. B. (Banjo) Paterson*, Lansdowne Press, Melbourne, 1965.

TOTTENHAM, S.E. *101 Great Australians. Biographies and portraits of famous men and women,* National Book Distributors, Brookvale, New South Wales, 1991.

UNAIPON, DAVID. *Legendary Tales of the Australian Aborigines,* edited by Stephen Muecke & Adam Shoemaker, The Miegunyah Press, Melbourne, 2001.

VESTEY, PAMELA. *Melba. A family memoir*, Pamela Vestey, Coldstream, Victoria, 2000.

WEIDENHOFER, MARGARET. *The Convict Years. Transportation and the penal system 1788-1868,* Lansdowne Press, Melbourne, 1973.

WILDE, W. H. & MOORE, T. INGLIS. *Letters of Mary Gilmore,* Melbourne University Press, Melbourne, 1980.

WRIGHT, DAVID MCKEE. *Poetical Works of Henry Lawson*, Angus and Robertson, Sydney, 1925.

Notes

Sir Joseph Banks

1 C. Lloyd (ed.), *The Voyages of Captain James Cook Round The World,* The Cresset Press, London, 1949, p. 18.
2 ibid, p. 18.
3 ibid, p. xvi.
4 J. Ross (ed.). *Chronicle of Australia.* Penguin, Ringwood, 2000, p. 73.
5 ibid, p. 78.

John Macarthur

1 Ross, op. cit, p. 123.
2 D. Blair, *The History of Australia*, McGready, Thompson and Niven, Glasgow, 1878, pp. 264.
3 ibid, loc. cit.
4 ibid, pp. 293-294.

Mary Reibey

1 Letter written by transportee Mary Haydock to her aunt Mrs Hope in Blackburn, Lancashire, in 1792. State Library of New South Wales Collection.

Francis Greenway

1 M. H. Ellis, *Francis Greenway, His Life and Times*, Angus and Robertson, Sydney, 1949, p. 3.
2 ibid, p. 3.
3 ibid, p. 4.
4 ibid, p. 12.
5 ibid, p. 13.
6 ibid, p. 15.
7 ibid, p. 18.
8 ibid, pp. 27-28.
9 ibid, p. 82.
10 ibid, p. 139.
11 ibid, p. 98.
12 ibid, p. 101.
13 ibid, p. 147.
14 ibid, p. 148.

Caroline Chisholm

1 M. Hoban, *Fifty-one Pieces of Wedding Cake. A biography of Caroline Chisholm*, Lowden Publishing Co., Kilmore, 1973, p. 6.
2 ibid, p. 4.
3 ibid, p. 26.
4 ibid, p. 27.
5 M. Kiddle, *Caroline Chisholm*, Melbourne University Press, 1950, p. 33.
6 Hoban, op. cit., p. 53.
7 J. D. Lang, *Popery in Australia and How to Check it Effectively*, Edinburgh, 1847, p. 21.
8 Hoban, op. cit., p. 178.
9 Kiddle, op.cit., p. 94.
10 Blair, op.cit., p. 363.
11 loc. cit.
12 Dickens, *Oliver Twist*, Chapter 8.
13 *Mount Alexander Mail,* 11 December 1854.

Sir Henry Parkes

1 A.W. Martin, *Henry Parkes. A Biography*, Melbourne University Press, 1980, p. 24.
2 ibid, p. 27.
3 ibid, p. 29.
4 ibid, p. 33.
5 ibid, pp. 44.
6 ibid, pp. 57-58.
7 Ross, op. cit, p. 291.
8 ibid, p. 57.
9 ibid, p. 309.
10 Martin, op. cit, p. 302.
11 Ross, op. cit, p. 413.
12 Martin, op. cit, p, 383.
13 C. M. H. CLARK, *Select documents in Australian History, 1851-1900,* Angus and Robertson, Sydney, 1955, p. 468.
14 Ross, op. cit, p. 439.
15 ibid, 402.
16 ibid, p. 439.
17 Martin, op. cit, p. 402.

Catherine Helen Spence

1 S. Margery, *Unbridling the Tongues of Women — A biography of Catherine Helen Spence,* Hale & Iremonger, Sydney, 1985. p. 12.
2 C. H. Spence, *An Autobiography,* Australia Facsimile Editions, Adelaide, 1975, pp 16-17.
3 Margarey, op. cit, p. 78.
4 ibid, p. 84.
5 ibid, p.85.
6 ibid, p. 86.
7 ibid, p. 142.
8 ibid, p. 47.
9 ibid, p. 56
10 ibid, p. 61.
11 ibid, pp. 161-162.

John Tebbutt

1 Ross, op. cit, p. 407.

William James Farrer

1 A. Russell, *William James Farrer, A Biography,* F.W. Cheshire, Melbourne, 1949. pp. 20-21.
2 ibid, p. 21.
3 ibid, loc.cit.
4 ibid, p. 27.
5 ibid, p. 28.
6 ibid, p. 33.
7 ibid, p. 31.

Lawrence Hargrave

1 G.V. Portus, *50 Famous Australians*, Colorgravure Publications, Melbourne, 1951, p. 413.
2 ibid, p. 414.
3 ibid, p. 416.

Dame Nellie Melba

1 J. Hetherington, *Melba. A biography*, F.W. Cheshire, Melbourne, 1967, p. 19.
2 ibid, p. 20.
3 ibid, p. 28.
4 N. Melba, *Melodies and Memories,* Thomas Nelson, Australia 1980. p. 9.
5 Hetherington, op. cit., p. 54.
6 loc. cit.
7 loc. cit.
8 ibid, p. 57.
9 Melba, op.cit., 28.
10 P. Vestey, *Melba. A family memoir,* Pamela Vestey, Coldstream, Victoria. p. 57.
11 ibid, p. 176.
12 ibid, p. 178.
13 Hetherington, op. cit., p. 28.
14 ibid, p. 47.
15 loc. cit.
16 loc. cit.

Banjo Paterson

1 R. Campbell & P. Harvie, *Singer of the Bush. A. B. 'Banjo' Paterson. Complete Works 1885-1900,* Lansdowne Press, Sydney, 1983. p. xxiv.
2 From *The Sport of Kings in Banjo Paterson tells his own story, Sydney Morning Herald,* 4 Feb - 4 March 1939, Five articles published on consecutive Saturdays.
3 Campbell & Harvie, op. cit., p. xiii.
4 ibid, p. 578.
5 ibid, p. xiv.
6 *Sydney Morning Herald,* 4 Feb - 4 March 1939, op.cit.

Sir John Monash

1 V. Northwood, *Monash,* State Electricity Commission of Victoria, Melbourne, 1961, p. 9.
2 A.K.Macdougall, *Australians at War, A Pictorial History*, The Five Mile Press, 2002, pp.116-117.
3 Northwood, op.cit, p. 18.
4 Macdougall, op. cit, p. 138.
5 ibid, p. 141.
6 *From* A. Wade, *The War of The Guns, 1936,* quoted in Macdougall *The Great Treasury of Australian Folklore,* The Five Mile Press, Melbourne, 2002, p. 370.
7 Macdougall, op. cit, p. 143.
8 Northwood, op.cit, p. 24.
9 ibid, p. 37.

Dame Mary Gilmore

1 W.H.Wilde and T. Inglis Moore, *Letters of Mary Gilmore,* Melbourne University Press, Melbourne, 1980. p. 13.

Henry Lawson

1 Portus, op. cit., p. 244.

2 A. Oldfield, *The Great Republic of the Southern Seas*, Hale & Iremonger, Alexandria, 1999, p. 230.
3 Oldfield, op. cit., loc. cit.
4 Portus, op. cit., p. 248.
5 Oldfield, op. cit., loc. cit.

Sir Douglas Mawson

1 Portus, op. cit, p. 59

Howard Florey

1 G. Macfarlane, *Howard Florey: The Making of a Scientist*, Oxford University Press, London, 1979, p. 92.
2 ibid, p. 62.
3 ibid, p. 91.
4 ibid, p. 86.
5 ibid, p. 151.
6 ibid, p. 255.
7 loc. cit.
8 ibid, p. 331.
9 ibid, p. 336.
10 ibid, p. 339.

Sir Ian Clunies-Ross

Records of the Australian Academy of Science, vol.3, no.3/4, Canberra, Australia, 1977. A memoir of Ian Clunies-Ross written by his son Anthony Ian Clunies-Ross, Senior Lecturer in Economics in the University of Strathclyde.

Index

Picture Credits

Page 21:
Sir Joseph Banks 1810
after Thomas Lawrence.
engraving 38.0 x 30.0 cm
photograph: David Paterson
Collection: National Portrait Gallery, Canberra. Purchased with funds provided by the Australian Decorative and Fine Arts Society, Canberra 2000.

Page 88:
Tom Roberts
Sir Henry Parkes, circa 1894
oil on canvas, 76.7 x 64 cm
Gift of Howard Hinton 1922
Art Gallery of New South Wales
photograph: Ray Woodbury for AGNSW [acc3 988]. Art Gallery of New South Wales Collection.

Page 110:
Charles Hill
The Proclamation of South Australia 1836
Charles Hill, Australia 1824–1915, c. 1856-76, oil on canvas, 133.3 x 274.3 cm. Morgan Thomas Bequest Fund 1936. Art Gallery of South Australia, Adelaide.

Page 192:
William Dobell
Dame Mary Gilmore, 1957
oil on hardboard, 90.2 x 73.7 cm
Gift of Dame Mary Gilmore 1960
© VISCOPY. photograph:
Christopher Snee for AGNSW. [acc#OA28.1960]. Art Gallery of New South Wales Collection.

Acknowledgements

I would like to acknowledge the generous assistance given me by the following public libraries, art galleries and individual collections: Antarctic Division, Hobart; Art Gallery of New South Wales; Castlemaine Art Gallery and Historical Museum; Hawkesbury Regional Library; La Trobe University, Bendigo; Melba Museum Lillydale; Monash University Archives; Museum of Victoria; National Gallery of Victoria; National Library of Australia; National Portrait Gallery, Canberra; National Portrait Gallery, London; Northern Territory Images; State Library of New South Wales; State Library of South Australia; State Library of Tasmania; State Library of Victoria; State Library of Western Australia; University of Adelaide; University of Sydney; VISCOPY.

There have been numerous occasions where I have had to rely on the generosity of many individuals who have made the effort to ensure that those items requested have been found, copied, scanned and delivered.

I would in particular like to express my gratitude to Mrs Melva Kartinyeri of Tailem Bend, South Australia who allowed me to reproduce the photographs of David Unaipon; Mr Max Rankine of the Raukkan Community Council who assisted in gaining permission to reproduce photographs of Point MacLeay Mission; Mrs Sally Garrett for permission to use her grandfather Harold Cazneaux's photograph of Reibey Place, Sydney; James Jackson for permission to reproduce Adelaide Perry's portrait of Mary Gilmore and Margaret McCredie for permission to reproduce her father Hardy Wilson's drawing of St James Church.

I would also like to thank all those librarians, curators and keepers of our nation's heritage, upon whom I have called time and time again, for your diligence, attention to detail — and above all your patience — in the face of the barrage of emails that shot back and forth as we tried to locate the hundreds of images used in this book. Once again, I thank you all — GEOFF H. 2004.